A CALL TO
HEROISM

A CALL TO

HEROISM

Renewing America's Vision of Greatness

Peter H. Gibbon

With a Foreword by Peter J. Gomes

Grove Press
New York

Photo Credits—page 14. Photo courtesy of the Hall of Fame for Great Americans on the campus of Bronx Community College of the City University of New York. page 36. Statue of John Bridge, Puritan, on Cambridge Common, Cambridge, Massachusetts. Photo by Mark Meatto. page 52. The Robert Gould Shaw Memorial on Boston Common, Boston, Massachusetts. Photo courtesy The Bostonian Society/ Old State House. page 70. Sports Bay Chapel Window, The Cathedral Church of St. John the Divine, New York City. Photo by Gregory Thorp. page 86. Detail of statue of George Washington. Horatio Greenough (1805–1852). Photo: Smithsonian American Art Museum, Washington, DC/Art Resource, NY. page 102. Bust of Benjamin Franklin. Jean-Antoine Houdon, French (active Paris), 1741–1828. Purchased with funds from the Barra Foundation, Inc., the Henry P. McIlhenny Fund in memory of Frances P. McIlhenny, with funds bequeathed by Walter E. Stait, the Fiske Kimball Fund, The Women's Committee of the Philadelphia Museum of Art, and with funds contributed by individual donors to the Fund for Franklin in honor of the 125th Anniversary of the Museum. page 116. View of Mount Rushmore. Photo by South Dakota Tourism. page 138. Martha Berry's school at Possum Trot. Photo courtesy of Berry College, Mount Berry, Georgia.

Published simultaneously in Canada
Printed in the United States of America

FIRST GROVE PRESS EDITION

Library of Congress Cataloging-in-Publication Data
Gibbon; Peter Hazen, 1942-
    A call to heroism: renewing America's vision of greatness / Peter H. Gibbon; with a foreword by Peter J. Gomes.
    p cm.
    ISBN 0-8021-4028-9 (pbk.)
    1. National characteristics, American. 2. Heroes—Mythology—United States. 3. Heroes—United States—Biography. 4. Idealism, American. 5. Idealism—Social aspects—United States. 6. United States—Civilization. 7. National monuments—United States. I. Title.
E169. 1 .G473 2002
920.02—dc21   2001056497

Design by Laura Hammond Hough

Grove Press
841 Broadway
New York, NY 10003

03 04 05 06 07   10 9 8 7 6 5 4 3 2 1

To Carol

There resides in us the motivating and civilizing force of the human spirit. It gives us the ability to think courageous thoughts, do courageous deeds, and give courageous sustenance to our fellows.

—Sherwin B. Nuland, 1988
Doctors: The Biography of Medicine

Contents

Contents

Foreword

FROM PLUTARCH TO KITTY KELLY AND BACK AGAIN: LIVES THAT MATTER

The Greeks tell us that people are known by the heroes they crown. If the Greeks are right, and they usually are, then a discussion about heroes and heroism is essentially an exercise in self-discovery and cultural introspection; and in choosing to honor certain persons as heroes and certain actions as heroic, we invest those persons and actions with ideals that we ourselves value and admire. Admiration and emulation are the qualities that heroes inspire. In the tradition of the hero, the qualities to be admired usually came down from on high, literally from Olympus, the mount upon which the gods of antiquity dwelt. Thus, literally, a hero was someone to be looked up to, someone to be observed from afar, who was, in fact, larger than life. In Greek mythology, a hero was the offspring of one mortal parent and one immortal parent, and this remarkable parentage accounted for the personality disorders and consequent struggles characteristic of those men and women who were made famous by Homer in *The Iliad* and *The Odyssey* (*Bloomsbury Guide to Human Thought*; ed. Kenneth McLeish; London, 1993; p. 343). The dilemma of a person of a split and warring nature set to persevering struggle in an impossible task, who nevertheless both overcomes the obstacles and accomplishes the desired end against all odds, is the classic formula of the hero. The Homeric gods and heroes were not themselves exclusively exemplary figures: their passions and their pettinesses contended with their admirable qualities

and made them recognizable to their fully human and thus more limited observers.

Thus, Plato, in constructing the ideal curriculum for his *Republic,* has
Socrates excise Homer from the reading list because the gods are immoral
and thus not fit for the emulation of the young. To Plato, the Homeric
gods, heroes, and myths are the stuff not of history but of poetry, and
hence in Book X of the *Republic,* the poets who publish and perpetuate
these tales are subversive to the state and deserved to be both thrashed
and banished. It would be first the Romans and then the Christians who
would rescue the concept of the hero from the reaches of poetic fiction
and place it at the disposal of history and morality. In the Roman tradition Plutarch, in his biographies, leaves poetry—with its propensity to
myth and fiction—and history—with its propensity for battles and what
he calls the "slanders" of the great historian Herodotus—for biography,
or lives. The lives he calls *paradiegmata,* which means "patterns, models, paradigms." In one of his introductions, Plutarch writes:

> I beg my readers not to hold it against me if I have not managed to work
> in every single one of the famous acts reported of these men, but rather
> have cut most of them short. The reason is that I am writing *Lives* not
> *Histories,* and the revelation of excellence or baseness does not always
> occur in the most conspicuous acts. Rather, some little thing, a witti-
> cism or a joke, often displays a man's character more clearly than battles
> with thousands of casualties, huge military formations, or sieges of cities.
> (Robert Lamberton; *Plutarch;* Yale University Press, 2001; p. 71)

Plutarch writes for the young that they may have examples of exemplary lives from antiquity to guide them in the present for the future. The purpose of biography is moral; the lives of the great and the
good are meant to make the reader better. The proof of admiration is
emulation, and even negative examples are exemplum of what to avoid,
what not to do.

Such a purpose is not far removed from the Judeo-Christian tradition, a world seemingly antithetic to the Greco-Roman concept of the
hero. In the Hebrew Bible, whose written text is the artifact of a much

earlier oral culture, we find the stories of great-souled people who did great deeds: greatness in the Hebrew Bible is always defined in terms of efforts to be faithful to the commandments of God. Psalm 78 is but one example of the singing of the heroically faithful:

> Give ear, O my people, to my teaching; incline your ears to the words of my mouth! I will open my mouth in a parable; I will utter dark sayings from of old, things that we have heard and known, that our fathers have told us. We will not hide them from their children, but tell to the coming generation the glorious deeds of the Lord, and his might, and the wonders which he has wrought. Psalm 78:1-4 (RSV)

The hero here is the collective "fathers," the notion of a faithful, good people whose heroism consists in fidelity to God when it would be easier either to despair or to disobey. The quality of the fidelity is directly proportionate to the quantity of conflict, both with external foes and inner demons. What is important in this tradition is not simply the fact of struggle, perseverance, and ultimately moral success, but the preservation of the stories and the transmission of them as *paradeigmata* to the generations yet to come. Psalm 78 became something of the paradigmatic psalm of Puritan New England. One of the most famous paraphrases of Psalm 78, adapted by Jeremy Belknap from Tate and Brady's *New Version of the Psalms* (1696), and first published in Boston in 1795, has been sung at Harvard Commencements since 1806:

> *Let children learn the mighty deeds*
> *Which God performed of old,*
> *Which in our younger years,*
> *We saw, and which our fathers told.*
> *Our lips shall tell them to our sons,*
> *And they again to theirs,*
> *That generations yet unborn*
> *May teach them to their heirs.*
> (*The Harvard University Hymn Book*; Harvard University Press, 1964; #249)

In the Christian Bible, the last three chapters of the book of Hebrews in the New Testament constitutes a catalogue of heroic lives to be emulated. The contemporary believers are surrounded by what the writer calls a "cloud of witnesses" whose righteous deeds have not been forgotten. Their deeds and sufferings are recorded, again as exemplum for the young community. The future depends upon the recall of this historic history transmitted not through theory or theology, but through lives. Hebrews has often been called the "book of heroes," and its readers are instructed:

> Remember your leaders, those who spoke to you the word of God; consider the outcome of their life, and imitate their faith. Hebrews 13:7 (RSV)

Just as the New England Puritans adapted Hebrew psalmody to their own circumstances, so too did they appropriate and combine the notions of Plutarchian lives and biblical exemplary biography to their own people. Cotton Mather, who claimed for himself the title of "Plutarch of New England," composed heroic biographies of the first settlers of New England, swathing Bradford, Winthrop, Cotton, and Dunster, among others, in the nomenclature and virtues of biblical and classical figures. Once again the purpose was not mere historical erudition, although this was always on ostentatious display in Mather's prose, but rather was that the past should teach the present and thus preserve the future. In the search for greatness in an uncertain present, once again heroic biography became the vehicle of choice. Before the American revolution, the first arrivals to New England—the Pilgrims of Plymouth and the Puritans of Boston—filled the primitive pantheon of the English new world, and the first recorded retrospective celebration of heroes and heroic enterprise occurred on the eve of the revolution itself.

In 1769, a group of young men in the old colony town of Plymouth, Massachusetts, determined to celebrate the anniversary of the landing of their Pilgrim ancestors in that place on December 21, 1620. They held a parade, shot a cannon, consumed a great dinner with many pious toasts, and celebrated the persevering qualities of their Pilgrim heroes.

The coming troubles in 1776 would disrupt these festival rites and split the club into loyal and revolutionary factions. By 1820, the two hundredth anniversary of the Pilgrims' landing, the stalwarts of Plymouth had been joined in the pantheon by the Founding Fathers, and a class of heroes worthy of the republic was invented.

The public rhetoric of such national figures as Daniel Webster, Edward Everett, John Quincy Adams, and the sermons and orations of countless lesser-knowns, combined in the period before the Civil War to create a syllabus of heroism and civic virtue designed to inculcate within the young and the young country both the sense of what historian Henry Steele Commager would many years later call a sense of a "usable past," and a sense of purpose and destiny both personal and manifestly corporate and public. The near deification first of George Washington, "first in war, first in peace, and first in the hearts of his countrymen," and then of Abraham Lincoln, the second founder of the Republic, at least in the North, served to personify the hopes and ambitions of a country with more of a future than a past. Until a half century ago, America's sense of greatness and its ambitions for the young could be seen in the fact that in nearly every schoolroom in every public school would be found prominently placed on the walls large framed reproductions of Gilbert Stuart's portrait of George Washington, and one of Mathew Brady's portraits of the bearded, melancholy Abraham Lincoln in profile.

The concept of the hero, with its appeal to an antique and essentially foreign exceptionalism, was always at risk in a culture fiercely independent, inherently suspicious of elites, and remorselessly democratic and inclusive. The concept of the heroic requires a cultural consensus as to what constitutes virtues and values worthy of admiration and emulation, and as the culture becomes more and more diverse, it becomes an increasingly demanding and difficult task to define the heroic and the worthy. So difficult is it to do so that many would abandon the project, arguing that not only is the search for new heroes fruitless, but that upon a more careful, critical examination, the old heroes were not so heroic after all. George Washington and Thomas Jefferson both held slaves, although Washington freed his at his death. Poor

Jefferson has been charged with hypocrisy, and with not only keeping slaves but of siring progeny by one of them, Sally Hemings, while proclaiming the universal rights of man. The very idea of "exemplary lives" fails if the lives prove to be less than exemplary, for there is nothing more unforgiving than a public that discovers that its expectations of its heroes are betrayed. Rather than risk such betrayal, many would argue that the search for the heroic, and the greatness it personifies, is an adolescent ambition beyond which a maturing republic should grow even as teenagers leave their idols and fixations behind them. This view, together with a cynical distrust of a pantheon filled with dead white males whose privilege and power challenges newer and more compelling notions of inclusion, equity, and opportunity, makes the notion of heroism in the twenty-first century as difficult to define as it is dangerous to advocate.

This might well have been the state of play when Peter Gibbon began his travels, researches, and lectures, the result of which constitute this book. Three years ago he was writing and reading against the tide, asking what would take their place if our old concepts of the hero were no longer adequate. An astute student of the cultural history and psyche of America, a professional schoolmaster, and a very good listener, Gibbon knew that American ideals depended upon a way to embody them, and so he went on what politicians nowadays call a "listening tour" of the schoolrooms of America to ask about heroes and ideals. Among the things he discovered was that while it was easy to desecrate the pantheon and, like the Vandals of ancient Europe and the Cromwellian Puritans of the English Civil War, destroy the idols and monuments of an earlier civilization at risk, it was not quite so easy to create new and enduring value systems. Gibbon visited more than one hundred fifty schools in twenty states, talked to anybody who would listen, and asked what they thought would be the ideals and values of the twenty-first century, and who would be its heroes and heroines. He was already well on the way to the substance of this quite remarkable book when the events of September 11, 2001, cast everything in a new light. Suddenly, under the experience of terror and devastating insecurity, the notion of the heroic was resurrected and redefined. The face of heroism was seen in the faces of heretofore anonymous fire fighters, police officers, and rescue workers who became the human response to the inhumane chaos that was New York City. Military service, for generations enduring a dubious legacy from Vietnam, again became a noble, honorable expression of civic responsibility. The flag was rediscovered as an acceptable icon of national identity, and the need to think as a people with both a common past and a common hope in the face of a common threat became the nearly spontaneous order of the day. *Renewing America's Vision of Greatness,* Gibbon's subtitle to his book *A Call to Heroism,* was no longer a pious abstraction but an essential act of national identity. In an early effort to answer the question "What is a hero?" Gibbon writes:

> As a society, we need to explore a more subtle, complex definition of the word *hero* for an information age, one that acknowledges weaknesses as well as strengths, failures as well as successes; but at the same time, one that does not set the bar too low. We need to portray our heroes as human beings but let them remain heroic. (p. 7)

In his encounters across America, Gibbon often had to deal with the distinctions between a celebrity and a hero. A celebrity is someone essentially famous or well-known, and while a celebrity can be a hero, being famous is not the same as being heroic. If it were the case that fame and celebrity were the criteria of heroism, then by the logic of Andy Warhol everybody would be a hero for fifteen minutes. The entertainment culture makes it difficult to maintain that distinction, yet the maintenance of it is essential to retaining the coin of the truly heroic that remains as Plutarch long ago insisted: exemplary, and worthy both of admiration and of emulation.

Gibbon also had to deal with the American tendency to personalize everything, and thus to declare as "my" heroes only those people whom we know. By this, he argues, we restrict our aspirations to the limits of our own experience. Why should we impose these restrictions upon ourselves, and, more to the point, upon our children? He replies:

Public heroes—or imperfect people of extraordinary achievement, courage, and greatness of soul whose reach is wider than our own—teach
us to push beyond ourselves and our neighborhoods in our search for
models of excellence. They enlarge our imagination, teach us to think
big, and expand our sense of the possible. (p. 13)

In the early days of the republic, the manufacture of heroes was a civic
industry; today the culture is as industrious in their defrocking. The twentieth century even gave a name to this process of de-divinization: "debunking," which is to reveal the falseness of something or someone,
doubtless from Henry Ford's famous aphorism that "history is bunk."
Rather than Ford, however, Gibbon cites Joyce Carol Oates's 1988 coin-
age of the word *pathography* to describe biography that focuses on aberration, Plutarch transformed into Kitty Kelly! What role is left to the
hero when the culture would rather be titillated than inspired and prefers gossip to gospel? What happens when the gossip is true? Martin
Luther King Jr. and Bill Clinton did cheat on their wives, as did John F.
Kennedy and Franklin Delano Roosevelt. Encountering a climate of cynicism and suspicion about public heroes among the young people he interviewed, Gibbon nevertheless concludes:

I have found a yearning among many students for something nobler than
what our culture is currently offering. And I have found that many are
still searching for heroes. (p. 170)

This is a timely book. It was not fashioned as an opportunistic screed
in the immediate aftermath of September 11, but rather its author's years
of careful reading and even more careful listening and analysis help us
to better understand our country as it lurches from its most recent en-
counter with mortality. Heroes and the search for greatness more often
than not emerge in times of adversity and crisis rather than in times of
prosperity and complacency: it is usually the crisis that forces the present
to examine both its past and its future. As we engage in this historic
moment of cultural introspection, we could not ask for a better guide
than this book, or a more companionable critic and mentor than Peter

H. Gibbon. Not only does he help us to formulate useful questions from out of our past and ambiguous present, but his hope for the future of the heroic in America's search for greatness is contagious:

> I cannot imagine a world without heroes, a world without genius and nobility, without exalted enterprise, high purpose and transcendent courage, without risk and suffering. It would be gray and flat and dull. Who would show us the way or set the mark? Who would inspire us and console us? Who would energize us and keep us from the darkness? (p. 184)

Who indeed!

Peter J. Gomes
Sparks House
Cambridge, Massachusetts
March 2002

Introduction

IN SEARCH OF HEROES

Human beings are deeply divided, eternally torn between apathy and activity, between nihilism and belief. In this short life, we wage a daily battle between a higher and a lower self. The *hero* stands for our higher self. To get through life and permit the higher self to prevail we depend on public models of excellence, bravery, and goodness. During the last forty years in America, such models have been in short supply. Except among politicians and Madison Avenue advertising firms, the word *hero* has been out of fashion since the late 1960s as a term to describe past or present public figures. We are reluctant to use it this way, doubtful as to whether any one person can hold up under the burden of such a word. After the September 11 terrorist attacks, *hero* was resurrected across the nation to describe the firefighters and police officers who lost their lives in the World Trade Center, rescue workers who patiently picked their way through the rubble, passengers who thwarted terrorists on a hijacked airplane, and soldiers who left on planes and ships. In difficult times, we turn to the word *hero* to express our deepest sorrow, our highest aspiration, and our most profound admiration. At the start of the twenty-first century, America was forced to question some of the attitudes of an antiheroic age: irony, cynicism, preoccupation with celebrities and sex, disdain for political leaders, and indifference to soldiers. Tragedy sobers a nation. It can also toughen a nation, encourage high-mindedness, and turn its attention to more permanent values.

* * *

IN 1992, I gave a commencement speech to high school students in which I described three women of extraordinary courage: missionary Eva Jane Price, who in 1900 was killed in the Boxer Rebellion; artist Käthe Kollwitz, who lost her son in World War I and transcended her grief by creating one of the most powerful sculptures of the twentieth century; and writer Eugenia Ginzburg, who spent eighteen years in Stalin's gulag. *Newsweek* picked up the introduction to the speech and called it "In Search of Heroes."

In the *Newsweek* piece, I argued that irreverence, skepticism, and mockery permeated the culture to such a degree that it is difficult for young people to have heroes and that presenting reality in the classroom is an empty educational goal if it produces disillusioned, dispirited students. The heart of the article was that we had lost a vision of greatness, in our schools and in our culture.

People responded from all over America. From a remote mining area of the Appalachian Mountains, a high school teacher wrote that in thirty-three years she had observed that "the more affluent students' vision of greatness" had been "clouded by materialism." From the University of Illinois an assistant professor of broadcast journalism commented that he had found "an increasing cynicism among my students that is most disturbing." A mother of ten wrote from Littleton, Colorado, a town most Americans had never heard of in 1993: "When I asked, several years ago, why the schools avoided any teaching of morality, I was told that the teacher could not enforce his/her morals on another. . . . how sad that this is what the world has become and even sadder that so many accept this as a lost cause."

Since writing the *Newsweek* article, I have plugged the word *hero* into every available database; read hundreds of biographies and books on heroism; traveled all over the country talking to Americans about heroes; and interviewed educators, historians, journalists, ministers, politicians, scientists, and writers asking questions that have given shape to this book: How did we lose our public heroes? Why does it matter? Where do we go from here?

As a historian, I have been tracing the changing face of the American hero, researching what has happened to the presentation of heroes in history books, and analyzing ways revisionist historians have shaped teachers' attitudes, which in turn shape the way students respond. I have been resurrecting historical heroes and testing them against a new definition of heroism. In an age of information, how are we to view Thomas Jefferson? What gives George Washington and Abraham Lincoln staying power? Has there been a connection between religion and heroism in our history? I have been looking at the role of celebrities, athletes, and journalists.

In my travels, I have been discovering and researching monuments and statues, plaques and inscriptions, roadside markers. On Commonwealth Avenue in Boston stands a historian hero of mine, Samuel Eliot Morison, a true believer in heroes. Not far from Morison stands abolitionist William Lloyd Garrison, who fought for emancipation in the 1830s. Encircling the base of Garrison's statue are his famous lines: "I will not retreat an inch and I will be heard." Next to him is a new monument: a raised stone semicircle engraved with the names of ten firefighters killed when the Hotel Vendome collapsed in 1957. On one side are the words "We are not heroes . . . we do our jobs." I also like the offbeat statues in Boston, such as the one honoring Edward Everett Hale, the nineteenth-century author of the once popular short story "The Man Without A Country," about a man who doesn't appreciate his country until he is exiled.

The word *memorial* comes from the Latin *memoria,* meaning remembrance. Memorials and inscriptions are primary sources in stone and metal, one way of reaching out to those who lived before us, of remembering those who built America, one way of honoring heroes and greatness.

The most rewarding part of this odyssey has been talking to students about heroes. In the last four years I have spoken to thousands of young people in schools all over America: in public and private schools, coed and single sex, urban and suburban, charter and parochial. I have been to both affluent and less affluent districts and to cities as different as San Francisco, Cincinnati, New Orleans, Milwaukee, Kansas City, New

York, and Boston. I have talked to students ranging in age from fourth grade to college, but most of my audiences have been in high schools —from a thousand students sitting on bleachers in a gymnasium to small classes in history and literature.

In my talks to high school students, I challenge the notion that they are too old, too jaded, or too cynical for heroes. I quote Ralph Waldo Emerson, another true believer in heroes and a writer most students still know: "Go with mean people and you think life is mean" and "with the great our thoughts and manners easily become great." In spirited debate, they agree, disagree, challenge, and probe. "Is Malcolm X a hero? John Brown? Why is Adolf Hitler any worse than Christopher Columbus?" They ask about celebrities, athletes, historical figures, politicians, and rescuers, and about such personal heroes as parents, teachers, and friends.

Discussions are often timely. I was in San Francisco not long after Joe DiMaggio died. Students asked about DiMaggio's relationship with Marilyn Monroe and why he was more of a hero than Mark McGwire. When the DNA verdict was delivered on Thomas Jefferson, students in Philadelphia pressed me on the personal lives of John F. Kennedy and Bill Clinton: "What's the difference?" they asked. When the movie *American Beauty* won the Academy Award for Best Picture, we talked about Hollywood. During the 2000 election squabbling, they brought up politicians. After September 11, students were more familiar with the word *hero*. Many asked about Osama bin Laden, whether suicide bombers are brave, and why we need a crisis to provide heroes.

"TIMES OF TERROR are times of heroism," said Emerson. America's new war reminded us of one kind of heroism, the brave deed, and of one kind of hero, the rescuer. My hope is that it will also encourage us to become more interested in past and present public heroes and that it will revive the qualities of admiration, gratitude, and awe too long absent from our culture. In a 1929 essay, "The Aims of Education," philosopher Alfred North Whitehead wrote, "Moral education is impossible apart from the habitual vision of greatness." What can we do to renew *and* sustain America's vision of greatness?

We can make the case for all kinds of heroes, to show how they have transformed America and how they can lift and improve our lives. We can honor our soldiers in peace as well as in war. We can look in new ways at old heroes and into the obscure corners of history for new ones. We can look back and learn from an age when the ideology of heroism was influential and imitation of the admirable was the norm. Immersed in the present, we need to pay more attention to our past. At the same time, we need to realize that a more mature society requires a more subtle and complex presentation of heroism—one that includes a recognition of weaknesses and reversals along with an appreciation of virtues and triumphs. And we need to recognize that an egalitarian multicultural society requires that the pantheon of heroes be expanded.

We can challenge the times and be combative. In a bureaucratic age, celebrate individual achievement; in an egalitarian age, praise genius; when everyone is a victim, stress personal responsibility. In addition to popular culture, high culture. In a celebrity age, caution young people about worshiping fame and beauty; in a society mesmerized by athletes, recall the moral language of sport.

We can teach our children and grandchildren that character is as important as intellect, that idealism is superior to cynicism, that wisdom should come before information. We can teach them to be realistic *and* affirming, to see life not only as it is but also as it ought to be. Heroes are a response to a deep and powerful impulse, the need to emulate and idealize. "The search after the great," said Emerson, "is the dream of youth and the most serious occupation of manhood."

I

One

WHAT IS A HERO?

Let me tell you they are out there—those of confounding selflessness and seeming immunity to fear. . . . They have eluded concise definition since the beginning of recorded history.

—Admiral James Stockdale, 1991
"On Heroes and Heroism"

It's a tricky word. It should not be thrown around easily, hero *or* heroism.

—Lance Armstrong, 2001
Union Square, New York City

Twentieth-century philosopher Joseph Campbell believed that all heroes take journeys, confront the unknown, endure trials, and return home transformed—as did Buddha, Muhammad, and Jesus. Christians believe heroes are humble and turn the other cheek. Friedrich Nietzsche believed heroes were proud and forceful. Who is a hero? "He who conquers his evil inclinations," according to the Talmud. "He who hangs on for one minute more," says a Russian proverb.

Hero is a difficult word. Is John Wayne a hero because he portrayed brave men? Is Babe Ruth a hero because he hit home runs? Can we look up to Charles Lindbergh after he accepted a medal from the Nazis, or to suffragist Elizabeth Cady Stanton, knowing she feared that immigrants would change American culture? Is General Dwight Eisenhower a hero even though he never risked his life? Can we admire Robert E. Lee when he fought to preserve slavery?

Nobody wants to be called a hero. After being widely acclaimed for his leadership in the Gulf War, General Norman Schwarzkopf called his book *It Doesn't Take a Hero* and passed along the glory to the men who served under him. When President Reagan saluted Mother Hale as "a true American hero" for taking babies with AIDS into her home, she replied, "I'm not an American hero. I'm simply a person who loves children." John F. Kennedy turned aside praise of his war exploits by saying, "My boat sank."

To many of today's intellectuals, the word *hero* is antique. They appreciate epic heroes like Achilles and Beowulf, mythological heroes like Hercules, tragic heroes like Antigone. But human heroes belong to a credulous prescientific age. Intellectuals don't have heroes; they have people they admire—some of the time.

Too male, too military, say feminists. *Hero* often means *oppressor*. In a patriarchal society, heroes have been warriors, cowboys, explorers. Our definition of *hero* reflects a "male model," poetry critic Helen Vendler told me in an interview. "I often wondered what happened to the children when the hero went away to war."

Deconstructionists find the word *hero* meaningless. In their view, no one is selfless or noble. Behind every altruistic act is self-interest. Social scientists tell us that human beings are not autonomous but conditioned by genes and environment, that we do what we are bred and trained to do, not what we believe is right. To some Americans today, the concept of a hero seems elitist and out of place in a democracy where all are equal.

"A hero is usually smug," Ned Rorem told me in his home on Nantucket. Rorem, a composer, won a Pulitzer Prize for his music in 1976 and had recently been named president of the American Academy of Arts and Letters in New York City. Rorem doesn't accept the word *hero* and has never had one. " I don't know what *noble* or *lofty* means."

Mother Teresa "is a fraud," he added; "she is in the hero business. . . . Abortion and birth control would help India."

It's hard to have confidence in the word *hero* when reputations rise and fall. At the World's Columbian Exposition in Chicago in 1893, visitors could stroll through a full-scale reproduction of the monastery where Christopher Columbus stayed in Spain before petitioning Queen Isabella for funding to sail to America. Life-size replicas of the *Niña*, *Pinta*, and *Santa Maria* floated across a man-made lagoon. On display were seventy-one portraits of Columbus and facsimiles of his ships' logs. Leading up to the 1893 exposition had been a year of parades and ceremonies commemorating the four hundredth anniversary of Columbus's first voyage. Almost one hundred years later, in 1992, demonstrators threw blood on the explorer's statue at Columbus Circle in New York City to protest the impact of colonization on Native Americans.

Besides, say skeptics, a skillful publicist can make an ordinary person great. Several patriots rode to Lexington on April 19, 1775, to warn Americans of the British attack, but Longfellow's 1861 poem "Paul Revere's Ride" made only one man a hero. Until John Filson mythologized Daniel Boone in the eighteenth century and Timothy Flint praised him in the most widely read biography before the Civil War, Boone was an average explorer, who in a moment of honesty confessed, "Many heroic actions and chivalrous adventures are related of me which exist only in the regions of fancy." Libby Custer wrote three best-sellers and gave hundreds of lectures around the country to assure posterity that in 1876 at the Battle of Little Big Horn her husband, George A. Custer, died a hero.

Names and stories linger in our memories and make a difference. Thomas Jackson became "Stonewall" Jackson during the Civil War, after he stationed his men in a strong defensive line and repulsed the Union troops at the Battle of Manassas in 1861. In the 1870s, Ned Buntline's dime novels transformed William F. Cody into Buffalo Bill.

Heroes can also be elevated by early death. Until the British hanged him as a spy at the age of twenty-one, Nathan Hale was an ordinary soldier in the Colonial army. Cartoonists mocked Abraham Lincoln until the night he was shot. "This thing of being a hero," said Will Rogers, "about the main thing to do is to know when to die."

What a Hero Is Not

The word *hero* comes to us from the Greek, meaning *demigod*. Offspring of a divine parent and a mortal parent, the heroes of Greek mythology were less than gods but greater than ordinary humans—and if their exploits in the mortal world brought honor to the gods, they could join them on Mount Olympus for eternity. Achilles, the quintessential classical warrior, who kills Hector on the fields of Troy at the end of the *Iliad,* was a great hero to the Greeks because he was courageous and handsome and valued glory in battle more than life itself.

Later in their history, the Greeks applied the word *hero* to human beings. The most renowned human hero in the ancient world was the conqueror Alexander the Great, who marched from Egypt to India and conquered the known world in nine years before he died at the age of thirty-two. In the Sackler Museum at Harvard University, there is a Greek coin that on one side depicts Alexander the Great as a human being and on the other side as a god. In Greece there were hero shrines where citizens could worship. Heroes seemed more accessible than gods. The bones of human heroes, the Greeks believed, had magical powers. From the Greeks comes the notion of the hero as extraordinary, superhuman, charismatic, godlike, as well as the beliefs that heroes are above all physically brave and that the crucible of courage is the battlefield, where decisions and actions mean life or death.

For most of human history, *hero* has been synonymous with *warrior.* Although we often link these words today, we do have an expanded, more inclusive definition of *hero* than the one we inherited from the Greeks. Modern dictionaries list three qualities in common after the entry *hero:* extraordinary achievement, courage, and the idea (variously expressed) that the hero serves as a "model" or "example"—that heroism has a moral component.

Today, extraordinary achievement is no longer confined to valor in combat. As well as military heroes, there are humanitarian heroes, cultural heroes, political heroes. Thomas Edison lit up the night. Harriet Tubman rescued slaves. Thomas Jefferson wrote the Declaration of Independence. Beethoven is a hero of music, Rembrandt of art, Einstein of science.

Likewise, courage means many things besides physical bravery: taking an unpopular position, standing up for principle, persevering, forging accomplishment out of adversity. After her life was threatened, activist Ida B. Wells continued to condemn lynching. Franklin Roosevelt battled polio. Helen Keller transcended blindness and deafness.

The moral component of the meaning of heroism—and, I believe, the most important one—is elusive. In French, *héros* is associated with generosity and force of character. And in Middle English, *heroicus* means noble. In dictionaries, *heroic* is an adjective of praise: some of its synonyms are *virtuous, steadfast, magnanimous, intrepid*. The *Oxford English Dictionary* uses the phrase "greatness of soul." It's an imprecise concept, like the word *hero* itself. There are many different ways to describe it, but I believe greatness of soul to be a mysterious blend of powerful qualities summarized by Shakespeare in *Macbeth* (IV.iii.91–94), where he describes the "king-becoming graces" as:

> ... *justice, verity, temp'rance, stableness,*
> *Bounty, perseverance, mercy, lowliness,*
> *Devotion, patience, courage, fortitude.*

When Nelson Mandela received an honorary degree from Harvard University in a special ceremony in September 1998, the seniors sat in the front rows. My son, who was among them, commented that there was an aura about Mandela, something about being in his presence that evoked a surprisingly powerful response. I believe the response he was describing is awe, which washed over many people attending the ceremony that afternoon and came from contemplating Mandela's extraordinary achievement, his profound courage, and his greatness of soul.

I find it significant that the heroes in American history with the most staying power, like Abraham Lincoln and George Washington, had this same greatness of soul. And I find it encouraging that the three people *Time* magazine picked as the most influential of the twentieth century—Albert Einstein, Mohandas Gandhi, and Franklin Delano Roosevelt—each had this quality.

Heroes, of course, do not have extraordinary achievement, courage, and the qualities that comprise greatness of soul in equal abundance, but I argue that the more of them one has, the higher one is in the pantheon. And if you take an antonym for each of Shakespeare's "king-becoming graces," you come up with a pretty good definition of what a hero is *not:* unjust, untruthful, intemperate, unstable, stingy, wavering, vengeful, arrogant, capricious, impatient, cowardly, and volatile.

THE GREATEST BURDEN the word *hero* carries today is the expectation that a hero be perfect. In Greek mythology, even the gods have flaws. They are not perfect but rather hot-tempered, jealous, and fickle, taking sides in human events and feuding among themselves.

The Roman historian Plutarch wrote some of the earliest biographies of heroes: *Lives of the Noble Grecians and Romans.* For hundreds of years these biographies were enormously influential in European and American education. Thomas Jefferson carried a copy of *Lives* in his knapsack. Ralph Waldo Emerson's essays and notebooks are sprinkled with quotations from Plutarch. For each of the biographies she read, Jane Addams's father paid her fifty cents. *Plutarch's Lives* was one of Harry Truman's favorite books, and it lingered as one of the staples of an Anglo-American classical education until the turn of the nineteenth century.

Plutarch's biographies were not hagiographies; in each he reminds us that an exemplary life has never been a perfect life, and we learn from his subjects' vices as well as their virtues. For example, in his treatment of the Roman statesman Cato the Elder (one of George Washington's heroes), Plutarch praises Cato for his frugality and integrity, and for being a good father and husband, but rebukes him for boasting about his achievements and mistreating his slaves. Plutarch acknowledged the flaws of the men he wrote about, but in the main he admired their many accomplishments.

In America today we have come to define the person by the flaw: Thomas Jefferson is the president with the slave mistress, Einstein the scientist who mistreated his wife, Mozart the careless genius who liked to talk dirty. These definitions lodge in our minds—especially if they relate to sex—and become the first and sometimes the only thing we remember.

As a society, we need to explore a more subtle, complex definition of the word *hero*, suitable for an information age, one that acknowledges weaknesses as well as strengths, failures as well as successes— but, at the same time, one that does not set the bar too low. We need to portray our heroes as human beings but let them remain heroic. Yes, Lincoln liked bawdy stories, was politically calculating, and suffered from melancholy. But he also exhibited astonishing political and moral courage, led our nation through its greatest crisis, and always appealed to the "better angels of our nature."

A realistic definition of *hero* does not mean we include in the pantheon those who are evil. Joseph Stalin and Mao Tse-tung were two of the most powerful men of the twentieth century, leading vast backward nations to global prominence while destroying millions of lives in the process. Though some in Russia or China still venerate them, few in America would call them heroes today. In his book ranking the one hundred most influential individuals in human history, Michael Hart observes, "It is not a list of the noblest characters." *Influential* does not mean *heroic*. Nor is *leader*—a word to which *hero* is frequently linked—a synonym for *hero*. Adolf Hitler was a leader; Nelson Mandela is a hero.

Among those who are not fond of the word *hero* was the philosopher Sidney Hook, because throughout history we have called so many leaders heroes who have been greedy and wicked. Reflecting a recurring criticism of heroes, one that becomes particularly pronounced after World War II, Hook noted that "on the whole, heroes in history have carved out their paths of greatness by wars, conquest, revolutions, and holy crusades." In his 1943 book *The Hero in History*, Hook suggested we take the word away from political leaders and soliders and give it to teachers.

A Hero by Any Other Name?

As I travel around the country talking to students, I have been asked many times, "Can't a celebrity be a hero?" A celebrity can be a hero but, by definition, a celebrity is simply someone who is famous. Are celebrities usually heroes? It is hard to combine the qualities of heroism with the values of today's entertainment industry.

In the media, the word *hero* is often used interchangeably with *legend, icon,* and *idol.* A 1998 cover of *Esquire* magazine featured Mr. Rogers and posed the question "Can you say . . . hero"? When Mr. Rogers retired in 2001, a television newscaster asked, "Can you say *icon*?" The name of a popular news magazine program that profiles famous people is *Headliners and Legends.* A recent issue of a pension fund magazine introduced a new advertising campaign with the headline "Icons, Thinkers and Everyday Heroes." Questions about distinctions among these words surface all the time in my audiences.

Legendary stories have always swirled around heroes. Since the age of Homer, legends flourished in societies that had low levels of formal education and slow means of communication. Often embroidered more elaborately after death, legends enhanced the status of mere mortals. Today newscasters and talk show hosts do use the word *legend* to describe a fanciful story that has been woven into someone's history but more often to describe some giant of the entertainment industry, like John Wayne, or some athletic superstar, like Babe Ruth. A legend is someone about whom stories have been generated by fans and publicists, someone who has become larger than life, someone around whom an aura of mystery has gathered.

Legends have a powerful emotional pull. We crave colorful, romantic stories. At the same time, an egalitarian, highly educated, information-rich society erodes legends and makes it harder to have heroes. Legendary history flourished in nineteenth-century America; contemporary historians believe it is their duty to distinguish legend from fact. We now have hundreds of books with titles like *Penetrating the Lincoln Legend* and *Stonewall Jackson: Soldier and Legend.* In a fact-based scientific society, people prefer their heroes to stand tall and strong without the help of legends.

Used liberally in advertisements and the entertainment industry, the term *icon* originally meant an image of a saint. This is still true in the Eastern Orthodox Church, but in our more secular world an icon need not be a saint. In computer listings under the keyword ICON are books on Saint Basil the Great and Sir Thomas More. There are also books on Che Guevara, Frank Sinatra, Mae West, and the Harley-Davidson motorcycle. *Icon* has become a fashionable word, applied to anyone or anything that some group will venerate, for whatever reason.

Less trendy, *idol* shares with *icon* the quality of worship. In the Bible, an idol is a false god, like the Golden Calf that Moses strikes down in the book of Exodus. *Idol* is often linked to immaturity; matinee idol, teen idol, rock idol are common blends. Idolatry implies slavish devotion, uncritical veneration, the kind of adulation found in cults.

Some Americans reject the word *hero* outright and insist on *role model,* which is less grandiose, more human. We search for role models in our daily lives, particularly as the American family disintegrates. We like to visualize these people—and, by emulation, ourselves—doing a particular job well, carrying out responsibilities, overcoming obstacles. People often ask me, "Why do we need heroes? Why aren't role models enough?"

I like Jill Ker Conway's distinction. Author of the best-selling autobiography *The Road from Coorain,* Conway recently ended a lecture on extraordinary women, such as nineteenth-century African explorer Mary Kingsley, with the statement "Women should have heroines, not role models." I asked her later what she meant. Women, she said, are as physically brave and as daring as men, and the routine use of *role model* to describe outstanding women conceals their bravery and diminishes their heroism.

Conway's distinction argues that *heroine* is a more powerful word than *role model* and that heroism is a reach for the extraordinary. Elizabeth Blackwell, who in the 1840s boldly persisted in her attempt to attend medical school for many years and later to find a hospital post at a time when few Americans—men or women—supported her efforts, is such a heroine. The woman physician who lives next door today is a role model.

Not all women are fond of the word *heroine*. Contemporary writer Maya Angelou has come up with a new word: *shero*. In library catalogs, *heroine* overwhelmingly refers to fictional characters, not to female figures in history. Even though dictionaries give *heroine* the same lofty definition as *hero*, to some it suggests the damsel in distress, the female in need of rescue, silent film star Mary Pickford tied to the train tracks.

Along with role model, the word *mentor* has lately become a strong competitor of *hero*. Like hero, the word *mentor* comes to us from the Greeks. In the *Odyssey*, Mentor was the tutor of Odysseus' son, Telemachus. Both in its origin and in contemporary use, *mentor* means teacher or adviser. A mentor is someone who has knowledge we would like to have or who, in corporate terms, can show us the ropes. A mentor "takes on" a novice: a student, a protégé, the junior associate in a law firm. We usually know our mentors and learn from them through conversation, imitation, and instruction. Beethoven is a hero of music, our music teacher a mentor.

Marian Wright Edelman, president of the Children's Defense Fund in Washington, D.C., told me in a phone interview that she was inspired by Sojourner Truth, who rescued slaves, and Alva Myrdal, who fought for peace and social justice. All groups of young people "are in desperate need of heroism," she said, but most of our heroes are "quiet role models working hard for their communities." Edelman has described how her life was molded by men and women she admired and wanted to imitate. She calls the book *Lanterns: A Memoir of Mentors*.

Many people, especially in schools, ask me about tragic heroes in fiction, like Macbeth, Hamlet, and King Lear. For most of the twentieth century, the reigning definition of the tragic hero in literature emerged out of a series of lectures given by British critic A. C. Bradley and published in 1904 in a book called *Shakespearean Tragedy*. Like the Aristotelian Greek tragic hero, according to Bradley, the Shakespearean tragic hero was a person of "high degree" whose fall from greatness and eventual death is brought about by a "fatal gift," eliciting "not only sympathy and pity but admiration, terror, and awe." As with Greek heroes and Plutarch's *Lives,* Shakespeare's tragic heroes were extraordinary but not by any means perfect. It was in fact the tragic hero's flaw and fall from greatness that elicited powerful emotions in Elizabethan audiences.

Modern playwrights have challenged this tradition. In 1949, a few weeks after the first performance of *Death of a Salesman*—one of the most popular and influential plays of our time—Arthur Miller wrote in an essay published in *The New York Times,* "I believe that the common man is as apt a subject for tragedy in its highest sense as kings were." In the play, still widely read in high schools today, the salesman Willy Loman struggles and suffers and becomes a casualty of the American Dream. His wife, Linda, says, "I don't say he's a great man. Willy Loman never made a lot of money. His name was never in the paper. He's not the finest character that ever lived. But he's a human being, and a terrible thing is happening to him. So attention must be paid." Willy Loman is not extraordinary. He does not fall from greatness. His suicide could be construed as an act of despair rather than courage. Some consider Loman a victim. Loman is the guy next door, someone we know, a new American tragic hero.

Just as, in the theater, Willy Loman has become a hero, so in their everyday lives Americans look to their neighborhoods for their heroes. Today, many Americans define heroes as decent people who sacrifice or try to make a difference. They name streets after local World War II veterans, parks after teachers, bridges after local politicians and philanthropists. Rejecting historical and public figures, who may have feet of clay or a skilled public relations expert, they democratize the word *hero* and jettison the Greek notion of the hero as superhuman and godlike.

When I wrote to John Updike to ask about his views on heroes, he referred me to a book of his, *Picked-Up Pieces,* where I found a statement he made in an interview for *Life* magazine in 1966: "The idea of a hero is aristocratic. You cared about Oedipus and Hamlet because they were noble and you were a groundling. Now either nobody is a hero or everyone is. I vote for everyone."

Emblematic of this transformation, John F. Kennedy launched his presidential campaign with the 1956 book *Profiles in Courage,* in which he writes about heroic senators throughout American history who put principle before party. In 1998, former Ohio congressman John Kasich launched his bid for the Republican nomination with *Courage Is Contagious,* a book about local heroes he met in his travels, people who are interested in "small victories," not "home runs."

THE DEFINITION OF *hero* remains subjective. What is extraordinary can be debated. Courage is in the eye of the beholder. Greatness of soul is elusive. Inevitably there will be debates over how many and what kinds of flaws a person can have and still be considered heroic.

Nevertheless, today we are reluctant to call either past or present public figures heroic. We are fearful they might be illusory, falsely elevated by early death or good spin doctors or the vagaries of history. The twentieth century has taught us well that leaders once thought heroes can turn out to be tyrants. And the tacit assumption that a hero is supposed to be perfect has made many Americans turn away from the word—and the concept—altogether. The contemporary preference for words like *role model* and *mentor* and the shift from the recognition of national to local heroes are part of the transformation of the word *hero* that occurred in the second half of the twentieth century.

There is something appealing about a society that admires a range of accomplishments, that celebrates as many people as possible, that looks beyond statues of generals on horseback into small towns and the obscure corners of history for its heroes. Making *hero* more democratic, however, can be carried to an extreme. It can strip the word of all sense of the extraordinary. It can lead to an ignorance of history, a repudiation of genius, and an extreme egalitarianism disdainful of high culture and unappreciative of excellence.

We need role models and mentors and local heroes; but by limiting our heroes to people we know, we restrict our aspirations. Public heroes—or imperfect people of extraordinary achievement, courage, and greatness of soul whose reach is wider than our own—teach us to push beyond ourselves and our neighborhoods in search of models of excellence. They enlarge our imagination, teach us to think big, and expand our sense of the possible.

THE HALL OF FAME
FOR GREAT AMERICANS

TAKE COUNSEL HERE OF WISDOM, BEAUTY, POWER.
—Inscription, south gate,
Hall of Fame for Great Americans

Standing on the highest hill in New York City, looking out over the Harlem and Hudson rivers, I am surrounded by heroes: Oliver Wendell Holmes Jr., Union soldier wounded at Antietam and Chancellorsville, Supreme Court justice, and author of *The Common Law*; Susan B. Anthony, crusader for women's rights; Walter Reed, army surgeon who discovered that mosquito bites cause yellow fever; educators Mary Lyon and Emma Willard. The founder of the American public school, Horace Mann, is here, along with painter John James Audubon, orators Daniel Webster and Patrick Henry, and inventors Robert Fulton and Alexander Graham Bell.

Designed by Stanford White at the end of the nineteenth century, the Hall of Fame for Great Americans has a sweeping 630-foot outdoor colonnade, which is open on the sides and covered by a terracotta tile roof. The colonnade has niches for 102 busts. Inside, a massive dome supported by gigantic green marble pillars covers an ornate library. Under the dome are statues of mythological heroes and the names of some of the creators of Western civilization: Plato, Aristotle, Copernicus, Goethe.

Walking down the colonnade, I see the faces of our most influential presidents and bravest soldiers. Opposite Stonewall Jackson is Ulysses S. Grant. Robert E. Lee looks into the eyes of Admiral David G. Farragut. Next to Theodore Roosevelt is pacifist William Penn. I pass Ben Franklin, and think about how much he accomplished in his long and happy life, and John Quincy Adams, and remember the slave ship *Amistad* and a life devoted to principle. Past Nathaniel Hawthorne is Ralph Waldo Emerson. Under Emerson is written THE DAY IS ALWAYS HIS WHO WORKS IN IT WITH SERENITY AND GREAT AIMS. Next to Franklin Delano Roosevelt is John Philip Sousa, under whom are etched the opening notes of "The Stars and Stripes Forever." Some of the heroes have become footnotes in history: William Morton, who discovered ether; Maria Mitchell, who spotted a comet from her Nantucket observatory; physicist Albert Michelson, who in 1907 was the first American scientist to receive a Nobel Prize. Michelson developed instruments to measure more accurately the speed of light.

The brainchild of New York University's chancellor Dr. Henry Mitchell MacCracken and paid for by financier Jay Gould's daughter, the Hall of Fame for Great Americans was dedicated on Memorial Day 1901, an expression in marble and bronze of the nineteenth-century idealization of heroes. MacCracken hoped to remind Americans that they lived in a nation of accomplishment and opportunity, and he believed in recognizing teachers and poets as well as soldiers and statesmen. The centerpiece of a new campus for New York University, the hall was envisioned as the counterpart to England's Westminster Abbey and France's Pantheon, a tribute to America's power and preeminence. It would unite a nation that still remembered the Civil War and revive idealism in citizens corrupted by the Gilded Age. And it would be democratic: Any citizen could nominate candidates dead twenty-five years, with a cross-section of one hundred notable Americans picking the winners every five years.

From the start the hall was a success. Newspapers urged readers to submit nominations, editorials lauded the achievements of candidates, and citizens tried to guess the winners. With trumpets, prayers, and eulogies delivered by eminent scientists, politicians, and lawyers, induction ceremonies were lavish and dramatic. The high point of the ceremony was the unveiling of the bronze busts and inscriptions. Sculptors competed for the commission. African American Richmond Barthé carved the bust of Booker T. Washington. Underneath is engraved THE HIGHEST TEST OF A RACE IS ITS WILLINGNESS TO EXTEND A HELPING HAND TO THE LESS FORTUNATE.

In the 1970s, the hall, grown rickety, was declared unsafe and closed for several years. Mark Twain's eye disappeared and his cheek fell off. Since 1976, there have been no nominations, no elections. There is no money for busts or inscriptions. Three empty niches await the heroes elected in 1976: Clara Barton, Luther Burbank, and Andrew Carnegie. In 1992 the colonnade was fortified and the busts cleaned, a restoration which led to awards for historic preservation.

I have climbed the hill to the Hall of Fame for Great Americans many times and have rarely met any other visitors, though I once caught a couple kissing between the statues of John Paul Jones and Stonewall Jackson.

Two

THE NINETEENTH-CENTURY
IDEOLOGY OF HEROISM

The faculty of love, of admiration, is to be regarded as the sign and measure of high souls. . . . Ridicule, on the other hand, . . . is a small faculty.

—Thomas Carlyle, 1829
Essay on Voltaire

The interests of a client are small compared with the interests of the next generation. Let the next generation, then, be my client.

—Horace Mann, 1837
Letter to a friend

I n some ages there is "an extravagant worship of great men," and in others "a disposition to disbelieve in their existence," wrote British historian James Froude in 1880, in an introduction to an elegant leather-bound eight-volume anthology, *The Hundred Greatest Men.* Attuned to the rhythms of history, Froude recognized that in some ages the predilection is to deny greatness. We live in such an age.

It was not always so. "Lives of great men all remind us/We can make our lives sublime, /And, departing, leave behind us/Footprints on the sands of time," wrote Henry Wadsworth Longfellow in an 1838 poem,

"A Psalm of Life," once familiar to generations of Americans. In Britain, philosopher Thomas Carlyle published *On Heroes, Hero-Worship, and the Heroic in History* in 1841, a book highly influential in England and America. Carlyle, a close friend of James Froude, believed "No sadder proof can be given by a man of his own littleness than disbelief in great men." In America, Ralph Waldo Emerson, influenced by Carlyle, became the chief apologist for heroes and delivered a series of seven lectures on "Representative Men" in the 1840s.

Until World War I, the ideology of heroism was intact and influential in American culture. It permeated parlors, schools, farms, and factories. It could be found in novels, newspapers, and eulogies; inscribed on statues, tombstones, and public buildings; and in the exhibits at the Philadelphia Centennial Exhibition of 1876 and the Chicago World's Columbian Exposition of 1893.

The ideology of American heroism formalized in the nineteenth century could be seen in the names parents chose for their children. The Marquis de Lafayette named his son after George Washington, as did the parents of George Washington Carver. After the battle of New Orleans in the War of 1812, thousands of Americans named their sons Andrew, after Andrew Jackson. Robert Frost was named after Robert E. Lee. Born in 1882, the year Emerson died, my grandfather was named Ralph Waldo Emerson Gibbon. In 1919, the year Theodore Roosevelt died, Jackie Robinson's parents named their first son Jack Roosevelt Robinson—in remembrance of the president who had invited Booker T. Washington to the White House in 1901, a politically daring thing to do at the time.

In their new nation, nineteenth-century Americans considered the defeat of England and the writing of the Constitution heroic acts, and they celebrated the founding fathers associated with these accomplishments. Pioneers moving west named their cities Washington, Franklin, Jefferson, and Hamilton. The state capital of Wisconsin was named after James Madison, often considered the brains behind the Constitution. The streets radiating out from the capitol building in Madison were named to honor the signers of the Constitution, including Rutledge, Dickinson, Blair, and Carroll. Americans also named cities Athens,

Rome, and Corinth, as many of the founding fathers had looked to classical models like Cicero and Cato for their heroes.

In 1824 the nation exploded in a burst of patriotism when, at the age of sixty-seven, the Marquis de Lafayette returned to America. As the old warrior slowly made his way from New York City to New Orleans, bands played, church bells rang, and cannons fired along his route, each city competing to honor the marquis in the grandest manner. Veterans of the Revolutionary War and schoolchildren lined the streets, hoping to catch a glimpse of him. Lafayette made extended stops at Mount Vernon, Monticello, and Yorktown, which by then had become shrines, and had emotional reunions with John Adams and Thomas Jefferson.

An expanding democratic America produced new heroes, men of modest education but brave and self-reliant. Known as "the Hero," Andrew Jackson was as admired as George Washington, better loved than Thomas Jefferson. Dying at the Alamo in 1836, Davy Crockett became a war hero. For the rest of the nineteenth century, plays, novels, biographies, and almanacs built up Crockett's legend as a backwoods superman.

Monuments reveal this fascination with heroes. Throughout the nineteenth century, in small towns and cities, Americans created memorials. Baltimore erected a huge marble column in 1829 to honor George Washington and a series of statues to commemorate soldiers of the War of 1812, prompting John Quincy Adams to name it "The Monument City." Boston followed with the Bunker Hill Monument in 1842, when Daniel Webster gave a famous oration on worthy ancestors.

The new rural Mount Auburn Cemetery in Cambridge, Massachusetts, designed in the 1830s, was intended to be healthier and less forbidding than the dark, crowded, cholera-infested church graveyards; and the tombs, said Supreme Court Justice Joseph Story, would teach "our destiny and duty." Thirty thousand visitors a year filed through the cemetery, and teachers urged young people to visit Mount Auburn to be inspired by the heroes interred there. Poet Henry Wadsworth Longfellow is buried at Mount Auburn, as well as reformer Dorothea Dix, jurist Oliver Wendell Holmes Jr., painter Winslow Homer, statesman Henry Cabot Lodge, historian Francis Parkman, abolitionist Charles Sumner, and sculptor Horatio Greenough. Near a small chapel on the grounds of the cemetery is a huge sphinxlike Civil War monument with this inscription: AMERICAN UNION PRESERVED, AFRICAN SLAVERY DESTROYED BY THE UPRISING OF A GREAT PEOPLE, BY THE BLOOD OF FALLEN HEROES.

Throughout the nineteenth century, Americans saved the Fourth of July to dedicate their grandest monuments. On July 4, 1848, President James Polk presided over the laying of the 24,500–pound cornerstone of the Washington Monument in the nation's capital. France officially presented the Statue of Liberty to America on July 4, 1884. In her left hand, the statue holds a law book inscribed *July 4, 1776*.

On May 30, 1868, our first official Memorial Day, children all over America picked wildflowers and placed them on the graves of soldiers. In Washington, D.C., people wore mourning scarves and decorated the graves of unknown men who had died at the Battle of Bull Run. Four thousand citizens marched to the National Cemetery in Richmond and marked each of seven thousand graves with a miniature American flag. In Baltimore, disabled veterans witnessed ceremonies from horse-drawn wagons. Across the nation, governors and generals extolled bravery and self-sacrifice. Cannons fired. Ministers gave thanks for a reunited nation and the abolition of slavery and searched for God's purpose behind the slaughter of 620,000 soldiers. From Nantucket to San Francisco, from North Carolina to Texas, in large and small towns, Americans honored their Civil War dead by creating statues and memorials on an unprecedented scale. The citizens of Richmond, Virginia, laid out Monument Avenue and erected gigantic statues of men on horseback. One hundred thousand people lined the avenue in 1890 for the dedication of Lee's statue.

In 1892, New Yorkers dedicated their 84-foot Italian marble statue at Columbus Circle, President Benjamin Harrison proclaimed Columbus Day a national holiday, and Francis Bellamy wrote the Pledge of Allegiance, which was recited by millions of schoolchildren for the first time to honor Columbus. In 1893, Anton Dvorák composed his *New World Symphony*. And, enchanted by the view at the top of Colorado's

Pike's Peak, Massachusetts educator Katharine Lee Bates wrote the text for what eventually became "America the Beautiful."

Near the end of the century, Bostonians chose architect Charles Follen McKim's plans for their new Boston Public Library, a building that celebrates greatness. Looking up to the granite exterior of the second story, one sees etched in stone the names of over five hundred artists, writers, inventors, and scientists of Western civilization. Inside, on the first floor, woven into the vaulted mosaic ceiling, are the names of American cultural heroes like Emerson and Henry David Thoreau. On the top floor are John Singer Sargent's huge painted murals of the ancient hero Sir Lancelot, seeker of the Holy Grail.

Entering the gates to the Chicago World's Columbian Exposition of 1893, thirty million people could look up and read inscriptions chosen or composed by educator Charles William Eliot, among them Eliot's tribute to America's pioneers: OF MANY RACES TONGUES CREEDS AND AIMS BUT ALL HEROES OF DISCOVERY.

True Believers

Francis Parkman, George Bancroft, and John Motley, the preeminent American historians of the nineteenth century, all shared an affection for grand heroes. Parkman retraced the route of explorer René de La Salle and dramatically described General James Wolfe's conquests in the French and Indian War. Bancroft celebrated our revolutionary heroes. Motley devoted his life to describing how William of Orange defied the tyrant Philip II of Spain. Before he became president, Theodore Roosevelt wrote about the naval heroes of the War of 1812 and coauthored a series of biographies for young people called *Hero Tales from American History*.

William James, the most prominent American philosopher of the nineteenth century, gave a speech to the nation's teachers defining the purpose of a liberal education: "that it should help you to know a good man when you see him." In an 1880 article, "Great Men, Great

Thoughts, and the Environment," he defended the view that exceptional individuals shape history; woven throughout his writings is the theme that heroism makes life more significant.

One of America's best-loved poets, John Greenleaf Whittier, believed verse should build moral fiber and encourage reform. Whittier wrote a poem, "The Hero," in which he paid tribute to the life of Samuel Gridley Howe, a New England doctor who, after fighting in the 1825 Greek War of Independence, devoted the rest of his life to the blind and the deaf, becoming a prophet in special education. "You must not think because you are blind that you cannot learn as much as other children," Howe told his students. A Quaker, Whittier eulogized Howe with these lines: "Peace hath higher tests of manhood/ Than battle ever knew." When educational crusader Horace Mann visited Howe's school and observed him teaching the blind to read through a new system of raised letters, Howe and Mann became lifelong friends.

Even so somber a realist as the artist Thomas Eakins believed in heroes. Working at the end of the century, Eakins was a renowned portrait painter. While Thomas Cole and Albert Bierstadt painted heroic landscapes intended to evoke awe and reverence in exhibitions that drew huge crowds, Eakins painted the bourgeois achievers of Philadelphia, celebrating endurance, discipline, and perseverance—qualities he believed necessary to cope with the anxieties of modern life—and offering new heroes for an expanding democracy: physicians, athletes, writers, musicians, bankers.

Not everyone in the nineteenth century joined in praise of heroes. Richard Hildreth, a sophisticated New England historian, wearied of celebration and called for the depiction of "living and breathing men . . . with their faults as well as their virtues." The tough-minded British scientist Thomas Huxley told philosopher Thomas Carlyle he believed neither in creationism nor in heroes. Edgar Allan Poe wrote, "That man is no man who stands in awe of his fellow man." And even in the nineteenth century, journalists mocked the exploits of Buffalo Bill, satirized the decisions of Abraham Lincoln, and questioned the reputed heroics of General George Custer. The dominant voice of the century, however, was affirmative and confident, even if sometimes sentimental.

Of course Longfellow and other nineteenth-century idealists knew their heroes were not perfect. Even so, they believed that heroes instruct us in greatness, that heroes remind us of our better selves, and that heroes strengthen the ordinary citizen trying to live decently. Perhaps our Victorian forebears were too stuffy and too sentimental, too credulous and too preachy, but today it is the scornful who prevail.

Thomas Carlyle

Born poor in 1795, Thomas Carlyle, through an iron will and a facility with words, escaped his background to become Victorian England's preeminent philosopher and constant critic, a friend of Charles Dickens, John Stuart Mill, Ralph Waldo Emerson, and Alfred, Lord Tennyson.

The son of a pious Scottish stonemason, Carlyle prepared for the church but came to doubt its Calvinist tenets. He wrote essays but couldn't find a publisher. In 1835 he wrote the first of his three-volume *The French Revolution.* Eager for approval, he lent his only copy of the manuscript to the philosopher John Stuart Mill. Thinking it scrap paper, Mill's servant burned it. "We must endeavor to hide from him how very serious this business is to us," Carlyle told his wife. Characteristically, he started over the next day, rewrote the entire volume, and by 1837 *The French Revolution* had made him famous.

Until he died in 1881, Carlyle lashed out against atheism and materialism. He had no use for Byron's poetry, Rousseau's *Confessions,* or Voltaire's mockery. To Victorians made anxious by science, skepticism, and change, Carlyle counseled resolution, belief, and courage. He had lost faith in a Calvinist God but insisted all the more vehemently on reverence and virtue.

Essential to Carlyle's vision were heroes. Carlyle believed that all society's advances were due to individuals supremely gifted in mind and character and sent by God to console and inspire us. According to Carlyle, we have a natural tendency to pay homage to these individ-

THE NINETEENTH-CENTURY IDEOLOGY OF HEROISM

uals and feel elevated when we do; in the "radiance" of great men, "All souls feel that it is well with them."

In 1840, Carlyle delivered a series of lectures on such men. He tried to describe what they had in common and why they were heroic. In his preface to *On Heroes, Hero-Worship, and the Heroic in History,* he wrote that the history of the world is "the Biography of Great Men." Along with a fervent defense of heroism, he offered profiles of, among others, Muhammad, Shakespeare, Dante, Samuel Johnson, Martin Luther, and Oliver Cromwell.

I first discovered Thomas Carlyle in a college course on Victorian prose, when I read his essays in a thick, blue volume I still own. Forty years later, I can turn the thin, yellowing pages and find underlined with a black ballpoint pen, "The battle of belief against unbelief is the never-ending battle." For my class, I typed out a passionate defense of Carlyle, studied portraits of him, and read a biography written by his friend, historian James Froude. My paper ends with a letter written by Carlyle to his mother in 1830 declaring that our hope lies in God and work.

I try to remember what Carlyle meant to me when I was twenty, why I wrestled with his knotty sentences and puzzled over his foggy metaphysics. Why, when many of my classmates concluded that Carlyle was impossibly obscure, did I find him so compelling? Carlyle appealed to me because he had suffered and struggled, because he shunned affectation and introspection, because he respected strong leaders. I liked his disdain for money, his concern for the poor, his reverence for his mother and father, and his advice, "Do the duty that lies nearest to you." I identified with Carlyle's earnestness, his dismissal of small talk, his contempt for self-pity, his fear of science, his hunger for God.

More than anything else, Carlyle rescued me from what had been a youthful fascination with antiheroes, such as the anonymous narrator of Fyodor Dostoyevsky's *Notes from the Underground.* I sat in my sagging red chair in my dormitory room late at night, reading the memoirs of an angry middle-aged clerk who a century before had given up normal life and ordinary values and allowed his mind to run free. In pursuit of self-knowledge, the narrator denounces reason and mocks love. His suspicion of pure motives and high ideals and determination to understand himself no matter what the cost appealed to me. Carlyle became for me an alternative to self-analysis, an incentive to action, a path to affirmation. Here was a writer who was realistic yet idealistic, a prophet who had wrestled with the devil but held faith, a lapsed Calvinist who clung to God and to work.

Reading Carlyle's biographies forty years ago, I saw Dante exiled from Florence, Cromwell dying without friends, Samuel Johnson lifting himself out of poverty. Carlyle's heroes suffered, saw deeply, and subdued their fears. They had different strengths: Dante is intense, Shakespeare farseeing, Cromwell earnest, Muhammad "a silent, great soul." Each had a vision to bring to the world; each had, according to Carlyle, "a deep, great, genuine sincerity," and Carlyle admired sincerity above all else. It is not surprising that his heroes were distinguished by this quality, driven to say what they believed and to do what they thought was right.

I have since discovered that I was not the first doubter to be uplifted by Thomas Carlyle. In his own century, he was enormously influential. Frederick Law Olmsted, who created Central Park, turned to Carlyle's essays when he couldn't decide on a career. Jane Addams drew strength from Carlyle in the middle of a nervous breakdown. In the coal fields of Belgium, Vincent van Gogh read Carlyle and drew inspiration for his missionary work. When Carlyle died, Walt Whitman mourned the passing of a great man.

Adolf Hitler dealt Carlyle's reputation a fatal blow in 1945. Slowly becoming squeezed between the Russian and American armies, Hitler took to reading from Carlyle's *Frederick the Great* and dreamed of eluding defeat as Frederick had in the winter of 1761–62. Unfairly, Carlyle became labeled a forerunner of fascism—though Carlyle always insisted that warriors and leaders had to be virtuous.

Today Carlyle does not find a ready reception in a skeptical age in which the very notion of the public hero is suspect. His tortuous style makes difficult reading. In a century that has suffered the savagery of Mussolini, Hitler, Stalin, Pol Pot, Mao Tse-tung, Saddam Hussein, and Osama bin Laden, we have reason to be suspicious of hero worship.

Carlyle was opinionated and uncompromising, not an easy man; but he was original and sincere, and we can respect his fervor and his resolute attempt to find meaning as democracy, science, and materialism transformed the century.

Ralph Waldo Emerson

Like Carlyle, Emerson spent his life searching for greatness. After his first wife died, Emerson traveled to England to meet Carlyle and later introduced America to his writings. Carlyle and Emerson both had religious fathers and were raised Calvinists. Each rejected Calvinism's gloom and fatalism and embraced heroes, but neither forgot its strenuousness and moral seriousness. Emerson believed that history was "the biography of a few stout and earnest persons" but did not place heroes on so high a pedestal as did Carlyle. Further, Emerson believed that ordinary citizens could acquire heroic qualities.

In his preface to seven lectures on *Representative Men*, Emerson is fervent in his plea that we think about heroes. He also tries to describe the qualities of the hero. Like Carlyle, Emerson says a hero must be sincere; Martin Luther and John Milton both radiated sincerity. Additionally, Emerson places a particularly high premium on persistence. "All men," says Emerson, "have wandering impulses, fits and starts of generosity." The hero perseveres and has complete self-confidence in his ideals, even when he is misunderstood.

Valuing intuition and enthusiasm, Emerson writes, "Heroism feels and never reasons." Both Emerson and Carlyle worried that too much introspection could preclude action and affirmation. To work, to act, and to believe were more important than to reflect endlessly. Both men also advised austerity. Their heroes value simplicity and scorn comfort and wealth.

One of the significant influences on Emerson's life was his aunt, Mary Moody Emerson, an eccentric visionary. She wrote many letters to Emerson when he was a young man that he copied into his journals. One of her favorite injunctions was "Always do what you are afraid to do." Emerson never forgot this and counted boldness chief among the heroic qualities.

Like everyone else in the nineteenth century, Emerson was mesmerized by Napoleon and wrote a long essay trying to understand him. He admired Napoleon as a soldier of courage, an intellectual, a reformer, and a rationalist but concluded that Napoleon did not have virtue. Emerson was not a pacifist. According to literary critic Edmund Berry, "Emerson's hero-worship always retained something of the admiration of the schoolboy for the hero of the battlefield." Emerson venerated the soldiers of Rome he read about in Plutarch's *Lives,* such as Cato and Marcus Aurelius. He also believed that war releases us from the ordinary, taps hidden reserves of bravery, and broadens our potential. But Emerson's unconditional love of virtue was stronger than his awe of military bravery, and in Emerson's worldview, Napoleon could not qualify as a hero.

In addition to sincerity, persistence, intuition, austerity, bravery, and virtue, the Emersonian hero has independence of thought. No one read more voraciously than Emerson in the pursuit of ideas, yet no one insisted more vigorously on the importance of originality and independence. Emerson's more popular essays are still included in the canon of American literature taught in most high schools, and students frequently cite them as evidence that having heroes is incompatible with being an individual. At a school I visited in Pittsburgh, a boy stood up and quoted this epigram: "Envy is ignorance . . . imitation is suicide." In Cleveland, a girl surprised her classmates by quoting perfectly: "The great man is he who in the midst of the crowd keeps with perfect sweetness the independence of solitude." Individualism is, of course, uneasy with the notion of emulation. And Emerson himself was ambivalent. While he copied in his notebooks quotations from great books and wrote essays on representative men, he also castigated intellectual servility. Emerson preached individuality and believed that in the end each of us must chart his or her own course, but he also believed that heroes guide us on our journey. It is curious how both Emerson and Carlyle combine hero worship with self-reliance.

Carlyle's heroes seem unapproachable. Reading Emerson, on the other hand, we feel we can appropriate the attributes of the great, make them our own, and become heroic in our own lives.

Heroes of Education

Charles William Eliot

In 1869, four years after the assassination of Abraham Lincoln and the same year Ulysses S. Grant became president of the United States, Charles William Eliot became president of Harvard College, at the age of thirty-five. Eliot would hold the office for forty years and become one of the most prominent educational reformers of the nineteenth century, not only at Harvard but across the nation.

Eliot pried Harvard College from its parochial Boston roots and carried it to national eminence, eliminating compulsory chapel, cutting back Greek and Latin, championing chemistry and physics, and building a prominent faculty, a national student body, an elaborate system of electives, and a graduate school. On the occasion of Eliot's seventieth birthday in 1904, the *Harvard Crimson,* in an uncharacteristic burst of praise, declared, "We are proud of him and glad of him, and to him we accord the reverence that even the worst of us in his heart feels for the good and great." In an age when college presidents had significant influence in America, Eliot was a national figure, a major voice in world affairs, an adviser to the nation's presidents. A commanding orator, he gave speeches to audiences all over America, and people who heard him reported they believed themselves to be in the presence of a great man.

Eliot worked throughout his life to improve public high schools and to make education both more rigorous and more democratic. He edited *The Harvard Classics,* an inexpensive fifty-volume edition of world literature, so that all Americans, especially those who could not afford a college education, would have the opportunity to read the works of great writers, scientists, and philosophers. "Fifteen minutes a day" with these books, said Eliot, would provide a person with "a liberal education." Marketed by Collier's Publishing as "President Eliot's five-foot shelf," the collection became a best-seller.

Americans in the nineteenth century turned to Eliot when seeking words to decorate their new buildings and monuments. Chiseled in concrete on the Samuel Dexter Memorial Gate leading into Harvard Yard

are Eliot's words, ENTER TO GROW IN WISDOM, and, leading out, DEPART
TO SERVE BETTER THY COUNTRY AND THY KIND. Words composed or
selected by Eliot are inscribed on monuments in Boston, such as the
Robert Gould Shaw Memorial, as well as on national public buildings,
such as Union Station in Washington, D.C. "Anyone who stops to admire a classical civic building in an American city," writes Brian Burrell
in his 1997 book *The Words We Live By,* "especially a building that
contains inspirational inscriptions, is contemplating the legacy of Charles
McKim, Daniel Burnham [architects], and Charles Eliot, three men who
nurtured an inspired vision of the nation's greatness."

Charles William Eliot was a nineteenth-century man: a true believer
in God, progress, and service, and the idea that leisure hours might in
part be devoted to education and reflection. Indifferent to radio and
motion pictures—the new inventions that would shape the culture of
the twentieth century—he preferred reading and rowing and climbing
the hills of Maine's Mount Desert Island. He died at the age of ninety-
two at his summer home in Northeast Harbor, Maine. In his eulogy to
Eliot, George A. Gordon of Boston's Old South Church said simply,
"He was our great moral hero."

Horace Mann

Horace Mann grew up on a farm just outside the small town of Franklin,
Massachusetts, a town named after Benjamin Franklin. From an early
age, Mann cut wood, raked hay, and pounded flax. "Industry, or diligence became my second nature," he later wrote. As a boy, he read
Noah Webster's *Grammar* and some of the 116 books Ben Franklin
had donated to the town. Mann also experienced sorrow. His father
died of tuberculosis, and his brother Stephen died four years later in
1810, when Horace was fourteen years old. Stephen had been swimming
on Sunday; according to the Calvinist minister, Nathanael Emmons,
he had desecrated the Sabbath and in his unconverted state would go
to hell. Bitterly, Mann turned against Calvinism and developed a lifelong antipathy toward ministers who preach a punishing God.

As a teenager, Mann decided that only nearby Brown University
could offer an escape from a life of farming. To prepare for Brown, he

studied Greek, Latin, and mathematics and in 1816 entered as a sophomore. He came to love books and revere knowledge. As valedictorian in 1819, he delivered a commencement-day oration titled "The Gradual Advancement of the Human Species in Dignity and Happiness," a speech that reflected his growing interest in humanitarian causes. After graduation, Mann studied law in Litchfield, Connecticut, moved to Dedham, Massachusetts, and was later elected to the state legislature.

When Thomas Jefferson and John Adams both died on the Fourth of July 1826, towns all over America solemnly took note of this amazing coincidence and paid tribute to the last of the founding fathers in the weeks following. In Dedham, the town leaders asked Horace Mann to prepare an address. Before a large crowd, which included Adams's son, President John Quincy Adams, Mann praised Jefferson as the author of the Declaration of Independence and Adams as a prophet and peacemaker. John Quincy Adams would later write that Mann's eulogy was "of splendid composition and lofty eloquence."

While a member of the State House of Representatives and later as president of the Massachusetts Senate, Mann learned how to craft legislation. He attended Emerson's lectures and heard the sermons of the well-known Unitarian minister William Ellery Channing, as well as those of Methodist minister Edward Taylor, the prototype for Father Mapple in *Moby-Dick*. At heart, Mann was an idealist, always on the lookout for good causes. He once said to a friend, "All my boyish castles in the air had reference to doing something for the benefit of mankind."

Mann's commitment to philanthropy was deepened by catastrophe. In 1832 Mann's wife, Charlotte, to whom he was deeply devoted, died at age twenty-three. Disconsolate, Mann isolated himself and sank into a depression that robbed his energy and sapped his idealism. He found it hard to believe in a benevolent God and an ordered universe. Only gradually did he recover. He vowed that he would honor Charlotte's memory by listening to his conscience, helping mankind, and working without respite.

In 1837, at age forty-one, Mann retired from politics, closed his law office, and accepted an appointment as secretary of the Massachusetts Board of Education, a job that paid a small salary and came with no

formal power. In his private journal, he wrote, "The path of usefulness is open before me. . . . God grant me an annihilation of selfishness, a mind of wisdom, the heart of benevolence."

For the next eleven years, from 1837 to 1848, Mann traveled all over
Massachusetts, peering into dilapidated schoolhouses, perusing anti-
quated textbooks, and listening to demoralized teachers. He made himself an expert on reading techniques and school construction and studied
the best ways to teach geography, science, bookkeeping, and hygiene.
To increase his knowledge, he traveled to Europe, observing how highly-
trained German schoolmasters maintained discipline without corporal
punishment and taught reading to very young pupils. He started the
Common School Journal, a professional biweekly that contained model
lesson plans for teachers. In speech after speech, he tried to convince a
skeptical citizenry that their schools were languishing and needed reform.

During his term as Massachusetts Secretary of Education, Mann produced twelve impassioned and detailed reports that were circulated all
over America and convinced other states to implement reforms. In these
reports, which eventually found their way to France, England, and South
America, he maintained that quality tax-supported public schools could
produce efficient workers, promote health, eliminate poverty, cut crime,
and unite a society fragmented by class and ethnicity.

Students, he argued, deserved a stimulating curriculum and well-
written textbooks adjusted to different age levels. Mann believed that
schools should teach students how to read, spell, and write, but their
more important goal was to build character. Early examples, he said,
were powerful examples, and lessons taught in classrooms would last
a lifetime. Mann made large claims for schools, frequently quoting from
Proverbs: "Train up a child in the way he should go; and when he is
old, he will not depart from it."

Like Jefferson, Mann believed that training in character would produce responsible and virtuous citizens who would make the republic flour-
ish. "Never will wisdom preside in the halls of legislation," he wrote,
"until Common Schools . . . shall create a more far-seeing intelligence
and a pure morality than has ever existed among communities of men."

To build character, Mann recommended that students study exemplary lives. He praised the study of "biography, especially the biography of the great and good, who have risen by their own exertions from poverty and obscurity to eminence and usefulness." In his second report to the voters of Massachusetts, he talked about how reading uplifting books could inspire the young student: "Sages imbue him with their wisdom; martyrs inspire him by their example; and the authors of discoveries . . . become his teachers." Rather than advocating vocational education for the poor and classical education for the privileged, Mann championed a revolutionary idea: a high level of general education for *all* citizens.

Mann's vision required that teachers have intellectual and moral power. They must not only know their subject thoroughly but command a wide range of pedagogical methods and be able to preserve order. He persuaded the state legislature to create teachers' colleges and to increase salaries. Regularly he celebrated the profession: "Teaching is the most difficult of all arts and the profoundest of all sciences," he wrote in his First Annual Report.

In his eleven-year campaign to improve public schools, Mann would make enemies: wealthy people who favored private schools, workers who depended on their children's labor, orthodox ministers fearful of a Godless curriculum, local politicians resentful of state control, teachers who believed in corporal punishment. But he consoled himself with the belief that "the molding of minds is about the noblest work that man or angel can do."

Mann was not perfect—and we know about his flaws because he kept a detailed journal. He complained, indulged in self-pity, demonized his enemies. On his way to Nantucket to give a speech, he admitted he was sick of education. And of course, like many crusaders, he made excessive claims for his cause. Behind the soaring rhetoric about the transforming power of education lay a melancholy man, unable to sleep, plagued by illness, morbidly attached to the memory of his first wife. Like many great individuals, even reformers and humanitarians, Mann was ambitious, sometimes egotistical. He liked being the center of attention and at times seems to have had a martyr complex. Emerson made this trenchant remark about genius in his journals: "Take egotism out, and you would castrate the benefactors. Luther, Mirabeau, Napoleon, John Adams, Andrew Jackson; and our nearer eminent public servants—Greeley, Theodore Parker, Ward Beecher, Horace Mann, Garrison—would lose their vigour."

But I find Mann heroic, worthy of the statue of him that stands in front of the Boston State House. Though born poor, he never craved wealth. He lived on a small salary in dank boardinghouses, traveled at his own expense, and gave his savings to the cause of education. Even though he rejected Calvinism and became a Unitarian, he retained his Christian charity. He had a conscience that could never be quiet and a belief in America's future that he never relinquished. Idealistic, he combined the incisive mind of a good lawyer with the politician's ability to maneuver.

Others had championed public schools. Horace Mann was the first to articulate a unified vision of how schools could transform, unite, and preserve the new republic. Most important, he tried to implement his vision. He traveled hundreds of miles by horseback and stagecoach, speaking in towns and cities until his body collapsed and his voice gave out. He roamed the halls of the Massachusetts State Capitol, asking legislators to support his educational bills. At night he wrote the reports that even today demonstrate an impressive range of knowledge, as he shifts from physical education to choral music to phonics.

At the end of Mann's crusade, schoolhouses had been improved, teacher salaries increased, the school year lengthened, and new high schools established. Mann was that rare hero, both practical dreamer and political idealist. To Carlyle, sincerity was the most important quality of a hero. To Emerson, it was perseverance. Mann had both.

Today Mann is remembered as the father of American public education, but his career did not end when he resigned his post as secretary. When John Quincy Adams died of a stroke on the floor of the House of Representatives in 1848, Mann was picked to fill his seat. Mann crusaded against slavery with the same zeal he had exhibited in his fight for public schools. Defeated in a bid for the Massachusetts governorship, he took over as president of Antioch College in Yellow Springs, Ohio, in 1853 and for five years fought an uphill battle to solidify a school committed to coeducation, equal opportunity for African Americans, and a non-sectarian Christian morality. Two months before he died, Mann gave a last speech in which he advised the senior class of Antioch, "I beseech you to treasure up in your hearts these my parting words: Be ashamed to die until you have won some victory for humanity."

JOHN BRIDGE, PURITAN

At the north entrance to Cambridge Common, a small park in Cambridge, Massachusetts, stands John Bridge, a Puritan who settled in the area in the early 1630s, supervised its first public school, and served as church deacon, selectman, and representative to the Great and General Court. According to the records of the Cambridge Historical Commission, the park is what is left of the land originally owned in common by the Proprietors of Cambridge. Throughout its history, dating back to 1630, the Common has served during various periods as a cow pasture, a site for military drills, and a place for holding elections, religious debates, and public ceremonies. In 1775, Minutemen assembled on the Common before the Battle of Bunker Hill. Today, veterans assemble here before the city's annual Memorial Day parade.

I have always been fascinated with artifacts that connect me to the past. I like to know where Washington stopped for dinner, where Lincoln attended church, where Stonewall Jackson was shot. On a recent car trip from Cincinnati to New Orleans, I read all the plaques along the Natchez Trace, the old Indian trail that runs from Natchez, Mississippi, to Nashville, Tennessee. Reading these markers, I think of horses and fur trappers, of tall forests and wild turkeys, of small churches and isolated farmhouses, of danger and disease and brief lives, of thousands of fellow human beings who walked the ground before automobiles, asphalt, telephone lines, fast food stands, and motels. I like to imagine lost worlds, vanished times.

Of course, one purpose of monuments and inscriptions is to bind us together as a nation. The inscriptions on Union Station and the adjacent post office in Washington, D.C., are intended to make us grateful for speedy rail transportation and communication. In New York Harbor, the Statue of Liberty reminds us that we are a nation of immigrants.

Memorials also reveal our conflicts. To get Arthur Ashe's statue on Monument Avenue in Richmond, Virginia, required long debates. In 1992, Congress changed the name of the Custer Battlefield National Monument to the Little Bighorn Battlefield. More recently, Americans argued about whether Franklin Delano Roosevelt should be immortalized in his wheelchair smoking a cigarette, whether women who fought in World War II merit a separate monument, and whether the faces in the photograph of three white firemen raising the flag at the World Trade Center should be changed in a statue to reflect a multicutural society.

Memorials show the changing face of the American hero. Beyond John Bridge, at the west entrance to Cambridge Common, are three cannons captured from the British during the Revolutionary War and a plaque commemorating the place where George Washington assembled the first Continental army. In the center of the Common stands Abraham Lincoln on the first level of a two-tiered monument, topped by an unnamed Union soldier who overlooks all of Cambridge. On the base of the memorial is the Gettysburg Address.

All but one of the memorials in the park were erected in the nineteenth century. Diagonally across from John Bridge is a new statue honoring the victims of the Irish potato famine. Underneath the gaunt figure of a father reaching out to his wife, who is clutching their sick child, are the words NEVER AGAIN SHOULD A PEOPLE STARVE IN A WORLD OF PLENTY. There is a movement in America today to honor the victims of history.

Nearly every day I walk by the statue of John Bridge. The inscription from Isaiah suggests that by waiting upon the Lord, we can have our energy renewed, our spirit lifted, our confidence restored. We can perform deeds undreamed of in uninspired hours.

In my speeches about heroes, I argue that by studying the lives of great men and women, we can improve and enlarge our own lives. I acknowledge that heroes are molded by parents and inspired by mentors, that they emerge out of crisis and are shaped by suffering. I do not mention religion. Yet as I read the biographies of great Americans, I keep bumping into God.

As I pull back the curtain on the lives of hundreds of heroic men and women, I see no easy victories. I see much suffering and many failures. I see courage emerging out of fear, confidence laced with doubt, nobility mixed with pettiness. I find achievement gained after great struggle, serenity after despair. More and more, I find heroes fortified by religious belief. Walking by the statue of John Bridge on Cambridge Common, I am reminded of how essential religion has been to our culture, of how powerfully it has molded our past, and I think about the many heroes of American history who turned to God to renew their strength and transform their lives.

Three

OUR HELP IN AGES PAST

On my arrival in the United States it was the religious aspect of the country that first struck my eye. . . . Among us, I had seen the spirit of religion and the spirit of freedom almost always move in contrary directions. Here I found them united intimately with one another; they reigned together on the same soil.

—Alexis de Tocqueville, 1835

It is one of my favorite thoughts, that God manifests himself to mankind in all wise, good, humble, generous, great and magnanimous men.

—Johann Lavater, circa 1790

O ur first American hero, George Washington, believed that God favored American independence. In his First Inaugural Address, he referred to Divine Providence five times. To his stepson he gave a copy of Sir Richard Steele's best-seller *The Christian Hero*. John Adams and his son, John Quincy Adams, devoured sermons. In office, each did what was right rather than what was popular. It is hard to imagine Theodore Roosevelt or Franklin Delano Roosevelt without religion. Theodore taught Sunday school and adopted "Onward, Christian Soldiers" as his campaign song. Sent to Groton at age fourteen, Franklin Roosevelt listened to the sermons of his headmaster, the Reverend Endicott Peabody, who extolled bravery, public service, and self-sacrifice. Can we talk about the idealism of Woodrow Wilson and ignore his Presbyterian upbringing? Can we understand the integrity of Harry Truman without knowing that one of his favorite books was *The Pilgrim's Progress?*

Many of our most influential presidents have been molded by religion. So have some of our greatest reformers. Because of God, Sojourner Truth took to the road and fought for emancipation and women's rights. Harriet Beecher Stowe believed divine inspiration drove her to write *Uncle Tom's Cabin.* The fervor of Lucretia Mott came from her faith in the Quaker inner light. Without God, Clara Barton would not have tended wounded soldiers in the Civil War and founded the Red Cross.

The most prominent educators of the nineteenth century were also devout. Noah Webster's *Blue-Backed Speller* and William McGuffey's *Reader*s mingled religious instruction with heroic biographies. Webster dedicated his dictionary to "That great and benevolent Being . . . who has given me strength and resolution." Driven by his Unitarian faith, Horace Mann worked to make education available to all Americans.

Many American capitalists were made more charitable by religion. An earnest Baptist, John D. Rockefeller accumulated money and then gave much of it away. In his essay "The Gospel of Wealth," Andrew Carnegie wrote, "He who dies rich dies disgraced."

In thinking about the relationship between heroism and religion in American history, we should not forget that for most of our history the Bible was our first textbook. Until World War I, many of the best-selling books in America, from *Ben Hur* to *In His Steps,* revolved around the Bible. Among other things, the Bible is a collection of hero tales: David slaying Goliath, Esther saving the Jews from the Persians, a father welcoming home the Prodigal Son, the Samaritan binding up the wounds of a man he does not know. The Bible is a collection of heroic biographies, maxims, and parables. Jesus was undoubtedly the most influential hero in early American history: an example of high achievement, self-sacrifice, and bravery. Later, even Unitarians and Deists, who doubted that Jesus was divine, honored and imitated him.

* * *

THE FIRST BIOGRAPHIES in America, written by Cotton Mather in the early eighteenth century, were tributes to preachers. The Puritans looked up to such ministers as the well-known theologian Thomas Hooker, with whom John Bridge first came to America. In a world in which men and women died suddenly and nature was only dimly understood, early Americans depended on preachers for explanations and consolation when diphtheria epidemics cut down their children and storms leveled their crops. Highly educated, preachers could read Hebrew and Greek, make sense of the Bible, distinguish between right and wrong, and set down guidelines for salvation.

Perceived by their parishioners as close to God, Colonial ministers had power unimaginable today. When the Anglican evangelist George Whitefield came to the colonies from England in 1739, people from New York to Charleston rushed to town squares and meadows to hear him preach in the open air. Whitefield was written up in local newspapers, and those who heard him speak reported that his voice could be heard over crowds of twenty thousand. In his fiery sermons, Whitefield warned of the dangers of sin and the need for a new birth. He ignited a religious revival known as the Great Awakening that swept through the colonies in the 1740s and thus became a hero to thousands of colonists. While Whitefield's emotional sermons and clear-cut answers alienated established ministers, who saw their authority questioned, his dramatic preaching style and his message that any sinner could be saved on the spot influenced future evangelists like Charles Finney, Dwight Moody, Billy Sunday, and Billy Graham. Whitefield intended to bring people to their knees and make them cry out for God, but he also insisted that acts of charity follow conversion, and he raised thousands of dollars for an orphanage in Savannah.

From the first, Colonial preachers had subjected their parishioners to a worldview favorable to heroism. The Puritans believed that work was a form of prayer. "Whatsoever thy hand findeth to do, do *it* with thy might." From a God who told Americans they were inhabitants of a City on a Hill, an example to the world, came a sense of destiny and a work ethic that produced extraordinary effort. Out of a sense of divine destiny came a belief in progress and an unshakable confidence. From a God who offered explanation for suffering and death came resilience. Most powerfully, Puritanism encouraged heroism by promising help. Through God, promised the preacher, we can end indifference, conquer fatigue, overcome pessimism, and transform our lives.

But Puritanism did more than encourage heroic effort. To the chaos of life, it gave moral order and immediate purpose, imposing meaning on the mundane and reminding Americans that life was short and serious, death certain, and the afterlife unpredictable. Each person had a calling, and at the end of life each person would be accountable; a watchful, judging God would reward the faithful, the brave, and the good.

Puritan ministers subjected Americans to an exacting, even punishing moral code, insisting on purity of thought and exemplary conduct. Eschewing frivolity and hedonism, they were relentless in demanding high-mindedness. Though commonly used in the nineteenth century, the term *high-minded* is not fashionable today. To the modern ear, it sounds self-righteous, even naive. I know of no better definition of high-mindedness and no more powerful antidote to cynicism than Paul's tribute to idealism at the end of his letter to the Philippians: "Finally, brothers, whatever is true, whatever is honorable, whatever is just, whatever is pure, whatever is lovely, whatever is gracious, if there is any excellence and if there is anything worthy of praise, think about these things." High-mindedness is another gift of religion to the ideology of heroism.

Puritan fervor had waned by the middle of the eighteenth century as Congregationalists in New England diminished in relative power and Baptists, Methodists, Quakers, Presbyterians, Episcopalians, and Unitarians competed for church members. By the end of the nineteenth century, America as a whole had become less Protestant, as Roman Catholics emigrated from Ireland, Italy, Germany, and Latin America; Eastern Orthodox came from Greece and the Balkans; Jews arrived from Russia and Eastern Europe; and Chinese came from Asia—bringing new traditions and new heroes to an increasingly diverse nation. But the spirit of Puritanism had given America its religious foundation.

When Alexis de Tocqueville visited America in the 1830s, he noted that the "spirit of religion" and the "spirit of freedom" coexisted. The Protestant preachers that he heard during his visit were enormously influential throughout the nineteenth century. Protestantism could be harsh and authoritarian but it also had a kinder democratic side, insisting that before God all are equal. Protestant egalitarianism called forth charity, stimulated idealism, and prompted humanitarianism. Many heroes of nineteenth-century America were motivated by religious idealism. Behind many of our reform movements— abolitionism, prison reform, and the creation of public schools—lay thousands of Protestant sermons. By providing a sense of destiny, an extraordinary work ethic, consolation, purpose, hope, high-mindedness, and charity, nineteenth-century Protestantism encouraged heroism.

Women Warriors

In patriarchal nineteenth-century America, women were free to marry, teach school, and work in factories. They were expected to have large families and often died young, due to the complications of childbirth. Those born privileged could patronize the fine arts and play uplifting music. If unusually daring, they crusaded. But they were not considered leaders or given center stage. Even in the early meetings of the American Anti-Slavery Society, women could only sit in the balcony and watch the debates. As Elizabeth Cady Stanton discovered, they could not speak or vote in male-dominated humanitarian organizations, much less in the U.S. Congress. Women could not be warriors, explorers, orators, or politicians—the normal routes to heroism in the nineteenth century.

Noah Webster and William McGuffey featured women as wives and mothers. When Mason Locke Weems looked for subjects for his best-selling juvenile biographies at the beginning of the nineteenth century, he did not think of women. Carlyle did not refer to women in his lectures in the 1840s. As its title indicates, no women are celebrated in Emerson's essays on heroism, *Representative Men*. New Yorkers at the dedication of the Hall of Fame for Great Americans in 1901 watched as twenty-nine plaques were unveiled, but not one celebrated a woman.

Unable to vote or hold office, generally excluded from the ministry, law, and medicine, and discouraged from speaking in public, women in nineteenth-century America—many of them motivated by their religious faith—channeled their heroic impulses into altruism and reform. Between the American Revolution and the Spanish-American War, America became a better nation, a more humanitarian nation, in part through the efforts of women of extraordinary achievement, courage, and greatness of soul, who tried to improve prisons, abolish slavery, and forge equality for women. Although not fully recognized in their time, these women not only reflected the ideology of heroism in nineteenth-century America but helped shape it.

Influenced by Unitarian minister William Ellery Channing, one of her heroes, Dorothea Dix wrote a book of uplifting poetry as a young teacher. In 1841, Dix was asked to teach a Sunday school class in a cold East Cambridge jail. Horrified by the conditions she found there, she undertook to visit every jail in Massachusetts, where she found mentally ill inmates "bound with chains, lacerated with ropes, scourged with rods." Dix reported her findings to the Massachusetts legislature and initiated a movement to reform treatment of the mentally ill and build new hospitals for them. She raised money from private donors in Massachusetts, then took her cause on the road, traveling ten thousand miles through other states in three years and going abroad in 1854 to meet with Pope Pius II and Queen Victoria. Dix volunteered during the Civil War and became the Union's Superintendent of Female Nurses. Accustomed to having her way, she alienated the Union medical establishment while managing to raise money and secure supplies. After the war, she continued to visit hospitals and prisons. By the end of Dix's forty-year crusade, the number of mental hospitals in America in 1881 had grown from 13 to 123.

Lucretia Mott grew up in Nantucket, where women had to be independent because men would disappear for years, chasing whales from

South American waters to the islands of Japan. After attending a Quaker boarding school in New York, Mott moved to Philadelphia with her husband (a reformer in his own right), whose encouragement helped make possible one of the great humanitarian careers in American history.

Unlike most religious denominations, Quakers permitted women to speak in meeting, and in 1821 Mott was officially recognized as a minister. She inveighed against slavery at Quaker meetings all over America, urging audiences to boycott products produced by slave labor. From 1825 until Emancipation, she refused to use cotton or sugarcane. Defying angry, sometimes violent mobs, she demanded an end to slavery and hid runaway slaves in her Philadelphia home.

Mott also advocated fair treatment of women—particularly after the World Anti-Slavery Convention refused to recognize her as a delegate. In 1848 she delivered the opening address at the first Women's Rights Convention in Seneca Falls, New York, and with Elizabeth Cady Stanton pushed though a Declaration of Sentiments that stated: "We hold these truths to be self-evident: that all men and women are created equal." Mott demanded for women equal pay for equal work, access to jobs and schools, and the right to vote and hold office. After the Civil War, she fought for the 15th amendment that gave African Americans the right to vote, helped raise money for Swarthmore College, and aided southern elementary schools that educated former slaves. Elizabeth Cady Stanton called Mott her mentor, noting in her diary, "I shall in future try to imitate her noble example." Frederick Douglass singled Mott out in his autobiography as a leading abolitionist and a woman of goodness and courage.

Before the Civil War, Harriet Tubman, who was called the Moses of her people, made nineteen trips south to rescue nearly three hundred slaves, wearing different disguises and carrying a pistol. So effective was she that Maryland planters offered $40,000 for her capture. She addressed abolitionist rallies, supported the radical John Brown, and condemned Abraham Lincoln for his initial refusal to free slaves. During the war, she served as spy, scout, and nurse and witnessed the attack on Fort Wagner, where Colonel Robert Gould Shaw's 54th

African American Regiment fell. While well-known in abolitionist circles, Tubman was never given the recognition in her lifetime that Frederick Douglass eventually received in his, and for many years the government denied her a pension for her service in the Civil War. In a letter in 1868, Douglass wrote to Tubman: "I have received much encouragement at every step of the way. You, on the other hand, have labored in a private way. I have wrought in the day—you the night. . . . The midnight sky and the silent stars have been the witness to your devotion to freedom and of your heroism."

As THE NINETEENTH CENTURY progressed, women did not gain access to the traditional hero-making professions, but those who became reformers and humanitarians received increasing respect and some recognition. Abraham Lincoln credited Harriet Beecher Stowe with starting the Civil War because so many Americans read *Uncle Tom's Cabin*. After calling Clarissa (Clara) Barton the Angel of the Battlefield, the chief Union Army surgeon at the Battle of Antietam wrote that Barton was more of a hero than General McClellan, the commander of the Army of the Potomac.

By the end of the century, suffragist Susan B. Anthony, once vilified, had traveled all over America giving interviews to hundreds of newspaper reporters. Anthony's friend and fellow reformer, Elizabeth Cady Stanton, had become a celebrity whom Americans compared to Martha Washington and Queen Victoria. In a letter Stanton wrote to her daughter, she remarked, "You would laugh to see how everywhere the girls flock around me for a kiss, a curl, an autograph."

At the start of the twentieth century, Jane Addams's efforts on behalf of immigrants gained her the accolade of heroine. Up until World War I, however, no woman commanded the adulation given Robert E. Lee or Abraham Lincoln. No woman in nineteenth-century America had the status of Joan of Arc in fifteenth-century France or of Queen Elizabeth in sixteenth-century England. In nineteenth-century America, heroism and greatness were linked to public life, physical bravery, war, and gender. Not until the feminist movement of the late twentieth century would American women be given full access to public life and fair representation in our history books. Not until then would altruists and reformers compete with soldiers and political leaders for the title of hero.

No Struggle, No Progress

Frederick Douglass was a true believer in Divine Providence, certain that God had saved him from a cruel master and guided him north to eliminate slavery. Also a true believer in heroism, Douglass took his last name from Ellen Douglass, the heroine of Sir Walter Scott's novel *The Lady of the Lake,* a book celebrating Scottish rebels. As a boy, he read the Bible and a school textbook, the *Columbian Orator,* reciting uplifting speeches, among them those of Cicero and William Pitt. From the *Columbian Orator,* he learned that some past leaders and philosophers thought slavery wrong. In 1852 he wrote a novella, *The Heroic Slave,* that extolled Madison Washington, the leader of a slave revolt.

Douglass never knew his white father or his slave mother. Raised by his grandmother, he learned to read and write while a house servant in Baltimore. When his master died, he was sent to a Maryland plantation as a field hand, where he was worked like an animal and beaten without provocation. He thought of suicide but instead retaliated, striking down a sadistic overseer and eventually escaping to New England. In New Bedford, Massachusetts, Douglass was influenced by William Lloyd Garrison's abolitionist newspaper, *The Liberator,* and joined the antislavery crusade.

Douglass wrote his autobiography in 1845. In chilling detail, he described cold and hunger, unremitting work, brutal floggings, casual murder. The book made him famous. Braving hostile crowds and threats to his life, he gave speeches in New England and the Midwest. In Indiana, a mob broke his arm. But in Great Britain, he was treated as a celebrity. When he returned to America, he bought his freedom and started his own newspaper, *North Star.* He also became active in the

Underground Railroad, hiding fugitive slaves in his Rochester, New York, home and forming a friendship with John Brown.

In the nineteenth century—an era of advancing democracy and idealism—heroism was linked to gender. It was also linked to race. None of the original twenty-nine plaques in the Hall of Fame for Great Americans honors an African American. Yet Douglass was an electrifying orator, the most famous African American of his time.

And he looked like a hero. Solid, well-built, and handsome, Douglass stood over six feet tall, dressed like a gentleman, and had the powerful voice and flamboyance of an actor. Elizabeth Cady Stanton described him as "an African prince." A newspaper reporter compared him to the Trojan war hero Ajax. Douglass also acted like a hero, standing before hostile mobs that called him a liar, speaking the truth about a life filled with struggle and suffering.

Douglass welcomed the Civil War, believing that only a violent struggle could end slavery. He met with President Lincoln and demanded emancipation and the creation of Negro regiments to fight in the Union Army. After the war, he continued to agitate, castigating an apathetic America for abandoning the slaves they had freed and denouncing disenfranchisement, segregation, and lynching. He died in 1895, collapsing after attending a women's-suffrage meeting.

In an era that looked up to the self-made man, Douglass rose from slavery to fame. In an America that was nationalistic, he was passionately patriotic, recruiting soldiers for the Union Army. An unsparing critic of racism, he believed in progress, in the Declaration of Independence, in the Constitution.

Though he seemed a middle-class gentleman, Douglass also had an edge. He castigated Christian ministers who condoned slavery, praised John Brown's attack on the U.S. arsenal at Harper's Ferry, and criticized Abraham Lincoln for waiting so long to issue the Emancipation Proclamation. When Robert E. Lee died, he did not mourn. He never forgave the South or forgot what the war was about. On Memorial Day 1878 he reminded the country that "there was a right side and wrong side in the late war which no sentiment ought to cause us to forget."

Even in the nineteenth century, when African Americans were kept out of public life and considered inferior, Douglass was eventually celebrated in his lifetime as an ex-slave who had suffered and triumphed, as a reformer who spoke truth to power, as a man who dined with presidents and kept to his principles. He operated as the conscience of America. After his death, both Booker T. Washington and W.E.B. Du Bois named him as a role model. As a young man, A. Philip Randolph, later head of the Brotherhood of Sleeping Car Porters and one of the most important civil rights leaders before Martin Luther King Jr., read Douglass's speeches and decided to become a reformer.

In contemporary America, Douglass's reputation soars and his influence remains strong, despite those historians who criticize him for embellishing his story. Douglass's autobiography is as widely read in schools today as Ben Franklin's. Not only did Douglass spend his life fighting slavery and racism, he was among the earliest and most persistent male champions of women's rights.

Though independent, aggressive, and ambitious, Douglass had a modest, gentle side, freely giving credit to the many people who aided in his ascent and helped his cause. Today Douglass can serve as a model for Americans who believe in family values and the importance of religion. Reformers can also emulate this man, who worked within the system yet was not corrupted, who held government offices yet denounced the racism of post–Civil War America. Even radicals find a model in Douglass. His fiery speeches give ample evidence that he believed in confrontation after the 1850 Fugitive Slave Act and before the Civil War. As he reminded Americans throughout his life, "If there is no struggle, there is no progress."

IN THE NINETEENTH century, philosophers and writers connected heroism to God. For a variety of reasons—science, materialism, mass culture—many Americans have lost the nineteenth-century conviction that man is a spiritual being, that life is a pilgrimage filled with joy and suffering, a cosmic drama in which one must fight evil, and that in helping the less fortunate we serve God. This conviction fortified the ideology of heroism and animated Dorothea Dix, Lucretia Mott, Harriet Tubman, and Frederick Douglass.

In our time, it also drove Martin Luther King Jr. King, who was shot fighting for justice and equality, a cause that continued the work of Abraham Lincoln and influenced other protest movements, the feminist revolution, and the apartheid crusade. King showed physical courage, refusing to back down when threatened with jail and death. He also showed moral courage. Born privileged, he could have lived a life of comfort and scholarship; instead, he was asked to lead the Montgomery bus boycott. Imprisoned in Birmingham jail, he wrote one of the world's most powerful letters. And he was a great speaker. King not only challenged white racism, he challenged members of his own organization by taking radical positions on poverty and the Vietnam War. After reading King's letters and speeches, I find he had an appealing humility; he listened, changed, and grew as a speaker, a preacher, and a person. Most of the people I talk to acknowledge that King, along with Nelson Mandela, is one of the few uncontested heroes of our time. But they often forget, I have discovered, that King was a minister. Christianity, he said repeatedly, was the force that drove his life, that gave him a passion for social justice and the capacity to find meaning in suffering.

There are are many reasons why, in the words of historian Barbara Tuchman, "Something about our time does not like the great." But we should not discount the steady growth of secularism among opinion makers and the highly educated. America remains more religious than European countries, but increasingly many of those who shape public opinion believe that faith is a relic from a superstitious past, that science is eliminating mystery, and that human beings can navigate the river of life alone, without divine assistance.

THE SHAW MEMORIAL

DEATH FOR NOBLE DEEDS MAKES DYING SWEET.

—Inscribed on Shaw memorial

I am standing on Beacon Street in Boston directly across from the State Capitol, looking up at lifesize figures in bronze relief of Colonel Robert Gould Shaw and the African American soldiers of the 54th Massachusetts Regiment. Shaw and more than half his men were cut down underneath the stone walls of Fort Wagner, South Carolina, in 1863. Short of food and water and under constant gunfire from well-protected gunners, the soldiers of the 54th showed extraordinary bravery in battle.

All the men on the memorial are in profile, Shaw on his horse with his sword drawn, the soldiers on foot with their knapsacks, canteens, and rifles as if marching past a reviewing stand. So it must have seemed on Memorial Day 1897 to the survivors of the 54th and to the thousands of Bostonians who attended the unveiling of this powerful memorial and heard orations from William James and Booker T. Washington. In his speech, James praised Shaw for his courage in defying public opinion by agreeing to lead a regiment of African American soldiers. Behind the Shaw Memorial, sculpted by Augustus Saint-Gaudens, on a stone wall facing the park, are etched the names of the soldiers who died at Fort Wagner. All over our country—on the sides of statues, underneath American flags, on granite walls, in chapels and cemeteries—are engraved the names of those once thought heroic.

Most American memorials were built to honor men who died in battle. We have a powerful impulse to recognize those who give their lives for their country. I stop at war monuments and read the names because I think we should remember people who suffered and sacrificed. I have climbed the steps at Bunker Hill, walked among the graves at Shiloh, and stopped my car to look at war monuments in cities and small towns all over America.

In Pittsburgh, I visited the Soldiers and Sailors Memorial Hall and Museum, a massive Greco-Roman building modeled after the mausoleum of Halicarnassus, one of the Seven Wonders of the Ancient World. The hall was dedicated in 1910 by the Grand Army of the Republic, a powerful veterans' organization formed after the Civil War, to honor veterans of Allegheny County, Pennsylvania. Two sixteen-foot bronze statues, a soldier and a sailor, stand at the entrance. Inscribed in stone on the left panel of the building is a quotation from Abraham Lincoln about the purpose of the Civil War: TO GIVE ALL AN UNFETTERED START AND A FAIR CHANCE IN THE RACE OF LIFE. Just inside the door, a frayed Union Army cap with a small hole blown through it sits in a display case. The cap once belonged to Lieutenant James Harbisen, shot in the head at the Battle of Salem Heights, Virginia. Not far from the cap is a cannonball embedded in an oak stump from the battlefield at Chickamauga, Tennessee. A bust of Jakob Brunn, the first Jewish officer killed in the Civil War, sits on a pedestal down the hall. Dozens of plaques list the names of Pennsylvania regiments. Originally constructed as a Civil War memorial, today the hall honors those who served in all America's wars. On display at the entrance is the book *Stolen Valor: How the Vietnam Generation Was Robbed of Its Heroes and Its History.* *Stolen Valor* argues that Vietnam soldiers were just as valiant as soldiers in other wars, not the homeless drug addicts depicted in the media.

A documentary on PBS, "Return with Honor," described American fighter pilots held as prisoners of war in North Vietnam. It is hard to withhold the word *hero* from men who were tortured, put in solitary confinement, and threatened with execution, yet refused to denounce their country. To keep sane, Lieutenant Commander Bob Shumaker built a house in his head. In solitary confinement, Commander James Stockdale recited the precepts of the Stoic philosopher Epictetus and memorized the names of his men in the prison compound. With the blood from his boils, Lieutenant John "Mike" McGrath painted on his cell wall a stag. In isolation, the American soldiers of the "Hanoi Hilton" invented a tap code to communicate with each other through the thick prison walls. Every Sunday, to keep up their morale, they faced east toward the United States and recited the Lord's Prayer and the Pledge of Allegiance. The message of "Return with Honor"—the motto the senior leaders chose to encourage their troops to survive—is that human beings in a crisis have unimagined reserves of courage and endurance.

Monuments reveal our ambiguity about war. Only over time have Americans come to understand the power of Washington's Vietnam War Memorial, so different is it from traditional American war memorials. Vietnam veterans, already defensive about an unpopular war and ingratitude from their own country, worried at first that without statues of soldiers the memorial would not be grand enough, would not measure up to other, more heroic testimonies. Controversy now swirls around the proposed World War II memorial on the Washington Mall, as Americans search for a way to honor the greatest generation without glorifying war.

Standing in front of the Shaw Memorial on the Boston Common, I am reminded of the 620,000 men who died in the Civil War, of lives cut short, of families bereaved, of the incalculable suffering the war brought. But I try to remember the war's achievements: a reunited nation and a nation without slavery. I remind myself that we do not have to love war to understand its brutal necessity, or to recognize the values of soldiers—loyalty, discipline, and endurance—or to honor those who lost their lives. I stand in awe of Shaw, who at a young age not only defied public opinion and chose to lead a regiment of African American soldiers but stood in front of his men under the cannons firing from Fort Wagner. And I stand in awe of the soldiers who followed him, expecting no glory and anticipating an anonymous death.

Four

THE AMERICAN WARRIOR HERO

If there be one principle more deeply rooted than any other in the mind of every American, it is that we should have nothing to do with conquest.

—Thomas Jefferson, 1791

All the great masterful races have been fighting races. . . . No triumph of peace is quite so great as the supreme triumph of war.

—Theodore Roosevelt, 1897

Isn't it time we destroyed the macho ethic? Where has it gotten us all these thousands of years? Are we still going to have to be clubbing each other to death?

—John Lennon, 1980

Throughout most of America's history, our heroes were warriors. We have extolled the preacher, the statesman, the capitalist, and the humanitarian, but until recently we reserved our highest status and most respected medals for soldiers. To generals who win went the greatest glory. Outnumbered and short of rifles, Andrew Jackson defeated the British professional soldiers at the Battle of New Orleans in 1815, losing only a dozen men while the English casualties numbered over two thousand. After Admiral George Dewey defeated the Spanish fleet in Manila Bay in 1898, New Yorkers built him a triumphal arch at Washington Square and Americans named their babies, racehorses, and yachts after him. Following World War II, General George Marshall—chief of staff during the Allied victory and architect of the financial plan to resuscitate Western Europe—became the most admired man in America. Generals George Washington, Andrew Jackson, Zachary Taylor, Ulysses S. Grant, and Dwight Eisenhower all became president.

In America, foot soldiers as well as generals are heroes. After World War I, we built the Tomb of the Unknown Soldier in Arlington National Cemetery, burying the unidentified remains of an American soldier exhumed from a grave in France. The tomb was intended to honor the nation's soldiers who had been denied glory and rendered anonymous.

For its living hero, Americans turned to a Tennessee farmer, Alvin York, who found himself behind the German lines on a foggy morning in 1918 when his patrol came under heavy machine-gun fire and half his men were shot. York alone—armed with only a rifle—attacked, killing over 20 Germans and capturing 132. Ferdinand Foch, the commander of the allied armies, described York's exploits as "the greatest thing accomplished by any private soldier of all the armies of Europe." York became an American hero because he had protected his men and had shot skillfully, but he garnered even further admiration when, in the spring of 1919, the *Saturday Evening Post* revealed that York, a pacifist, had gone to war reluctantly.

America typically has made heroes out of soldiers who do not like war. The colonists praised George Washington when he defeated the British but were relieved when he gave up his sword at the end of the Revolutionary War. The founding fathers, fearful of a military dictatorship, wrote into the Constitution that only Congress—not the military—could declare war and that the president—a civilian—would be the commander in chief. Unlike the ancient Romans, we do not glorify war. We have, for the most part, always been reluctant warriors.

Heroes of Peace, Heroes of War

In the nineteenth century, even as the ideology of heroism flourished, doubts about warriors surfaced among educators, philosophers, and influential Americans. William James articulated the paradox: Americans recognized the importance of soldiers and honored them—but disliked killing. James believed that men needed an outlet for inherent aggression, a "moral equivalent of war," and recommended some sort of national service that would call forth bravery and self-sacrifice. Yet James always admired, maybe even envied, his brother Wilkie, who joined Shaw's 54th Regiment in the Civil War and helped lead the assault on Fort Wagner, where he was shot through the side and almost died. Later James wrote, "In heroism, we feel life's supreme mystery is hidden . . . if yet we cling to life and he [the war hero] is able to fling it away like a flower as caring nothing for it, we account him in the deepest way our born superior." But James opposed the 1898 Spanish-American War and supported the peace campaigns that preceded World War I. While he distrusted aggression, extreme masculinity, and imperialism, he believed that some wars are necessary.

The Carnegie Hero Medal

A contemporary of James, industrialist Andrew Carnegie, took a more extreme position. Ruthless and competitive, Carnegie built the largest steel company in America, drove away all rivals, worshiped Herbert Spencer (who preached that only the fittest, most aggressive human beings prosper), and became one of the richest men in America. Carnegie also became an ardent antiwar activist and created the first medals in America to honor bravery off the battlefield.

Carnegie came to America in 1848 from Scotland, where his Uncle George had filled his young mind with stories of Robert Bruce, William Wallace, Rob Roy, and other Celtic soldiers. But in America, Carnegie's heroes were not soldiers. He hated war, calling it "the foulest fiend ever vomited forth from the mouth of hell." He even found football too bloody and in 1903, at the urging of Woodrow Wilson, built for Princeton University a $400,000 artificial lake so undergraduates could work out their aggressions rowing boats instead of maiming classmates on the football field.

Because his heroes were entrepreneurs, scholars, reformers, and, above all, peacemakers, Carnegie established libraries, concert halls, schools, and pension funds for aging professors—and crusaded against war. During the second half of his life, he traveled the world, pleading for disarmament, urging kings and presidents to reconcile their differences. In the Netherlands, he built the Hague Peace Palace so diplomats would have a majestic building in which to settle disputes among nations. Carnegie would have been devastated to know how many soldiers and civilians would die in the wars of the twentieth century.

While Carnegie accepted the idea of male aggression, he believed it could be channeled into rowing, competing in business, and, most significantly, into reading books. So ardent was his faith that enlightenment would lead to peace that he built libraries all over America. Then, in 1904, he found a new way to honor heroes who were not warriors.

On a cold morning in January, the Allegheny Coal Company's Harwick Mine near Pittsburgh exploded, killing 179 men. Eminent mining engineer Selwyn M. Taylor heard about the explosion, rushed to Harwick, and went down the wrecked mine shaft looking for survivors. At the bottom he found Adolph Gunia, seventeen years old, badly burned but alive. Hoping that more miners might be saved, Taylor descended farther; instead of more miners, he came upon afterdamp, a deadly gas produced by the explosion. Early the next morning Taylor died, leaving a widow and stepson. Another miner, Daniel A. Lyle, also responded to the call for rescue workers and went down into the rubble-filled mine. Like Taylor, Lyle suffocated, leaving a widow and five children.

In New York, Carnegie read about the disaster. "I can't get the women and children of the disaster out of my mind," he wrote. Haunted by the image of Taylor and Lyle felled by gas while groping for men they did not know, Carnegie sent money to their families and ordered two gold medals struck to recognize the dead miners' bravery. The Carnegie Hero Fund Commission was born.

Of his many charities, Carnegie was proudest of the Hero Fund. From the beginning, it had been his idea to honor civilians who "preserve and rescue instead of soldiers who maim and kill" and to call them "heroes of civilization." Selwyn Taylor and Daniel Lyle were the first "peace heroes" to be recognized by Carnegie's five-million-dollar gift.

Every year since 1904, the commission has read accounts of thousands of Americans who have calmed runaway horses, run into burning buildings, dived into swollen rivers, fought off attacking dogs, and pried open cars to save people. Since 1904 the commission has considered over 75,000 rescues, trying to calibrate and weigh valor. How great was the risk? How wise the act? How unselfish? From hundreds of files each year, the commission selects its heroes. Each receives $3,500 and a medal. On the back of the medal are the words of John: "Greater love hath no man than this, that a man lay down his life for his friends." The Commission passed a resolution to confer a group award on all the heroes of the September 11 terrorist attack and gave $100,000 in relief for the victims' families.

Scientists study rescuers. Some skeptics think the rescuer, like the courageous warrior, merely responds to a surge of adrenaline or a sudden impulse. Other researchers talk about altruism and unusual empathy and rescuers having had compassionate role models. But even the Carnegie Hero Fund Commission investigators are baffled by their honorees. We do not know why in a moment of crisis and danger some act with resolution and courage while others hesitate and shrink back. Andrew Carnegie celebrated the mystery.

Roosevelt's Rough Riders

While Carnegie was thinking of ways to make the world more peaceful, Theodore Roosevelt was charging up San Juan Hill in front of his men. In 1899 Roosevelt wrote *Rough Riders,* a description of his military career in the Spanish-American War, which made him a hero at the time and helped him win the presidency. Roosevelt believed the youth of America had become weak and coddled and a war would make them strong. In *Rough Riders,* he described Princeton polo players and Arizona cowboys becoming brothers through battle: their training in Florida for the attack on Cuba, the heat of combat, and the bravery of wounded soldiers who fall without complaint and refuse to retreat to field hospitals. In *Rough Riders,* there are no reluctant warriors. Roosevelt put into words an ethos atypical in American history and antithetical to the views espoused by James and Carnegie, an ethos that temporarily captured the imagination of many Americans before World War I. With the memory of the Civil War growing dim at the turn of the century, *Rough Rider*s provided the nation with new warrior heroes.

World War I

In June of 1914 the Great War began. In the cities of Europe, citizens cheered and young men flocked to recruiting stations. Everyone believed the war would be short and glorious. But the impersonal, seemingly senseless, and catastrophic losses of trench warfare shattered the beliefs that man is rational and inherently good and that progress is inevitable, influencing a whole generation of European and American intellectuals.

Before he died in France at age twenty-five in 1918, Wilfred Owen wrote antiwar poems like "Dulce et Decorum Est," describing the horror of a gas attack and mocking the Roman notion that it is sweet and decorous to die for your country. In Ernest Hemingway's *A Farewell to Arms,* Frederick Henry, a medic on the Italian front, concludes that he was "embarrassed by the words sacred, glorious, and sacrifice and the expression in vain." After the horrors of the war, Sigmund Freud would write, "The world will never be again a happy place."

By the 1920s the idea that the war in Europe—with all its losses— had not made the world safe for democracy settled into the American mind. To many, the war vindicated the antiwar crusades of James and Carnegie. In *Rough Riders,* Roosevelt had spoken for an age that had not seen over 300,000 men die in the battle of Verdun.

In 1931, Jane Addams, once a pariah for her opposition to the war, was honored with the Nobel Peace Prize for her lifelong crusade for peace. The 1933 movie *Heroes for Sale* portrays a World War I veteran, down on his luck and unappreciated by his country, who goes to a pawnshop to sell his Congressional Medal of Honor. The owner of the pawnshop shows him a case full of similar medals and turns him away. World War I was a watershed in the decline of the soldier hero in American history.

The evils of fascism ended the pacifism of the 1930s, resuscitated the warrior hero, and made icons of generals like Douglas MacArthur and George S. Patton Jr. But the greatest generation dispensed with the ardor of Theodore Roosevelt and entered World War II reluctantly, only after the attack on Pearl Harbor, when they volunteered in greater numbers. They fought Japan and Germany without sentimentality and returned home gratefully, chastened by the blitz, Auschwitz, Hiroshima, and civilian deaths unprecedented in human history.

The Legacies of Vietnam

Since World War II, a constellation of factors—primary among them the Vietnam War—has given rise to a skepticism about warrior heroes that persists even today, especially among many young Americans. Following the carnage of the two world wars came the conflicts in Korea and Vietnam. Korea ended in a draw, Vietnam in defeat. Vietnam was our longest war, our first televised war, and our most bitterly contested war.

During the Vietnam era, large sections of the American population, particularly college students threatened with the draft, turned against the war. Nightly television news coverage of violence in Vietnam and protests at home steadily eroded America's confidence in the military. In 1968, at My Lai in South Vietnam, an estimated five hundred Vietnamese civilians, among them women and children, were slaughtered under the command of Lieutenant William Calley. When news of these atrocities was reported back home, the image of the

American soldier—already seriously damaged by participation in a widely unpopular war—took on a sinister cast. Two years later, in 1970, Ohio National Guardsmen opened fire on students at Kent State University who were protesting American involvement in Cambodia. Four students died and several others were seriously injured. Film of the tragedy played over and over on television, imprinting an image in the minds of Americans that our soldiers were killing our college students. *Time* magazine published an article on Kent State and called it "At War with War." The concept of the American soldier as hero reached an all-time low.

Fifty-two thousand Americans and over a million Vietnamese died in the Vietnam War for a cause nobody could explain. For the soldiers who returned home, there were no ticker tape parades, no heroes' welcome. No Alvin York or Audie Murphy, no Douglas MacArthur or Dwight D. Eisenhower emerged out of Vietnam. The media depicted the returning Vietnam veteran as angry, depressed, and homeless—unlike the veterans of World War II, who were celebrated by their countrymen and settled down and got on with their lives. The few heroes to emerge in time from Vietnam were prisoners of war, like John McCain, who endured captivity with courage; conscientious objectors like Muhammad Ali, who was punished for his opposition to the war but is now considered by some a seer; and soldiers who tried to protect civilians, like Hugh Thompson, the helicopter pilot later profiled in *U.S. News & World Report* for his effort to stop the massacre at My Lai.

After Vietnam, Hollywood produced a series of antiwar movies, like *Full Metal Jacket, Platoon,* and *Born on the Fourth of July.* In *Full Metal Jacket,* soldiers smoke marijuana and rape Vietnamese women. In *Platoon,* they burn peasant villages and kill each other. The protagonist of *Born on the Fourth of July* becomes a hero not by having his legs blown off but by recanting his misguided patriotism and joining the war protest movement.

Born on the Fourth of July was based on the true story of Ron Kovic, who grew up in an idealistic working-class family in the suburbs of Long Island, New York. Before the Vietnam War, he saluted the flag, prayed to God, looked up to the president, honored his father and mother, and believed that communism threatened America. In his 1976 autobiography, Kovic described how he made heroes out of Audie Murphy and John Wayne, watched *Sands of Iwo Jima* over and over, and dreamed of becoming a marine. Then he went to Vietnam and lost his idealism.

In post–Vietnam War movies, violence is depicted more graphically than ever before. Women and children are butchered; soldiers die slowly, screaming in pain. Realistic and powerful, these movies are sympathetic to soldiers, who are not, however, depicted as heroes because they are caught in a war without purpose. Unlike popular war movies of the 1950s, such as *To Hell and Back* and *Sands of Iwo Jima,* there is no trace of glory.

In an unprecedented way, American writers and filmmakers have removed romance and glamour from war, and the fall of the warrior hero has been one consequence of this movement toward realism in our information-rich world. *Saving Private Ryan,* which won Best Director and other Academy Awards in 1998, is in part a tribute to the soldiers who fought on the beaches of Normandy and liberated villages in France, but the first twenty minutes of combat footage is so graphic that students have told me it turned them into pacifists.

After Vietnam, American history textbooks gave less space to military heroes and more to reformers and humanitarians. In literature classes, students learned about war through antiwar novels, like Erich Maria Remarque's *All Quiet on the Western Front,* Joseph Heller's *Catch-22,* and Kurt Vonnegut's *Slaughterhouse-Five.* As the curriculum in American schools became profoundly antiwar, it also became antimilitary, making it difficult for students to honor the men who fought and died for America and hard for them to think about volunteering for the armed forces.

Robert Cormier's 1998 book *Heroes* was on display in the library at one of the schools I visited. Cormier, who recently died, was known for bringing the grim realism of contemporary fiction into the young-adult novel. His best-known novel, *The Chocolate War,* published in 1974, featured Brother Leon, an assistant headmaster who conspires with some of his students to brutalize a freshman who dares to refuse to sell chocolate for a school fund-raiser. After *The Chocolate War* came Cormier's novels about amoral government bureaucrats, psychopathic terrorists, and serial killers. In an interview Cormier said the teen years are not "a peppermint world of fun and frolic" and added, "I am not in the business of creating role models or sending out lessons. I am a storyteller."

Cormier's *Heroes* is set in World War II and describes two boys who live in the same town, returning from the front. Francis Joseph Cassavant has fallen on a live grenade, ostensibly to save his platoon, and had his face blown away. But Cassavant knows he is no hero; his motive was to kill himself, because before he enlisted, he had caught his idol, Larry LaSalle, raping his childhood sweetheart and had done nothing. In the Pacific, Larry LaSalle charged a Japanese machine gun nest, lost the use of his legs, and received a medal; but he, too, lost his self-respect and thinks of suicide because he has used his hero status to prey on young girls. Cassavant returns from Europe to kill LaSalle, but, unable to pull the trigger, he leaves his hometown and looks up Nicole Renard, the rape victim, who now lives alone, bitter and disillusioned. Cassavant confides to Renard, "I don't know what a hero is anymore."

Vietnam did more than tarnish the military in our culture and schools. It contributed to a value shift harmful to heroism. Many who protested the Vietnam War concluded that a society that could start and pursue such a misguided war was fundamentally flawed. Young people refused to say the Pledge of Allegiance, burned the American flag, took over buildings in elite colleges, and denounced corporations and capitalism. *The New Yorker* writer Nicholas Lemann remembers growing up in the 1970s believing "that America could do nothing right"; that it was "a force of evil in the world . . . and that the whole idea of order and authority was probably wrong too." Vietnam contributed to the rise of a counterculture that questioned authority, disparaged patriotism, and ridiculed conventional values.

For most of the twentieth century, Americans looked up to their leaders and deferred to a foreign policy establishment thought to be impartial and wise. Vietnam shattered that confidence. In *The Best and the Brightest,* published in 1972, David Halberstam argued that the hubris of America's ruling elite lured us into the war and insisted that generals, diplomats, and cabinet officials lied about our involvement in it. The war, argued Halberstam, transformed men who were loyal, decent, and self-sacrificing—men like Robert S. McNamara, General Maxwell D. Taylor, and Dean Rusk—into fanatics.

As a result of Vietnam, Americans not only challenged the idea of an establishment that could confidently lead a nation but also looked with skepticism upon the ethos of masculinity that helped define that establishment. Critics of the war wondered whether President Lyndon Johnson had a "John Wayne complex"—too much machismo that caused him to ignore advice and escalate the war and that prevented him from admitting he might be wrong.

Before Vietnam, most Americans accepted gender roles and praised masculinity, which was equated with exploration, physical bravery, competition, and risk-taking. In 1958, *Gunsmoke* was the nation's most popular television show and Marshal Matt Dillon epitomized the calm, confident, tough male hero. By the 1970s, the Western hero was seen as unconnected to community and family, as uncommunicative, and as a killer rather than a protector. Books appeared suggesting that society could be improved if men became more gentle.

Typical of "male liberation" books is Mark Gerzon's 1992 *A Choice of Heroes,* in which he argues that society should discard such "masculine archetypes" as the soldier and replace them with new archetypes, such as companions and healers. Three years later John C. Robinson, in his book *Death of a Hero, Birth of the Soul,* suggested that men should abandon the search for sex and status and concentrate on self-knowledge: "Men see that the Compulsive Warrior mentality now has no more value to the soul and, in fact, must be discarded for the soul to be born." The debate over Vietnam has led to a critique of conventional masculinity and, indirectly, to a critique of conventional heroism.

At the start of the twentieth century, Theodore Roosevelt had worried that American boys were becoming feminized and called for a reemphasis on masculinity. Roosevelt celebrated "the great virile virtues—the virtues of courage, energy, and daring: the virtues which beseem a masterful race—a race fit to fell the forest, to build roads, to found commonwealths, to conquer continents, to overthrow armed enemies." He supported the Boy Scouts, which offered ethical training, a constructive outlet for aggression, and experience in the wilderness. By the end the century, Roosevelt's rhetoric of masculinity was associated not with exploration, boldness, and bravery but with the urge to dominate and destroy.

Thirty years after the fall of Saigon, anger over the Vietnam War has dissipated. Today, millions of Americans file by the Vietnam War Memorial in Washington, D.C., reading the names inscribed on the low black wall. Many weep out of sympathy for the young soldiers sent to fight overseas who died in a war that still seems pointless to many Americans. Families travel from all over the country to search for the names of children and siblings honored at last.

One of the many legacies of the Vietnam War is the end of the draft and an all-volunteer military. Just as most college graduates avoided going to Vietnam, many of our highly trained young men and women have avoided the armed forces since Vietnam. Consequently, those who now influence public opinion—politicians, business leaders, lawyers, editors, columnists, talk-show hosts, professors, and teachers—have had no first-hand experience with the military. Without basic training, it becomes easier to forget the skill and daring of pilots, easier to lose sight of the many soldiers who have won the Congressional Medal of Honor. And the gap widens between a civilian culture that values comfort and individualism and a military culture that stresses sacrifice and discipline.

As warfare became more technological—dominated by satellites, computers, and long-range rockets—the idea of the traditional courageous, self-sacrificing hero soldier seemed remote. In 1999, *The Wall*

Street Journal wrote an article on the air war against Bosnia. The reporter described how early in the morning American pilots took off from an air base in St. Louis, Missouri, refueled from planes flying beside them over the Atlantic, dropped bombs on Serbian targets they couldn't see, and returned to base in time for a game of golf. An article in *The New York Times* predicts that future wars will be plotted by defense intellectuals making decisions from command stations in space and implemented by laser cannons.

The status of the American warrior has never been high in times of peace. At the end of the Cold War, it was easier for Americans to dismiss the value of the military. With the collapse of the Soviet Union and the retreat of communism, the American military lost its enemy of forty years and started to downsize. Salaries lost pace with inflation, recruits became harder to find, and many people highly trained in technical fields left the military for the more lucrative private sector. As world trade expanded and democracy spread, nationalism seemed less important and globe-trotting capitalists became more powerful than generals. But the September 2001 terrorist attack against America provided a new, if shadowy, enemy; and a nation that once felt secure at the end of the Cold War turned with fear and gratitude to the warrior heroes whom, until recently, it had taken for granted.

SAINT JOHN THE DIVINE'S
SPORTS BAY

*What could be happier or more appropriate, more wholly in accord with
the ideal of the cathedral. . . . Clean, wholesome, well-regulated sport
is a most powerful agency for true and upright living. It calls out and
develops just those qualities which are essential to noble manhood and
womanhood.*

—The Right Reverend William T. Manning, 1928

The Cathedral Church of Saint John the Divine in New York City
is a cathedral of heroes. Begun in 1892, it is still not completed.
I like to walk down Broadway, with its stores and crowds, turn left on
112th Street, and suddenly see a block away the huge bronze doors
topped by statues of disciples and prophets. Before I enter the cathedral, I circle it and check out the gargoyles and gardens. This takes me
fifteen minutes. Once inside, I am propelled back to a simpler world.
In a noisy irreverent age, cathedrals still evoke serenity and purpose.

The heroes depicted in the Cathedral Church of Saint John the Divine
are not just the martyrs of the church carved in stone on the portals or
the heroes of the Old and New Testaments set in bronze on the front
doors; in stained glass we see Abraham Lincoln at Gettysburg, George
Washington at Valley Forge, Florence Nightingale in the Crimean War.

Depicted in the many windows are heroes of science, art, literature, and music: Louis Pasteur, Rembrandt, Shakespeare, Palestrina. Also honored in the windows are those who are known only to God: mothers and fathers, farmers, artisans, laborers.

Just inside and up on the left is a twenty-five-foot stained-glass window dedicated to sports. In bright colors and jewel tones in this vast and solemn vaulted cathedral are, among many other athletes, a downhill skier, a football player, an ice skater, a batter, a boxer, an auto racer, three women riding a toboggan, and a tennis player. Miscellaneous pieces of sports equipment—billiard cues, golf balls, a fishing pole—are scattered along the borders. In all, twenty-eight sports are symbolized. It is an interesting collection—archery, car racing, baseball, basketball, bicycling, billiards, bowling, boxing, cricket, curling, fencing, figure skating, fishing, football, golf, hunting, ice hockey, marksmanship, polo, running, sailing, sculling, skiing, soccer, swimming, tennis, tobogganing, and wrestling—a representation of American athletics in the 1920s in fourteen thousand pieces of stained glass. Biblical heroes from the Old and New Testaments dominate the eight larger medallions that run the length of the window, among them David conquering Goliath, Jacob wrestling with the Angel, and Paul encouraging the citizens of Corinth to run the good race.

Inspired by the Summer Olympic Games of 1924 (the games that introduced to the world runners Eric Liddell and Harold Abrahams, heroes of the movie *Chariots of Fire*), Elizabeth Manning, daughter of the Episcopalian bishop of New York, returned from Paris with the idea of building a sports chapel in the cathedral as a tribute to the connection between religious ideals and athletic values in America. Bishop Manning embraced the idea, defended it against purists who saw in it secularism and materialism, and established the Sports and Games Committee of the Cathedral, under the direction of Julian S. Myrick. Grantland Rice, preeminent sportswriter of the era, supported the project, noting that religion and sport "stand against hate, greed, trickery, fouling, and muckerism of any sort."

Twenty-seven years later—after solicitations appealing to sports organizations all over the country and after Bishop Manning's death, the Great Depression, and World War II—the surviving members of the committee gathered in the cathedral chapel on a Sunday afternoon in 1951 for the unveiling of the window and the dedication of the bay. They heard a Handel anthem and words from the book of Isaiah. Myrick delivered the main address. Extolling "the value of courage and self-sacrifice, within clean, strong bodies," he dedicated the bay to four athletes—Walter Camp, Robert D. Wrenn, Christy Mathewson, and Hobart A. J. (Hobey) Baker—whom the committee believed symbolized "the highest ideals of character and sportsmanship."

The nineteenth-century conviction that good character was formed on the playing fields of America prevailed well into the twentieth century. The moral language of sport could be found in newspapers, magazines, and books; among coaches and teachers; inscribed on athletic trophies and memorials; and at athletic ceremonies, such as the dedication of the Sports Bay in 1951. Looking up at the athletes portrayed in the window of the Cathedral Church of Saint John the Divine recalls a time when athletes stayed with one team, respected their fans, and wore uniforms without logos—a time when sports at least seemed clean and special, before cameras and dollars obliterated the magic and mystery.

Five

THE FALL OF THE HERO ATHLETE

A LIFE IS NOT IMPORTANT EXCEPT IN THE IMPACT IT HAS ON OTHER LIVES.
—Inscribed on Jackie Robinson's tombstone, 1972

I don't give a rat's turd about what adults think of me.
—Brian Bosworth,
The Boz: Confessions of a Modern Anti-Hero, 1988

When Walter Camp played football for Yale in the mid-1870s, players wore knitted caps and had no pads in their uniforms. Little more than a free-for-all, football had few rules, no professional coaches, and no forward passing. Serious injuries were common. The *Chicago Tribune* calculated 159 injuries and 18 deaths in 1905. From the 1880s through the turn of the century, there were fierce national debates about the brutality of football and whether it should be banned from college campuses. Leading the campaign to ban it was Harvard's Charles William Eliot, who called it "a spectacle more brutalizing than prizefighting, cockfighting, or bullfighting." Eliot, however, was up against President Theodore Roosevelt, and Roosevelt and football prevailed in the end. Nevertheless, out of the debates and deaths came reform.

Leading the campaign for reform was Walter Camp, who was by then Yale's legendary football coach. In his thirty-three-year career, Camp's teams lost only fourteen games. Like Roosevelt, Camp believed football instilled the heroic virtues of courage and endurance. At the same time, knowing that "No game so tries the temper as does football," Camp invented the quarterback, the line of scrimmage, four downs, and penalties for unnecessary roughness and helped establish the All-American team. An ardent competitor, he insisted in speeches and articles and books—as well as by personal example—that, through sports, society fosters the qualities of honor, dedication, fair play, and sacrifice.

When Camp learned that nearly half the men examined for service during World War I were rejected as unfit, he introduced to the navy a series of stretching exercises, "the daily dozen," which quickly spread to the army and the air forces and, after World War I, throughout the country. Camp became America's first guru of physical fitness. He persuaded President Wilson's cabinet to work out, warned businessmen about the dangers of stress and anger, and urged schools to teach physical fitness and to build fields and playgrounds.

Prophetically, Camp opposed recruiting, fearing that a marriage of commerce and sport would encourage egotism, diminish idealism, and compromise the love of the game. When Camp died in 1925, American newspapers paid tribute to "the father of American football," and fans from high schools and colleges all over the country sent donations for a fifty-foot colonnade, the Walter Camp Memorial Gateway, which stands at the entrance to the Yale Bowl.

During Walter Camp's tenure as Yale's coach, a spare 148-pound five-foot-ten-inch junior, Robert Wrenn, was the star quarterback on the Harvard team, Yale's arch rival. In his last game against Yale in the 1894 season, Wrenn was by far the lightest athlete on the field and the only Harvard starter to play the entire game, a feat of unusual courage and endurance, as the contest between the two schools that day was so brutal it resulted in a two-year moratorium on their rivalry. Wrenn went on to achieve national fame in a new racquet sport, winning the U.S. lawn tennis singles four times between 1893 and 1897.

One of Roosevelt's Rough Riders in 1898, he saw action in the Spanish-American War and later volunteered again for service in World War I at the age of forty-six, piloting a plane and commanding an aviation camp. After a battle against Bright's disease, Wrenn died, like Camp, in 1925. Twelve thousand people attended the unveiling of a bronze plaque in the Forest Hills Tennis Stadium the following year. The inscription on the plaque reads COURAGEOUS IN COMPETITION—GRACIOUS IN PERSONALITY—INSPIRING IN LEADERSHIP.

The most influential athlete of the nineteenth century had been the fictional Frank Merriwell of Yale. Merriwell excelled in lacrosse, track, golf, and billiards; he rejected alcohol and cigarettes, fought bullies, preached fairness, exuded robust health. Like his name, Merriwell was endlessly cheerful, the creation of writer Gilbert Patten, aka Burt L. Standish. Millions of young Americans, including boxer Jack Dempsey and future president Woodrow Wilson, read about Merriwell in *Tip Top Weekly* and aspired to be like him. One of these young Americans was Christy Mathewson, growing up in Factoryville, Pennsylvania, in the 1890s. With Merriwell as his role model, Christy Mathewson was to become America's first baseball hero.

At Bucknell College, Mathewson was a standout in football, basketball, and baseball, an honors student, class president, and (during the summer) a pitching phenomenon in a newly formed Virginia baseball league. In 1900, he was "discovered" and joined the New York Giants. With a blazing fastball and a new pitch called the "fadeaway," Mathewson was formidable, winning thirty or more games a season from 1903 to 1905 and going on to win 373 games with the Giants.

When America entered World War I, Mathewson volunteered, returned home with his lungs permanently scarred by mustard gas, and died, like Camp and Wrenn, in 1925. In its eulogy to Mathewson, the New York *Herald Tribune* declared, "If baseball will hold to the ideals of this gentleman, sportsman, and soldier, our national game will keep the younger generation clean and courageous and the future of the nation secure."

While Christy Mathewson was finishing his career with the New York Giants, Hobey Baker was becoming a legend at Princeton. As captain of the football team in 1913, and named All-American, Baker, a speedy and elusive runner, could kick soaring punts and crucial field goals. As supple and superbly coordinated as he was fast, he could also swim, dive, sprint, and—to the delight of his dorm mates—walk up and down the stairs on his hands. Baker had learned to play hockey late at night on the black ice at St. Paul's School in Concord, New Hampshire, and later became one of the top players in the United States. Fans admired him for his selflessness as much as for his stick handling—passing to the player with the best chance to score—and he was rarely penalized. Baker joined the first group of American pilots sent overseas in World War I and won the French Croix de Guerre. He wrote home, "You handle your machine instinctively just as you dodge instinctively when running with the ball in an open field." After the Armistice, his plane, which he insisted on taking for a test flight even though it was having engine trouble, stalled five hundred meters above a field in France and crashed. Al Lang of the New York *Herald Tribune* wrote of Baker, "He was a sort of legendary hero like Sir Galahad, Richard the Lion-Hearted, and even Paul Bunyan."

The New Gladiators

On a Sunday afternoon in late January, the streets are quiet and the shopping malls deserted. Americans are watching the Super Bowl. In late March, they will put money into office pools and prepare for the college basketball championship. In May come the pro-basketball playoffs, in October the World Series. Capitalism and advertising, Stone Age imperatives and childlike fantasies, powerful cameras and a mysterious but urgent appreciation for physical grace and power—all combine to make sports dominant at the beginning of the twenty-first century.

Sports make cities proud and colleges prominent. Athletic stars can make a shoe company rich and cause its stock to soar. With more teams, modern stadiums, and distant satellites, never before in American history have spectator sports been so powerful and influential, a multibillion-dollar business. Better equipped, better conditioned, and skillfully coached, our athletes excel and break records. Better informed, today's spectators look into locker rooms and hear more than press releases. They know about the players' feuds, the coaches' moods, and everyone's salary.

Through sports, Americans of all ages, races, and occupations find a common language. Now this language includes talk of fines, probations, pending court appearances, fights, and freebasing. Fans are as familiar with contract provisions and strike disputes as they are with touchdowns and batting averages. There is less talk of teamwork and more of the high-flying dunk, the long bomb, the fastest puck, the most powerful serve. Spectators insult as much as they applaud. Among players, trash talk prevails.

Of all our heroes, none have fallen so fast and so far as our athletes. Consider a few highlights from the last forty years: Yankee Stadium is renamed "The Halfway House that Ruth Built," as repeat drug offenders Daryl Strawberry and Steve Howe circle its bases; Pete Rose is banned from the Baseball Hall of Fame for gambling; Wilt Chamberlain boasts about sleeping with twenty thousand women; Jennifer Capriati wins twenty million dollars before the age of twenty and is arrested in Miami for shoplifting and drug use; Barry Bonds signs a multimillion-dollar contract with the San Francisco Giants—and then, as he hits one of his many home runs, hoists his middle finger to the crowd.

Before 1995 is over, a total of 220 college athletes appear in court, charged with offenses ranging from manslaughter to illegal gambling to rape. In 1996, Dennis Rodman's *Bad As I Wanna Be* hits the bestseller lists, and Roberto Alomar spits at an umpire. During the 2000 World Series, pitcher Roger Clemens throws the jagged barrel of a broken bat at runner Mike Piazza.

BEFORE THE 1960S, athletes did not make astronomical salaries, and billions of dollars did not slosh around sports arenas, tempting everyone. Professional and college athletes behaved better. And behavior counted. In fairness, however, Americans were never invited into the dugouts and locker rooms of their heroes. They had little information about how athletes behaved off the field or what went on behind the events they cheered for.

Jim Bouton changed all that. A winning pitcher with the New York Yankees, Bouton developed a sore arm and in the 1968 season was dropped to an expansion team, the Seattle Pilots. From February to October of 1968, Bouton kept a notebook in his pants pocket. When "The Star-Spangled Banner" played and his teammates roamed beneath the bleachers to look up women's skirts, he wrote down: "beaver shooting." When players squabbled with managers over money and rules, he recorded the acrimony. Ted Williams swore; Bouton wrote down every word. Mickey Mantle slammed down the window of the bus to avoid autograph seekers; Bouton recorded it.

"I think we are all better off looking across at someone, rather than up," philosophized Bouton, as he casually described how his teammates "take pep pills, get drunk, stay out late, talk dirty, have groupies, and are rude to fans." Any qualms he may have felt about demythologizing baseball were alleviated by the wisdom of psychologist Sheldon Kopp, who assured him, "There are no great men. If you have a hero, look again: you have diminished yourself in some way." Packed with memorable anecdotes and aided by a condemnation from Baseball Commissioner Bowie Kuhn (who declared Bouton had done the game "a great disservice"), *Ball Four* hit the best-seller lists.

"It was not our purpose to offend," insisted Leonard Shecter, the editor of *Ball Four*. Bouton's colleagues disagreed. From the day of publication, *Ball Four* produced controversy. In a later edition, Bouton describes some of the reactions. The San Diego Padres burned a copy of the book and left the ashes in his locker room. From the top steps of his dugout, reports Bouton, Pete Rose screamed, "F_ _ _ you, Shakespeare." A cousin, Jeff Bouton, a good college pitcher, was told to change his name if he wanted to pitch in the big leagues. Jim Bouton never expected to be invited back to Yankee Stadium for "Old Timers' Day." Vilified by owners and players, Bouton was consoled by lecture fees and steady sales and by letters from young fans who enjoyed the scatological humor and liked seeing ballplayers as human beings.

Bouton dedicated *Ball Four* to his wife, Bobbie, who looked up to him and believed in the book. It was Bobbie who insisted he dictate the day's events, even late at night when he was tired. For a few years the Boutons were celebrities and enjoyed success. Then Bobbie discovered that fame can make men arrogant and her husband had been unfaithful, like the teammates he had exposed. Divorced, Bobbie Bouton kept her husband's name and wrote her own inside account, this one about baseball marriages, *Home Games*. Included in her book were letters she had written to a friend, describing her famous philandering husband.

Bouton notes that *Ball Four* changed the nature of sportswriting. Instead of spouting platitudes, jocks told "raunchy stories." Now, in a new kind of one-upsmanship, they competed to give reporters the juiciest anecdote—an increasingly profitable commodity for both athlete and reporter.

In 1988, Brian Bosworth perfected the technique with his book about college football. A 240-pound All-American linebacker with the Oklahoma Sooners, Bosworth was banned from the Orange Bowl in 1987 for using steroids. After he left Oklahoma University and its football team, the Seattle Seahawks gave him an $11 million contract. Later, Bosworth wrote *The Boz: Confessions of a Modern Anti-Hero*.

In his book, Bosworth details the escapades of his former Oklahoma teammates, including their firing a machine gun in a fraternity and freebasing cocaine on game days. He confides he likes to hurt people, pick fights on the football field, and autograph the breasts of groupies. *The Boz* stayed on *The New York Times* Best Sellers list for ten weeks. At the age of twenty-five, Bosworth retired from the Seahawks and subsequently appeared as an undercover cop in the movie *Stone Cold* and as a rogue detective in the television series *Lawless*.

The profitable genre begun by Bouton and Bosworth continued in sports books throughout the 1990s with titles like *Shark Attack* (on the short and bitter career of college coaches), *The Dark Side of the Game* (about the mercenary world of pro football), *The Courts of Babylon* (on the venality of the women's pro tennis circuit), *Breaking the Surface* (about exploitation and sex abuse in the swimming and diving world), and *Public Heroes, Private Felons* (on college athletes who break the law).

In a 1991 *Sports Illustrated* article, Ron Fimrite looked back to the Hobey Baker code. "A star player must be modest in victory, generous in defeat. He credits his triumphs to teamwork, accepts only faint praise for himself. He is clean-cut in dress and manner. He plays by the rules. He never boasts. . . . And, above all, he is cool and implacable." This code, suggests Fimrite, influenced an entire generation of athletes, among them Lou Gehrig, Joe DiMaggio, and Joe Louis.

Passed from one generation to the next well into the 1950s, the language of sport and the public behavior of athletes reflected the values of the Baker code. Christy Mathewson looked up to the mythic Frank Merriwell. Joe DiMaggio looked up to Lou Gehrig. Athletes of the fifties looked up to Jackie Robinson. Contemporary sports historian Benjamin Rader describes the mind-set. "Nurtured on Frank Merriwell stories and traditional values, nearly all of the athletes of the forties and fifties conceived of themselves as role models for the nation's youth."

Following the slaughter which took place in World War I, we banished heroic language from war; now we have dropped heroic language from sport. With steroids and painkillers, can we still talk about endurance? Is it sentimental to bring up love of the game with multimillion-dollar contracts? Can we use without embarrassment words like *selflessness, dedication,* and *loyalty?*

The Nostalgia Trap

It is easy to succumb to false nostalgia when discussing sports heroes of the past. Coming from privileged backgrounds, the four heroes celebrated in the Sports Bay of the Cathedral Church of Saint John the Divine had obvious advantages. Some sportswriters accused Christy Mathewson of being egotistical and thought Hobey Baker reckless. Sports columnist Grantland Rice wrote hyperbolic prose about the athletes he covered, and the fictional Frank Merriwell of Yale was of course impossibly perfect.

During what we now think of as the Golden Age of sport, Babe Ruth was America's premier athletic hero. Ruth could pitch, hit, and field with effortless ease. Connected to Ruth all over the country by radio, Americans made their "Sultan of Swat" larger than life. Far from perfect, Ruth fought with managers and owners, stuffed himself with hot dogs, chased women, and wrecked cars. Protected by reporters, he could remain godlike, and those who knew his flaws overlooked them. Even today, Ruth triumphs over biographies that make him human and movies that portray him as a lout.

Women athletes of the era are often unjustly forgotten. Mildred "Babe" Didrikson was arguably the greatest all-around athlete in the history of American sports. Nicknamed after Babe Ruth because of the prodigious number of home runs she hit in softball, Didrikson set records in track, basketball, baseball, and golf, and won gold medals in the 1932 Olympics in Los Angeles in the javelin throw and the 80-meter hurdles. Only 5 feet 6 inches tall and 140 pounds, Didrikson formed her own basketball team, played billiard matches, and excelled in swimming and diving before taking up competitive golf in 1940 and winning the U.S. Women's Open in 1948 and 1950. Didrikson also coped with virulent sexism (once at a baseball game, a woman spectator shouted, "Where are your whiskers?"). And Didrikson publicly combated breast cancer in 1952, rebounding in 1954 to win the U.S. Open a third time. When she died at the age of forty-two in 1956, President Eisenhower eulogized her in a press conference and *The New York Times* paid her this tribute: "She didn't know the meaning of the word quit, and she refused to define it, right to the end."

Sports were not free of scandal before 1960. Eight players for the Chicago White Sox accepted bribes to throw the 1919 World Series. The Carnegie Commission denounced intercollegiate sports in 1929 for greed and an obsession with winning and documented "illegal subsidies for players, grade tampering, the exploitation of athletes, and the violation of admissions requirements." In his autobiography, *Basketball Is My Life,* one of my heroes, Bob Cousy, reminds us that in the early 1950s, "many top stars, several of them All-American players, confessed to throwing games or shaving points." And sports were not fair to minorities. Major-league baseball was not integrated until the late 1940s; when he played for the Brooklyn Dodgers, Jackie Robinson was subjected to jeers and death threats.

When nasty sports episodes dominate newspaper headlines, it is also easy to forget such heroic athletes of our time as Arthur Ashe: the excellence and integrity of his tennis career, the quiet but insistent activism, a heart attack followed by AIDS, a death preceded by courage and acts of charity. Under Ashe's statue on Monument Avenue in Richmond, Virginia, is this inscription from the Bible: "Since we are surrounded by so great a cloud of witnesses, let us also lay aside every weight, and the sin which ensnares us and let us run with endurance the race that is set before us."

Lance Armstrong came down with testicular cancer in his twenties. The cancer spread to his abdomen, lungs, and brain. With hope disappearing, Armstrong chose a radical procedure involving two operations and chemotherapy, a treatment his doctors warned could kill him. For six months he lingered between life and death. But just eighteen months after his cancer was diagnosed, Armstrong started training again. He won the Tour de France in July 1999 and again in 2000 and 2001. In his autobiography, *It's Not About the Bike,* Armstrong describes how suffering made him a better person.

We could also recall Cal Ripken, Jr., who played in 2,131 consecutive games to break Lou Gehrig's record. And the courage of Jim Abbott, who pitched for the Yankees and threw a no-hitter, even though he was born without a right hand. Athletes, I always suggest to my audiences, ought to have something beyond extraordinary athletic skill to be heroes.

COULD WALTER CAMP, Robert Wrenn, Christy Mathewson, and Hobey Baker have survived the era of *Ball Four* and the age of the shocking ad? Could they have resisted steroids, drugs, groupies, and contracts with advertising agencies? How would Jackie Robinson and Bob Cousy have fared if subjected to the inquisition of the modern media? In a time intent on eradicating myths, legends, and illusions and committed to the inside story and the intimate detail, could they have triumphed? If reporters had followed their every move, printed their every word, would they have been heroes?

Athletes before the 1960s were far from perfect, but most of them felt a responsibility, at least *on* the field, to pass down to the next generation some measure of idealism. At a banquet for sportswriters in 1922, New York State Senator Jimmy Walker (soon to be mayor of New York City) publicly admonished Babe Ruth, saying that his carousing had cost the Yankees in the 1922 World Series and that Ruth had an obligation to be a role model. "Will you not give back to those kids their great idol?" Walker asked. "So help me, Jim, I will," Ruth answered. Ruth loved children, autographed thousands of baseballs for them, and sat by their hospital beds. In the 1926 World Series, he promised eleven-year-old Johnny Sylvester, critically ill in a hospital bed in Essex Falls, New Jersey, that he would hit a home run. He hit three, and his legend grew. "Boys worship the muscle hero," wrote Marshall Smelser in his 1975 biography of Ruth, *The Life that Ruth Built.* "A boy can imagine himself a champion athlete much easier than he can imagine himself President."

In his preface to *When Pride Still Mattered,* his 1999 biography of Green Bay Packers coach Vince Lombardi, David Maraniss notes that fans also make heroes of coaches. "[Lombardi's] bronze bust at the Pro Football Hall of Fame in Canton, Ohio, has the shiniest nose, touched more than any other by the faithful, the sporting equivalent of rubbing Saint Peter's foot in Rome."

I have found that students are very protective of their sports heroes. At a school outside Pittsburgh, a boy vigorously defended DiMaggio against Richard Ben Cramer's recent biography, *Joe DiMaggio: The Hero's Life,* firing off a series of questions: "Did he ever hit an umpire? Did he brag? Do you remember the scene where Marilyn Monroe's skirt gets blown up in the air as she stands over a sidewalk grate? That would have made me jealous—and he took roses to her grave every day!"

Joe DiMaggio may have been a flawed hero, but he did believe that being gifted and revered entailed responsibility. "There is always some kid who may be seeing me for the first time or the last time. I owe him my best." Some modern sports commentators suggest that we as a society should give up the idea that athletes need to be anything more than skilled professionals who are paid to tackle, pitch, and score. Nowhere is this better expressed than in Charles Barkley's Nike ad: "I am not paid to be a role model . . . I am paid to *wreak havoc* on the basketball court." This argument, however, ignores the fact that young people have a powerful inclination to look up to athletes who excel in familiar games and to imitate in sports, as well as in their lives, the behavior of their physical heroes.

GREENOUGH'S STATUE
OF WASHINGTON

The Washington is nearly done. I assure you it surpasses my expectations as a likeness, but what will be its reception as a work of art I know not.

—Horatio Greenough, 1839
Letter to his brother Henry

In 1833, sculptor Horatio Greenough received the commission of a lifetime. He would be paid by Congress to create a statue of America's first hero to be placed in the center of the rotunda of the Capitol. Greenough read Washington's letters and diaries and studied portraits of him. He traveled to Europe to study classical models, fretted for eight years, and in 1841 finally produced his statue: a huge likeness, over eleven feet high, sitting like a god on a marble pedestal. From the waist up, except for the toga draped over his shoulder, Washington was nude.

Greenough waited for applause. Instead, Americans rose up in anger. Citizens called the sculpture obscene and insisted that picturing George Washington without his clothes desecrated the new nation and its founder. Too heavy for the newly constructed rotunda—as well as controversial—the statue was removed and placed outside on the Capitol grounds, exposed to rain and snow. Eventually it was carted away to the Smithsonian.

Greenough modeled his creation on Phidias' gigantic ivory and gold statue of Zeus, which sat in the Greek temple at Olympia and was considered, in the fifth century B.C.E., one of the Seven Wonders of the Ancient World. Washington's right finger points to heaven, as if entrusting America to the care of a favoring God, and his left hand holds a sheathed sword, as if returning it to the nation he had led in battle.

Some Americans in 1841 liked the statue: artists and writers praised it, satisfied that Greenough was the equal of any classically trained European sculptor. Citizens who objected felt that America should not rely on Greece for models of artistic excellence. Nor, complained some, should a founding father be compared to a Greek god. Some said Greenough's rendition of Washington made him look as if he were getting ready for a bath. Many mocked his sandals. More thoughtful critics felt Washington should be holding the Constitution instead of a sword.

The controversy over Greenough's statue in 1841 had nothing to do with the way most Americans felt about Washington at the time. Even as they criticized the statue, they revered the man—as a brave general, a visionary president, and a hero. Forty years after Washington's death, no journalist was suggesting he owned too much land, had too many slaves, made military blunders, or fought the British to protect his tobacco profits. In fact, some Americans wanted Washington's body removed from Virginia and placed underneath Greenough's statue in the Capitol rotunda.

But the controversy did reveal that, in a rapidly evolving democracy, everyone could give opinions on statues, particularly those paid for by taxpayers. And for most Americans, Horatio Greenough was out of step. The American farmer and tradesman had no interest in Phidias, Zeus, or the temple at Olympia. His soul was not stirred by togas, cloaks, sandals, and an ornate chair. Critics did not object to the marble perfection of Washington's face, nor to his finger pointing to heaven, but they were accustomed to seeing their hero dressed in uniform on his horse in battle, accustomed to seeing him as an extraordinary human being. Greenough's Washington came from an alien and aristocratic world, one believing that heroes were divine. This statue suggested European monarchs, luxury, and the world Americans had just rejected in their Revolutionary War.

Greenough's statue of Washington now sits on the second floor of the American History Museum of the Smithsonian Institution, a colossal marble representation of hero worship. Looking up at it today, we are not bothered by Washington's bare chest as our ancestors were in 1841, but we too find it odd to see the head of an American president on the body of a Greek god. Unlike our ancestors, however, our response to Greenough's statue *is* connected to the way we now see Washington. Conditioned to seeing all the founding fathers as fundamentally flawed, we are reluctant to consider any of them heroes. On their empty pedestals we have placed celebrities, trading hero worship for celebrity worship, and jettisoned the very idea of having public heroes.

Six

HEROES TO CELEBRITIES

You no sooner set up an idol firmly, than you are sure to pull it down and dash it into fragments . . . any man who attains a high place among you, from the President downwards, may date his downfall from that moment.

—Charles Dickens, 1842

The men with the muck-rakes are often indispensable to the well-being of society; but only if they know when to stop raking the muck, and to look upward to . . . the crown of worthy endeavor.

—Theodore Roosevelt, 1906

You're not anybody in America unless you're on TV. On TV is where we learn about who we really are, because what's the point of doing anything worthwhile if nobody's watching?

—Nicole Kidman, 1995
In the movie *To Die For*

In the beginning, some of the founding fathers talked about the dangers of hero worship. "Let us not make a *god* of him!" cried one ardent republican, fearful of the adulation given George Washington. "Beware of great men," warned the champion of egalitarianism,

Samuel Adams. Nevertheless, fifteen different artists painted Washington, many coins bore his image, nearly every home had a painting or print or bust of him by 1814, and 198 places had been named Washington by 1859.

Ignoring the warnings of Sam Adams, Americans started their history with heroes, looking up to the founder and protector of their nation and paying homage to the general who had saved them from British invaders. At the same time, Americans also heeded Sam Adams and from the beginning criticized the heroes they elevated, calling Washington ignorant, Adams arrogant, Jefferson cowardly. Thus we started our history by simultaneously idealizing and denigrating. We have continued this pattern for two and a half centuries. In America we are eternally torn between a profound need to idealize and emulate, and the democratic message that everyone is equal and our rulers need to be watched.

Democracy can destroy deference, abolish privacy, and offer an outlet for envy. It is, as Winston Churchill noted, "the worst form of government—except for all those other forms that have been tried from time to time." But think of its achievements: Democracy liberated us from tyranny, ended slavery, and gave African Americans and women the right to vote.

Democracy fights discrimination and privilege, makes us more tolerant, and protects us from tyrants. It also promotes achievement by promising equality of opportunity. America has never been completely egalitarian, however, because the Declaration of Independence and the Constitution proclaim only political rights, legal rights, and equality of opportunity. A radical egalitarianism would not only eliminate heroes but banish all distinctions. We would confiscate the money of entrepreneurs, abolish valedictorians, ban medals and generals, and open medical schools to all. As Thomas Jefferson cautioned his countrymen, American democracy did not promise equality of talents, virtue, or wealth; it was to be a meritocracy in which anyone could rise.

A democracy characterized by equality of opportunity promotes one aspect of heroism: extraordinary accomplishment. Thomas Edison became a hero of science because he invented the phonograph, the electric light, and the movie camera. Henry Ford became a business hero because he produced millions of cheap cars. Babe Ruth became the preeminent sports hero for the twentieth century because he hit home runs. In all fields America seeks out and rewards excellence, not only propelling forward its own citizens but attracting talent from around the world and leading all nations in Nobel Prize awards.

From the beginning, John Adams predicted that democracy would favor "Strength, Hardiness, Activity, Courage, Fortitude and Enterprise." Alexis de Tocqueville and other early visitors to America did note energy, movement, industriousness, hope. They praised enormous ambition, unreserved effort, unusual creativity. On his first visit in 1831, de Tocqueville, however, observed a component of American democracy hostile to the notion of heroism. He observed that Americans did not venerate their ancestors or worry about their descendants; they did not believe their first loyalty was to nation, family, or community but to themselves. They celebrate the unencumbered self, and this individualism, according to de Tocqueville, throws a man "back toward himself alone and threatens finally to confine him wholly in the solitude of his own heart."

At the end of his second term as president, Washington was tired and wounded. He did not enjoy reading in pamphlets such statements as the "essentials of his education" had been "gambling, reveling, horse racing and horse whipping." Thomas Jefferson did not relish the label "effeminate," nor did Abraham Lincoln enjoy being portrayed in cartoons as a baboon.

Some elements of our culture have always made us skeptical of heroes. Democracy has always been suspicious of distincition. To democracy, we have added information and openness on an unprecedented scale. To information and openness, we have added nihilism, a value vacuum in which there are no fixed beliefs and forms. Added to all these factors is modernism: an artistic movement that is suspicious of religion, that repudiates structure, form, and conventional values, and that negates didacticism, affirmation, and optimism.

In contemplating the future of a democratic America, the founding fathers had assumed that leaders needed to be watched. But more important than constitutional checks and balances, more significant than free speech, was a democracy based upon the hope that citizens would be *educated*—and that educated citizens would be virtuous and wise. George Washington, John Adams, and Thomas Jefferson did not foresee the rise of political parties fiercely contending for power, with newspapers taking sides. Nor did they expect that in a republic guaranteeing free speech, the right to criticize would leave us with so few past and present public heroes.

Heroes and the Fourth Estate

Should we blame journalists? It is certainly tempting. But just as teachers are not responsible for poverty and disintegrating families, journalists are not responsible for satellites, fiber-optic cables, transistors, and microprocessors—the inventions that make instant information possible. Journalists didn't invent celebrity worship or our appetite for gossip. Many of the people I talk to blame the media, convinced that the contemporary journalist is out to topple, but journalists didn't create the leaders who let us down. And of course we get the news we want. We dial the programs. During the Clinton-Lewinsky scandal, everyone said it was terrible that the media were covering it in such detail. Meanwhile, cable channels were doing very well, their ratings high.

At the same time, journalists are not innocent, and they know it. Cover-ups like Watergate made reporters more aggressive and more cynical. And reporters are quick to pull down the high and mighty. As *New Yorker* writer Adam Gopnik commented, "The reporter used to gain status by dining with his subjects; now he gains status by dining *on* them."

Just after she had delivered a speech at Stanford, on privacy and the press, "Politics: Up Close and Too Personal," journalist Ellen Goodman told me in a telephone interview that she once believed you could discover a leader's character by delving into his personal life. Now, she said, we have gone too far. We have invaded privacy rather than revealed character. And psychological interpretations make us suspicious of heroes' motives. We think they are all driven by demons. We gossip about our public figures, she had told her audience at Stanford, "the way we used to gossip about the people next door."

Journalists, like all professionals, are now reviled more often than revered. Editor James Fallows notes in his 1996 book *Breaking the News* that movies once portrayed journalists as heroes, but now portray them as rogues "more loathsome than . . . lawyers, politicians, or business moguls."

How much of this is new?

Since the founding of America, reporters have been harsh critics of public figures; throughout our history, reporters have also been the targets of harsh criticism. Harriet Beecher Stowe claimed after the Civil War that the press had become so vicious, no respectable American man would ever again run for president. In 1883, the British critic and poet Matthew Arnold toured America and concluded, "If one were searching for the best means . . . to kill in a whole nation . . . the feeling for what is elevated, one could not do better than take the American newspaper."

In the early decades of the twentieth century, *yellow journalism, muckraking,* and *debunking* became household words to describe newspaper stories that exaggerated and distorted events to make them more sensational. "No man ever quite believes in any other man . . . after all, the scoundrel may have something up his sleeve," wrote H. L. Mencken. Between 1925 and 1947, millions of Americans read Walter Winchell's columns in the *New York Mirror* and listened to him on the *Lucky Strike Hour* on the radio. Winchell hung out at the Stork Club, collecting gossip from tipsters. He helped break the news about Mayor Jimmy Walker's affair and let Americans know who was making whoopee with whom. He urged that newspaper offices post these words on their walls: TALK OF VIRTUE AND YOUR READERS WILL BECOME BORED. HINT OF GOSSIP AND YOU WILL SECURE PERFECT ATTENTION.

Media critics have always called reporters cynical. Reporters have always collected gossip and featured celebrities. And high-minded Americans have always warned that journalists can lower the moral tone of the nation.

From the outset, no one expected journalists to be purveyors of admiration for those in authority, particularly after the formation of political parties in the 1790s. Thoughtful critics in early America knew journalists had an obligation to inform and expose. But those same critics were afraid that reporters would eliminate privacy and slander leaders; that by repeating gossip and emphasizing crime and corruption, newspapers would coarsen citizens; and that journalists would become more influential in shaping our national character than ministers, artists, professors, and politicians.

They were right. Today's journalists preside over an empire of information unimaginable to our ancestors, an empire characterized by staggering choice, variety, technological sophistication, and speed. With recorders and cameras, reporters freely enter locker rooms, boardrooms, hotel rooms. Aggressive and eager for ratings, talking heads are quick to judge and prone to offer easy solutions for complex problems. Many talk shows feature hosts and guests who come with hardened opinions, argue, yell, interrupt, and rarely make concessions. In an age of instant communication with little time for reflection, accuracy, or balance, the media can misinform us and make us cynical.

This empire of information is slick, quick, hard-hitting, entertaining, and inescapable. It makes us more knowledgeable, but it can also leave us overwhelmed. Early critics were right to worry that by pandering to public appetite for sensationalism, journalists could contribute to a decline in taste and judgment, could help eliminate an appetite for the admirable.

At a school I visited in New Jersey, one boy argued that the media have always been vicious and political parties have always fought, using as his example the 1828 election between Andrew Jackson and John Quincy Adams. Jackson blamed the untimely death of his wife, Rachel, on political invective and hostile reporters who cast doubt on the legitimacy of their marriage. Certainly, journalists of the early nineteenth century were as unrestrained as they are today, political partisanship was as intense, and interest in sexual gossip as keen. But in the nineteenth century, history, biography, literature, and education fostered a belief in heroism. And, most significantly, the print media of the past lacked the power of today's electronic media.

The Rise of Celebrity

In 1926, newspapers across the nation reported the deaths of two famous Americans within a day of each other. On the afternoon of August 26, while several hundred people attended a memorial service for Charles William Eliot in Harvard's Appleton Chapel, crowds began to gather around Campbell's Funeral Parlor in New York City to mourn the death of silent screen star Rudolph Valentino, who had succumbed to a perforated ulcer at the age of thirty-one following a week-long deathwatch broadcast on radio and chronicled in the newspapers. At midnight, the doors to the funeral parlor had to be forcibly closed by a troop of mounted police, who pushed back thousands of angry fans, many of them rioting and fighting for a last look at Valentino as he lay in his bronze and silver casket dressed in formal evening attire. Made famous by the movie *The Sheik,* Valentino had become the first sex symbol of the silent screen.

For two weeks after Valentino's death, radio and newspaper coverage continued unabated, describing the riots around the funeral parlor, relating rumors of foul play, and following the journey of the train that carried his body from New York City to a marble crypt in Hollywood's Memorial Park Cemetery. In the newspaper analysis following Eliot's and Valentino's deaths, the *Boston Transcript* commented that we had "come to a pretty pass, when a man like President Eliot evoked such scant notices, and a man like Valentino such torrents of type." And the *Chicago Tribune* lamented, "The idealist gazes, groans, and despairs of the republic. The cynic smiles at another proof that mankind cherishes those who entertain rather than those who instruct; those who help us to dream rather than those who waken us to truth."

Heroes and celebrities have always competed for our attention, but Valentino's death and the hysteria surrounding his funeral revealed the magic and the power of the motion picture and forced some Americans to contemplate a new world, one in which, by the end of the twentieth century, stars on a screen would become more widely known and paid more homage than scientists, writers, presidents, artists, educators, soldiers, or reformers.

In the 1920s, Americans began to turn away from traditional heroes and look up to entertainers. They came to believe that to be young and beautiful is better than to be old and wise, that sexuality lurks behind all behavior, and that living for the moment is preferable to planning for the future. With the growth of movies and the omnipresence of newsreels, celebrities penetrated and influenced the culture and gained a lasting hold on the American psyche.

When Princess Diana was killed at the age of thirty-six in an automobile crash and Mother Teresa died of heart failure less than a week later at the age of eighty-seven, the debate buried in the 1926 newspaper stories about Valentino and Eliot resurfaced: Why did we pay so much attention to Diana and so little to Mother Teresa? Students today regularly ask me about these two women. Diana tried to abolish land mines and help babies with AIDS. Wasn't that heroic? Mother Teresa gave her entire life to helping the poor and didn't seek publicity. Wasn't that more heroic?

Princess Diana was the quintessential celebrity: young, beautiful, aristocratic, with a shy, magic smile. She appeared on the cover of *People* thirteen times, more often than any other person in the history of the magazine. Diana's problems—depression, bulimia, and an unfaithful husband—made her even more alluring. She showed a certain courage by defying the royal family and rebuilding her life, and she died suddenly, tragically, and young. Mother Teresa spent most of her life on the streets of Calcutta and in dank hospitals, cleaning lepers and feeding emaciated babies. Dying in her eighties, she evoked respect and admiration but did not call up the primal emotions generated by a pretty princess who in the prime of life died in a Paris tunnel surrounded by paparazzi.

Celebrities satisfy urgent needs. To make up for ordinary faces, we seek beauty. To compensate for humdrum lives, we crave adventure. To forget ourselves, we escape to the movies and leaf through glossy magazines whose pages release alluring scents. In a hardworking country with few holidays and rituals, celebrities provide relief. They stand for whatever it is we want and do not have; they seem to have it all in a society that honors winners.

During the second half of the twentieth century, technology made it possible for us to spend more and more time with celebrities. In the 1950s, television brought them into our living rooms. Today we have eighty-one TV sets for every hundred Americans; in the typical household, the television runs over seven hours a day. Satellite dishes offer a hundred channels or more, and VCRs allow us to replay shows and movies. *Entertainment Tonight* and *Inside Edition* compete with the evening news. Many serious news programs have given in to the celebrity culture they sometimes criticize, routinely including celebrity clips.

Today, celebrities are omnipresent, giving the news, selling products, commenting on world affairs, endorsing politicians. *Reader's Guide to Periodical Literature* lists twelve articles under the heading of CELEBRITIES between 1955 and 1960 and over a thousand between 1995 and 2000. *People* magazine has a higher circulation than *Newsweek,* and *Forbes* magazine reports a multibillion-dollar industry for celebrity collectibles at Sotheby's.

On our computers, we can press a few keys and chat with the stars, enter famous names, find unlimited information, and join fan clubs with people all over the world. Celebrity Service International has a database of over 650,000 names and will release information for a yearly retainer of over $3,000. There are celebrity cruises, resorts, dolls, criminals, weddings, sightings, trials, tattoos, madams, and stalkers; forty thousand celebrity look-alikes are registered with their agents. A Massachusetts couple collects celebrity trash and calls it art.

We know who wins Academy Awards, Golden Globe Awards, and the Heisman Trophy but not who wins the Carnegie Hero Medal, the

Congressional Medal of Honor, or the Presidential Medal of Freedom. Our children know more about the life of Madonna than the life of Abraham Lincoln. Instead of finding heroes in fairy tales and adventure stories and biographies, many look to models, pop singers, and athletes.

IN CHICAGO, I took a city bus tour with an articulate twenty-eight-year-old guide. He showed us where the *Jerry Springer Show* and the *Jenny Jones Show* are filmed and told us how to get tickets to join a studio audience. We drove by Michael Jordan's restaurant and Oprah's apartment building. Would we like to know more about the cast of *Chicago Hope?* he asked. Did we want to see the subway line featured in the movie *Risky Business?*

In a culture increasingly more visual, we have become obsessed with beauty, youth, and sex appeal. Inundated with images of the famous, some people conclude you do not matter unless you make it in front of a camera. On the *Jerry Springer Show,* guests routinely humiliate themselves, yet they report their moment on national television as the high point in their lives. On the tape of the Columbine murders eventually released by the police, Eric Harris and Dylan Klebold speculate about who will compete for movie rights to their story after their death.

Not only has the delivery system become more powerful and expanded the celebrity pool; our values have shifted. The belief in a high culture to which educated citizens might aspire and the notion that our leisure hours might in part be devoted to instruction and self-improvement have given way to a new ethic of entertainment. "Americans spend 58 percent of their waking time interacting with media," according to writer and industry consultant Michael Wolf in his 1999 book *The Entertainment Economy.* In a *New Yorker* interview, Wolf says, "I really believe that entertainment in a lot of ways has become a way for people to come together . . . a replacement for religion. And I think that in the same way people used to quote scripture, they're now quoting *Seinfeld.*" A society tipping toward entertainment, one that believes in popular culture and values fame per se, is a society comfortable with celebrities and uneasy with heroes. "Face it, Dr. Gibbon, we believe in Hollywood," a student told me politely in a New Jersey high school.

Most significantly, celebrities have become more powerful today not only because of technological advances and shifting values but because of a fundamental change in the way we treat them. Fifty-four million people—approximately 83 percent of the entire television audience at the time—watched the *Ed Sullivan Show* on January 6, 1957, when the camera was not allowed to roam below Elvis Presley's waist. Still, no serious journalist in 1957 considered asking Elvis his opinion on Sputnik and civil rights or whether he endorsed Eisenhower.

In the late 1960s, celebrities ceased to be merely entertainers. They became spokespersons, enlightening us about war and telling us what was wrong with America. Quick to echo the criticism of the counterculture, celebrities found America moralistic and materialistic. Wavering and confused—after race riots, assassinations, Vietnam, and Watergate—we embraced our celebrities as philosophers. Today celebrity interviews are routine on *20/20, Prime Time,* and *48 Hours.* Political candidates condemn Hollywood and then seek celebrity endorsements. As early as 1961, historian Daniel Boorstin in his book *The Image* cautioned Americans they were confusing fame with greatness: "The hero is distinguished by his achievement; the celebrity by his image or trademark." Boorstin could not, however, have imagined that, by the beginning of the twenty-first century, celebrities would have become our philosopher kings.

HOUDON'S BUST OF FRANKLIN

If to be venerated for benevolence, if to be admired for talents, if to be esteemed for patriotism, if to be loved for philanthropy can gratify the human mind, you must have the pleasing consolation to know that you have not lived in vain.

—George Washington, 1789
Letter to Ben Franklin

When Franklin arrived in Paris in 1776, the gendarme who kept tabs on distinguished foreign visitors had this to say about him: "Dr. Franklin lately arrived in this country. This Quaker wears the full costume of his sect. He has an agreeable physiognomy; spectacles always on his eyes; but little hair; fur cap is always on his head. He wears no powder; tidy in his dress; very white linen; a walking stick his only defense." Almost immediately Franklin's portrait was everywhere in Paris: on rings, watches, snuffboxes, medallions, bracelets, and chamber pots. World-famous French sculptor Jean-Antoine Houdon pursued Franklin around Paris, hoping to do a bust, but could not persuade Franklin to sit for him. Instead, relying on previous portraits and studying Franklin at parties, Houdon produced the startling likeness that now sits in the Philadelphia Museum of Art.

Although not a great believer in the possibility of seeing character in faces, I find in Houdon's masterpiece of Franklin humor, wisdom, humility, and a touch of melancholy, as if this energetic optimist knew his life was winding down. How do we reconcile this evocative bust of Franklin against a poster advertising the 2000 History Channel's series *Founding Fathers*—a portrait of Franklin with "skirt chaser" written across his face? How might we look at Franklin, our first homegrown secular hero before the Revolutionary War? Of course we suspect that anyone, like Franklin, who declared his goal was to improve his character and serve mankind had to be a hypocrite.

To make Franklin more human, I tell my audiences that when he was twenty-one he almost died of pleurisy, that he lost his four-year-old son, Francis, to smallpox, that he had to take opium for gout. His son William probably was illegitimate, but—with his common-law wife, Deborah—Franklin raised the boy, who became his father's closest companion, a scientific colleague, governor of New Jersey, and later—much to Franklin's sorrow—a famous Tory.

Still familiar to Americans today are maxims from Franklin's Colonial best-seller, *Poor Richard's Almanac,* like "God helps them that help themselves" and "Fish and visitors stink in three days." As a humorist, he wrote satirical essays mocking religious hypocrisy, the pretensions of a Harvard education, and the follies of the British Empire; *Drinker's Dictionary,* listing one hundred words for *inebriation;* and a famous unpublished pamphlet, "Advice to a Young Man in the Choice of a Mistress."

The more I get to know Franklin, the more I like him. To his children he wrote affectionate letters, for his wife a poem of praise. He eschewed backbiting and freely gave credit to fellow scientists and diplomats. Franklin was also happy, serene, and modest—rare qualities in a hero. Historian Samuel Eliot Morison noted in an essay that he had read thousands of letters written by Franklin and never found him either mean or vindictive. Still, Franklin was not naive. In a 1780 letter looking ahead to a utopia where lives would be long and food abundant, he implied that men would probably still "be wolves to one another."

Franklin is the only founding father to sign the three key documents of early American history: the Declaration of Independence, the Peace of Paris that ended the Revolutionary War, and the Constitution—all of which might not have happened without him. Never quick to praise a colleague, John Adams said that Franklin's reputation had surpassed that of Sir Isaac Newton, Frederick the Great, and Voltaire.

In 1748, at the age of forty-two, Franklin gave up a lucrative printing business to devote the rest of his life to seeking knowledge and doing good works. He invented the lightning rod and bifocal lenses, studied whirlwinds and waterspouts, speculated on the nature of sunspots, and charted the Gulf Stream. In his spare time, he set up a laboratory and, through a series of ingenious experiments, made profound discoveries in electricity.

During the revolutionary crisis, Franklin gave up his scientific research to serve his country. He fought the Stamp Act, wrote 126 newspaper articles defending American rights, and became a delegate to the Continental Congress. Congress sent him to France in 1776, where two years later he helped negotiate a treaty that provided money and troops for a Colonial army badly in need of supplies. At the end of the Revolution, Franklin returned from France and retired to Philadelphia, where in his eighties he helped shape the new Constitution and form the American Anti-Slavery Association.

In 1790, over twenty thousand people—the largest crowd ever assembled in Philadelphia—followed Franklin's funeral cortege from his home to Christ Church Burial Ground. Bells tolled, militia fired their guns, and ships in the harbor flew their flags at half mast.

Way ahead of his time, Franklin was an advocate of daylight saving time, penal reform, an international organization of nations, good ventilation and frequent bathing, and electric shock treatment for mentally ill patients. Looking into the future, he predicted aerial navigation by dirigibles, a longer life span, and America's explosive growth in population.

In Cambridge, I spoke with I. Bernard Cohen, whose course on the history of science in the Western World I had taken in 1961. Over the last forty years, Cohen has written over forty books, including several studies of Franklin, and countless articles exploring and celebrating scientific genius. In *Science and the Founding Fathers,* he demonstrates how scientific knowledge formed Franklin's political ideas. Cohen said that Franklin is one of his heroes, that few Americans recognize Franklin was a genius, making profound discoveries in electricity, and that Americans, in picking their heroes, have paid more attention to soldiers and politicians than to scientists.

Who influenced Franklin? In his autobiography, he mentions Cotton Mather's best-selling *Essays to Do Good*. He also cites John Bunyan's *The Pilgrim's Progress* as key to his development, and he devoured Plutarch's *Lives*. Nor should we discount Franklin's father, who, after a long day of making candles, gathered his large family around the dinner table to encourage conversation about useful topics. Sadly, we know little about Franklin's mother, as the historical record is usually silent on the contributions of women.

Our first Colonial secular hero reflects emerging American values: tolerance, idealism, curiosity, pragmatism, humor. He also helped create these values. Franklin's influential autobiography injected into the American psyche a belief in the self-made man, a passion for self-improvement, the importance of philanthropy and public service, and, one might add, the value of simple lucid writing. To the Puritan values Franklin inherited from his parents—thrift and hard work—he added the Enlightenment values of tolerance and reason. And in addition to being a scientific genius and an astute diplomat, he was a wise and kind man.

Franklin would be amused to know that in contemporary America he is known as "skirt chaser" rather than "kite flyer." Of all the founding fathers, he would most welcome our openness about sexuality. (Washington would be embarrassed, Jefferson reticent, John Adams outraged.) Franklin talked openly about lust and admitted youthful indiscretions. His enemies concluded he was a lecher, but the historical record leaves no evidence of promiscuity, indicating only that Franklin loved the company of women and treated them with an ease and equality rare in the eighteenth century. His core values were reason and moderation, his ruling passions, science and the improvement of society.

Seven

THE LIVES OF HEROES

Formerly we used to canonize our heroes. The modern method is to vulgarize them.

—Oscar Wilde, 1891

In 1858, impatient with Victorian prudery, tired of the glorification of George Washington, and familiar with the debate over Horatio Greenough's statue, novelist Nathaniel Hawthorne asked, "Did anybody ever see Washington naked?" Today we need not ask such a question. The spectacle of an American president evading questions about oral sex in the Oval Office in front of a leering world in 1998 was just one more sign of a revolution so sudden and pervasive that we take it for granted, the culmination of America's forty-year experiment with sexual freedom.

During the last half of the twentieth century, the United States overcame prudery, eliminated censorship, and forged a revolution. No longer is sex secret, shameful, sordid, and sinful; absent from books, magazines, television, and movies; ignored by schools and teachers; or whispered about in front of children. Abandoning Puritan guilt and Victorian inhibition, Americans have taken sex out of the bedroom, away from church and state, and put it at the very center of our culture.

The sexual revolution has a healthy side. Out of dark corners it has brought child abuse, rape, harassment, gay bashing, incest, and domestic violence. It has diminished the power of patriarchy and the double standard and increased tolerance.

But the sexual revolution also has an unhealthy side. It has obliterated privacy, increased illegitimacy, made children less innocent, and devalued marriage and the family. It has also relentlessly stimulated the most powerful part of our brain while negating the rules for regulating our appetites.

Viewed through the lens of sexuality, the American past is personal. Frederick Douglass had a mistress. Neither Douglas MacArthur nor Dwight Eisenhower, it is said, resisted temptation when defending their country overseas. Franklin and Eleanor Roosevelt's intimate life is not off bounds, nor is the love life of Henry James, Woodrow Wilson, or Emily Dickinson.

THIS BUSINESS ABOUT sex and the hero is complicated. "If a man's public record be a clear one . . . I do not inquire what his private life may have been," said Susan B. Anthony in the nineteenth century. One can say, like Anthony, that it is none of our business, or as Alfred, Lord Tennyson said to Lord Byron's many critics, "What business has the public to want to know all about Byron's wildnesses? He has given them fine work, and they ought to be satisfied." We can be agnostic and say that we can never really know the intimate lives of others, or blasé and say that sex is unimportant. Or we can claim that sex is crucial, that without this intimate knowledge we can neither understand leaders nor fairly evaluate our past heroes—not our geniuses, humanitarians, musicians, soldiers, statesmen, or scientists, not even our fictional heroes. This is the stance that America assumed in the second half of the twentieth century. It is an alluring premise, but translating it into reality is dangerous—and has been devastating to the notion of the heroic.

"Heroism," said the Swiss writer Henri Amiel in the mid-nineteenth century, "is the brilliant triumph of the soul over the flesh." Conversely, the triumph of the flesh over the soul makes it hard to have heroes. So powerful is sex, so quickly does it lodge in the brain, that even if we aim to be impartial, if we sincerely want to balance the human and the heroic, we slide inexorably toward the human. When the first question asked about past and present heroes is "What did they do in bed?" it is easy to forget extraordinary acts of bravery, accomplishment, and nobility.

Students often ask me about John F. Kennedy. I point out that Kennedy rescued his men in World War II when his torpedo boat was cut in half, that for much of his life he suffered in hospitals, and that historians generally credit him with peacefully settling the Cuban missile crisis. We will never know (and perhaps never should know) all the facts of John F. Kennedy's sex life. In the White House, he was not monogamous. Many Americans, myself included, find this upsetting—given his marriage vows, his religion, his two young children, his obligation to set an example, and his potential vulnerability to blackmail. Still, we are so inundated with sexual revelations about John F. Kennedy, so many salacious books have been written, so many tell-all movies made, that it is now difficult to visit his presidential library—in the soaring shiplike building overlooking Boston Harbor—and see in the photographs anything other than a sexual predator.

In the 1994 movie *Immortal Beloved,* Gary Oldman plays a Ludwig van Beethoven more intent on chasing women than in composing music. That Beethoven ardently sought love and failed is true. That Beethoven read Plutarch and Goethe, denounced Napoleon, and, through unremitting effort and genius, produced some of history's most memorable music is also true—and essentially ignored. Viewers of the film may never learn that Beethoven's heroes were Socrates and Jesus. Hearing his music as the background score for temper tantrums and seductions, they will have difficulty understanding biographer Maynard Solomon's assessment that Beethoven's symphonies "hold out images of beauty, joy, and renewal." In *Immortal Beloved,* a genius of the Age of Reason is "made human," his sexuality highlighted, his heroism set aside.

At the Paine Music Center at Harvard, I talked to Professor Lewis Lockwood, who has spent his life studying Beethoven's symphonies, string quartets, and piano sonatas. We discussed a new path of research: analyzing locks of the composer's hair to determine whether he had syphilis. The interest now, said Lockwood, is on the ways Beethoven failed. Nathaniel Hawthorne's 1850 novel *The Scarlet Letter* is still widely taught in high schools today. In the novel, Hester Prynne becomes an adulteress, believing her older husband lost at sea. She and her daughter, Pearl, are cast to the edge of the Puritan community. A woman of courage, depth, and complexity, Hester is passionate yet pious, rebellious yet penitent, defiant yet stoic. "Shame, Despair, Solitude! These had been her teachers—stern and wild ones—and they had made her strong," writes Hawthorne. Several movies have been made of *The Scarlet Letter* since the 1920s. In the most recent version, Demi Moore plays Hester Prynne as sensualist. Early in the movie, she watches the young minister, Arthur Dimmesdale, swim naked in a pool. While making love to Dimmesdale in her barn, she is spied on by a female servant; at the end of the movie, a lecherous Puritan tries to rape her. As Demi Moore cavorts from scene to scene, a complex heroine of American literature becomes one-dimensional, a sybarite in Puritan clothing.

Hawthorne spent his life peering into the dark corners of the human soul. No friend of Puritanism, he eschewed repression and self-righteousness. He would, I think, applaud today's openness, tolerance, and honesty about sex—and our attempts to combat sexual abuse and exploitation. But Hawthorne also knew that the appetite for sexual gossip is insatiable. Impatient as he was with hero worship in 1856, he would easily understand that scholarly desire for personal information and "truth" can quickly degenerate into voyeurism. Hawthorne hoped Americans would be able to see George Washington as a human being, but he did not envision a time when hedonism and cynicism would replace sublimation and idealism.

Champions of the sexual revolution hoped that it would set us free and make us more tolerant, not that, in opening doors once closed and seeking knowledge once forbidden, we would use sexual information to slander, titillate, sell books and movies, and bring past and present heroes to heel.

Pathography

To give verisimilitude to his best-selling book *The Oregon Trail,* nineteenth-century historian Francis Parkman traveled extensively in the West in the 1840s, living among fur trappers and Sioux tribes. In the process, he ruined his health. Defying partial blindness and chronic illness, he turned out many more books, tracing the exploits of his heroes, René de La Salle and Samuel de Champlain. Theodore Roosevelt dedicated *The Winning of the West* to Parkman. Oliver Wendell Holmes Jr. found Parkman's travels extraordinary, his portraits of explorers riveting.

Contemporary critics claim, however, that Parkman intentionally became an invalid to make himself heroic and projected on his explorer heroes his own visions of grandeur.

In 1843, Isabella Van Wagenen, a tall raw-boned freed slave, had a vision that she should take to the road and preach. An ardent revivalist, she called herself Sojourner Truth and traveled all over America. "I cannot read a book, but I can read the people," she declared. In time she joined with the abolitionists to become an eloquent crusader for emancipation and, after the Civil War, for women's rights. In the late 1840s she publicly rebuked Frederick Douglass when the usually peaceful reformer advocated violent revolution. After hearing his incendiary speeches in Boston's Faneuil Hall, Truth, always the believer, asked, "Frederick, is God dead?"

Truth was unable to read or write, say modern biographers, and dictated her narrative in order to maximize sales and embellish her own legend.

In contemporary America, men and women like Francis Parkman and Sojourner Truth are transformed into spin doctors who carefully crafted their own stories to impress future historians. Skeptics allow that an explorer like Parkman was admirable to live with the Sioux but condemn him for not rising above his chauvinistic Boston Brahmin upbringing to surmount every bias of his century. And Parkman made the mistake of putting in writing in the 1880s what most Americans believed at the time, that women should not participate in politics. People once considered heroes are fast forwarded and put on trial in our century, with no excuses for those who do not measure up. Biography today is rarely about greatness. At best, it displays a dispassionate balance. More often, it focuses on failure, compromise, and weakness and unveils the intimate life—slighting artistic accomplishment, scientific discovery, and political achievement. At worst, contemporary biographers self-righteously excoriate any hint of impurity, prejudice, sexism, or hypocrisy.

General Douglas MacArthur was not an easy or uncomplicated man, but he was heroic. By the time we finish Geoffrey Perret's biography of MacArthur, *Old Soldiers Never Die,* we forget MacArthur's return to the Philippines, his rebuilding of Japan, and his daring amphibious landing in Korea. Gone are the soaring speeches and the medals earned during World War II. Instead, Perret concentrates on MacArthur's vanity and self-promotion.

Scientists also feel the scalpel. Marie Curie discovered radium, won two Nobel Prizes, and became known worldwide. In 1937, her daughter, Eve, wrote a biography of her mother, *Madame Curie,* that became an inspiration for young women considering a career in science, and the 1943 movie of Marie Curie's life starring Greer Garson moved audiences all over the world. In *Marie Curie,* contemporary biographer Susan Quinn peels away what she considers to be mythology and stresses the scientist's duplicity, adultery, and neglect of her children.

When I was young, I thought the core of T. S. Eliot's life was arresting poetry and original criticism. I did not read Eliot's bawdy poems, which he requested be burned. Today we can relish the poems, recently unearthed, and speculate about whether Eliot was impotent and if his wife had an affair with Bertrand Russell. We can debate whether Eliot was anti-Semitic. We can forget haunting and memorable and musical lines and irony and insight and wit. No longer do we remember a man who helped countless young writers. In her 1999 biography of Eliot, Lyndall Gordon writes, "Biographers, of all people, know it is naive to expect the great to be good." Her title is *T. S. Eliot: An Imperfect Life.* Routinely, contemporary biographers add deflating subtitles.

Joyce Carol Oates coined the word *pathography* in 1988 to describe biographies that focus on aberration. Oates was prophetic. What was a dangerous drift in 1988 has now become the norm. Today, we are all tempted by pathography and conditioned to look for the worst in people. Focusing on the mundane and the neurotic, pathography offers an outlet for resentment and envy and eclipses extraordinary achievement. Modern psychology is quick to discount noble motives but fails to scrutinize our capacity for envy.

Even well-intentioned biographers are conditioned by the times and, like us, are tempted by pathography. Our biographers are also human. They must compete for readers and money and status. They know that the intimate life will sell and a juicy revelation might make their book stand out.

Hagiography

At the beginning of the nineteenth century, the *Monthly Anthology* noted, "The design of biography is to celebrate useful talents, to record patriotick labours, and to exhibit characteristick traits of virtue." When Mason Locke Weems wrote *The Life and Memorable Actions of George Washington,* he was determined to inspire young people and a young country. Weems made up stories, deleted unpleasant facts, and freely drew moral lessons. His goal, he said, was "to exalt human nature." It was Weems who had young Washington try his new hatchet on a cherry tree and Weems who invented the father's reply to George's honesty: "Such an act of heroism is worth more than a thousand trees." His biography went through seventy editions and inspired thousands of Americans, including a young Abraham Lincoln. Uplifting biography that errs on the side of the fanciful and mythic, known as hagiography, can be useful, even therapeutic.

But hagiography's goal, to elevate the subject and inspire the reader, is difficult to defend. Pathography, however, is equally false and even more damaging, particularly to young Americans today, who are raised on nastiness and told that all leaders are hopelessly flawed.

Hagiography does not permit heroes to be human. Pathography does not permit humans to be heroic. Hagiography hides blemishes; pathography magnifies them. Hagiography promotes a shallow patriotism; it also produces cynicism. Pathography induces self-righteousness; it also produces despair. Each is harmful to heroes: the one routinely romanticizes, the other denigrates.

In the tradition of the nineteenth century, some biographers today write about people they admire. They search for truth but exercise charity. In his biography of explorer Meriwether Lewis, *Undaunted Courage,* Stephen Ambrose says, "If I was ever in a desperate situation . . . I would want Meriwether Lewis for my leader." In a telephone interview, Ambrose told me he is a professional hero worshiper and is not ashamed to be labeled a triumphalist. Once, he said, he spent an entire night next to Lewis's grave in a Tennessee cemetery.

David McCullough likes to find heroes, particularly among scientists and engineers. In *Brave Companions,* he celebrates the naturalist Louis Agassiz and the builder of the Brooklyn Bridge, John Roebling. In today's world, he told me in an interview, people think believing in heroes is naive, but the need for heroes is "built into us." Heroes "show us the possibilities in life and enlarge the experience of being human . . . and give us the capacity to endure the tragic." McCullough boldly concludes his biography *Truman* by declaring Truman "a figure of world stature, both a great and good man, and a great American president."

William Manchester is not ignorant of Douglas MacArthur's flaws, but in *American Caesar* he asks us to consider MacArthur "at his best, which is how he deserves to be remembered." Blanche Wiesen Cook may be at times overly interested in Eleanor Roosevelt's intimate life, but she is refreshingly appreciative of her achievements. In *Eleanor Roosevelt* she depicts the First Lady as brave, spiritual, and optimistic.

Richard Brookhiser proudly imitates Plutarch's *Lives* in *Founding Father,* in what he describes as a "moral biography" of George Washington. Brookhiser praises Washington's courage and physical presence, but he finds even more appealing and instructive Washington's commitment to civility and self-control, values rare today. Brookhiser points out that where we are wavering, Washington is certain; where we believe in openness and self-exploration, Washington praises restraint and virtuous action.

DEBUNKING BIOGRAPHIES ARE not new. In 1904, muckraker Ida Tarbell savaged John D. Rockefeller in *The History of the Standard Oil Company.* In 1918, Lytton Strachey shocked readers with *Eminent Victorians,* mocking Florence Nightingale for becoming fanatical about reforming the British military and General Charles Gordon for fighting to the death at Khartoum. In the 1920s, William E. Woodward coined the word *debunking* and wrote revisionist biographies of George Washington, Ulysses S. Grant, and the Marquis de Lafayette. In *George Washington: The Image and the Man,* Woodward concludes that, while possessed of a certain animal courage, our founding father was intellectually dull and personally vain.

What is new about these biographies is their number and the lack of debate about accepting them. What is new is the attitude that past and present heroes are ordinary people benefiting from a few good breaks. What is new is the relentless concentration on personal and sexual lives. Committed to the notion that every aspect of private life may influence public action, scientific discovery, or artistic creation, we have enshrined the intimate life.

Might we not recognize that even great men and women have their bad days and cannot surmount every prejudice of their time? Could some areas of their private lives be off bounds and some of our prurient impulses controlled? As historian Barbara Tuchman prophetically asked, before she died in 1989, "Do we really have to know of some famous person that he wet his pants at age six and practiced oral sex at sixty?"

RUSHMORE REVISITED

It is to be lamented . . . that great characters are seldom without a blot.
—George Washington, 1786

None of us, no, not one, is perfect, and were we to love none who had imperfections, this world would be a desert for our love.
—Thomas Jefferson, 1790

The author of the life of his hero paints him as a perfect man—magnifies his perfections and suppresses his imperfections—describes the success of his hero in glowing terms, never once hinting at his failures and blunders.
—Abraham Lincoln, circa 1857

It is not having been in the Dark House, but having left it, that counts.
—Theodore Roosevelt, 1916

Mount Rushmore was intended to be a monument to western explorers, a way to attract tourists to the natural beauty of the Black Hills of South Dakota. In the mind of then state historian Doane Robinson, it would celebrate Lewis and Clark, John C. Frémont, and Sacagawea. Robinson tried his idea out on sculptor Gutzon Borglum, who liked the idea of mountain carving and had recently chiseled a figure of Robert E. Lee into a towering granite rock in Georgia. But Borglum saw in the mountain the faces of presidents rather than explorers, a celebration of the founding and expansion of the nation, a tribute to democratic ideals.

Borglum had trained in Paris under Auguste Rodin and produced statues celebrated for their fidelity to life. Returning to America, he carved angels and apostles for the Cathedral Church of Saint John the Divine in New York City and patriots for Statuary Hall in the nation's capitol. Borglum was also a boxer, fencer, and orator who had campaigned for Roosevelt's Bull Moose Party in the election of 1912. When World War I broke out, he reported on the state of the American aircraft industry for Woodrow Wilson. A restless, energetic man, Borglum courted reporters and patrons, offering opinions on everything and offending many, but his patriotism was sincere. Mount Rushmore offered Borglum the supreme challenge: a chance to create a tribute to America that would rival the pyramids.

Of course the monument needed money, and its backers turned to President Calvin Coolidge, who decided to take a short vacation in the Black Hills in 1927. Knowing the president was an ardent angler, local officials made certain the trout streams were well stocked, and Coolidge extended his visit, giving Robinson and Borglum time to persuade him that a national monument in the Dakotas had merit. They were successful. At the groundbreaking on August 10, 1927, President Coolidge celebrated George Washington for founding America, Jefferson for expanding it, Lincoln for preserving it, and Roosevelt for reaching out to the world. After he finished speaking, Coolidge handed Borglum a set of drills, and the artist climbed to the top of the mountain and started to work.

Three years passed, as four hundred miners and rock carvers blasted and chiseled a granite peak. On July 4, 1930, amid fireworks and speeches, Washington's head was unveiled. It took another eleven years to produce Jefferson, Lincoln, and Roosevelt. Each face is sixty feet high, each nose twenty feet long, each eye eleven feet across. Borglum said about his creation that "we believe a nation's memorial should, like Washington, Jefferson, Lincoln, and Roosevelt, have a serenity, a nobility, a power that reflects the gods who inspired them and suggests the gods they have become." Today we no longer consider the four presidents on Mount Rushmore gods. In an age skeptical of greatness, inundated with information, and cynical about politicians, how might we see them?

George Washington

In 1927, Borglum had no doubt about whose face he should carve first, but in 2001 George Washington is not an easy sell. Washington was a soldier and an aristocrat. He owned slaves. Students today want to know about Washington's fierce temper and wooden teeth, whether he grew marijuana at Mount Vernon, and why he and Martha had no children.

It helps to remind my audiences that Washington was human. His father died when he was eleven; his mother was dour. He didn't attend college or travel to Europe, couldn't marry the woman he loved, and didn't get from Britain the commission he thought he deserved. In an age when disease killed capriciously, he watched his half brother, Lawrence, die from tuberculosis and his stepdaughter, Patsy, succumb to epilepsy. His own face was scarred by smallpox, his body at times weakened by malaria and dysentery.

Washington liked to play cards, drink wine, dance, and watch cock-fights. He was happiest on horseback, chasing foxes, hacking trails, and improving his estate. Although he achieved a measure of fame for his military actions in the French and Indian War, until 1775 he seemed ordinary. Then the war came. He did not seek to be commander, and he should have lost. Great Britain was confident and formidable, wealthy and well-equipped—an eighteenth-century superpower. Washington had few soldiers and they were untrained. Short of boots and bullets, they grew bitter. Many Americans bet on Great Britain.

Washington failed at first, at Brooklyn Heights and Brandywine. And he suffered—as his men went without pay, Congress squabbled, his army melted away, and defeat seemed increasingly certain. He wrote in a letter, "I never was in such an unhappy divided state." In 1776 he told his brother he would gladly quit.

But he didn't. He dodged and retreated and somehow kept an army in the field and endured the harsh winter at Valley Forge. He took risks, attacked at Trenton and Princeton, and forced himself to appear confident and indomitable before his men, despite fatigue and frustration. And he grew—as a general and a politician and a human being.

Washington learned to use America's wilderness and to exploit England's arrogance. Patiently, he extracted authority and supplies from a divided Congress. Stoically, he shook off critics. Above all, he endured—until the French sent money and Great Britain grew weary of their losses of men and material.

I tell my audiences that Washington is great because he showed extraordinary courage, not just the courage to face bullets but the courage to stick to a cause no matter how great the odds, the courage to shake off failure and transcend pain, the courage to take risks, to change, to grow.

When the war was over, Washington gave up his sword and returned to Mount Vernon to tend his estate. His magnanimity astonished the world. He was happy at Mount Vernon and would have preferred to stay there, but the Confederation was weak. The same sense of duty that made him give up his sword forced him to return to Philadelphia for the Constitutional Convention and then to serve eight years as our first president, putting his country's welfare above his personal happiness.

It is not hard to understand why, two hundred years ago, Americans revered Washington. A soldier and superb horseman, he was tall, athletic, imposing, gentlemanly, mysterious. Tested by crisis and war, he endured and prevailed.

Washington also inspired respect from those who knew him best. Washington was not brilliant like Hamilton or eloquent like Jefferson. He lacked Franklin's originality and Madison's insight. But our first president had character. Like the Stoics whose words he read, he exercised self-control. Imitating the famous Roman general Cato, he valued honor and reputation above wealth and power. He believed in conscience, in kindness, and in a caring and watchful God. With a few simple but powerful influences, a few key enduring convictions, he was a man who eschewed extremes, a man with a center, who could not be budged by catastrophe or success.

In these skeptical times, when we are more interested in reality than in mythology, it is important to recognize Washington's humanity. In a crowd, he seemed shy. On the podium, he was inarticulate. Contemporaries found him courteous but cold. Recognizing Washington's humanity, however, should not blind us to his heroism. In a crisis, he stood firm. Through willpower, he turned himself into an able general, a masterful administrator, and a prudent statesman. He learned from his mistakes, coped with despair, and demanded no reward.

After Washington died, Americans mourned for weeks. Biographers described Washington as superhuman, perfect. Painters portrayed him ascending into heaven. Future leaders Daniel Webster, Robert E. Lee, and Abraham Lincoln adopted Washington as a personal hero.

In all cultures, the founders and protectors of nations have been considered preeminent heroes. But Washington is more than the father of his country. He believed the president should be an example to the nation, he injected majesty and humility into the office, and he became a symbol of incorruptibility. Into American political life, he infused the Roman notion of self-control and the ancient belief that the state comes before the self. By giving up his sword and disbanding his armies, he established at our founding the principle of civilian control. By backing the Constitution and agreeing to serve as president, he made it possible for us to start our history as one nation instead of thirteen squabbling states. In 1789, before his inauguration, he wrote, "Integrity and firmness are all I can promise." Thomas Jefferson thought him great and good. So might we.

Thomas Jefferson

Unlike Washington, Jefferson never fought in a battle or led troops. But Borglum and his South Dakota patrons agreed that the man who wrote the Declaration of Independence and acquired almost half the

United States from France should stand next to the nation's founder on the mountain.

A man of letters, Jefferson read compulsively and wrote fluently. Also a scientist, he invented a new plow, speculated about dinosaurs, and corresponded with intellectuals all over the world. Jefferson was our most learned and versatile president, probably a genius. While Washington's victories made possible the founding of our country, Jefferson's words gave expression to our credo: belief in equality and liberty and devotion to freedom of conscience. Washington is the warrior hero, Jefferson our intellectual one.

Jefferson could name his heroes: John Locke and Francis Bacon, one the theorist of limited government, the other the champion of scientific empiricism. Jefferson believed in mentors and in the idea that, by imitating admirable and accomplished individuals, one can improve both mind and character. He particularly idealized Dr. William Small, professor of natural philosophy at William and Mary College, who taught him science, introduced him to mathematics, and instilled in him a fervor for learning. In his autobiography, Jefferson wrote, "Under temptations and difficulties, I would ask myself what would Dr. Small do in this situation." Losing his father when he was fourteen, Jefferson looked for substitutes, such as Governor Francis Fauquier of Virginia and, of course, George Washington. Jefferson in turn served as father figure and hero to future presidents James Madison and James Monroe.

By challenging English power before it became fashionable and defending radicals like Thomas Paine, Jefferson displayed courage. As president, he defied public opinion and made himself unpopular with both political parties by closing American ports rather than risking the unprepared young nation in a world at war.

Of the four presidents on Rushmore, Jefferson is the most complex. He detested politics, hated to speak in public, and escaped to Monticello whenever he could, planting trees and expanding his estate. Like his companions on the mountain, Jefferson was extraordinarily disciplined, ambitious, and idealistic, believing that integrity was as important as intellectual excellence. Like them, he determined early in life that he would play a role on the world's stage. But then begin the paradoxes: a man who craved friendship yet was intensely private; an aristocrat who detested privilege; an urban intellectual who feared cities; a slave owner who preached equality; a peaceful man who sanctioned violent rebellion; a dreamer and philosopher who served as a hard-nosed and cunning diplomat.

One would expect a genius to be complicated and a politician to appear inconsistent. But one would not necessarily expect to discover underneath the genius and politician a sweet-tempered, affectionate human being. Early in life, Jefferson, like Ben Franklin, decided not to be disputatious but always to listen to his opponent. Serving as minister to France, secretary of state, vice president, and president, Jefferson made enemies, yet invective against him did not make him nasty. He craved love and gave it freely, was devoted to his wife and daughters, and cherished his friends. At the end of his life, he reconciled his differences with John Adams, his former rival, to whom he wrote poignant, graceful letters.

Jefferson was familiar with loss. In addition to losing his father, he lost his wife, Martha, after ten happy years of marriage, when she died just after giving birth to their sixth child. During her last illness, Jefferson nursed Martha until her death and afterward shut himself in his room for weeks, refusing to talk to anyone. In 1803, during his first term as president, his daughter Patsy died at age twenty-three, leaving only his daughter Martha. Later in life he wrote to John Adams, "There are . . . even in the happiest life, some terrible convulsions."

In 1998, I attended a weeklong conference on Jefferson and read hundreds of his eighteen thousand letters. I came away impressed by his humanity and complexity, sympathetic to his pain and personal losses, and above all astounded by the range of his interests. Jefferson moves easily from Italian vineyards to yellow fever, from the bones of mammoths to Indian vocabularies, from whale oil to *King Lear,* from Epictetus to Jesus.

Of course, today what makes Jefferson an embattled hero, the most controversial figure on Mount Rushmore, is the fact that he owned slaves and probably fathered children by one of them, Sally Hemings. Though Jefferson hated slavery, he profited from it, and unlike Washington he did not free his slaves in his will. Early in life, Jefferson drew up proposals to eliminate slavery; later he threw up his hands in despair, passing on what he considered to be an intractable problem to future generations.

Who can read *Notes on the State of Virginia* and not admire Jefferson's catholic learning and scientific precision, yet who today can read him without wincing at his derogatory comments about African Americans? Jefferson was far in advance of many of his contemporaries in his views on slavery, but today he seems reactionary. And the strong evidence that he fathered Sally Hemings's children makes him appear hypocritical, since he condemned miscegenation, even though apologists remind us he was not married at the time and suggest the relationship with Sally Hemings may have been an affair of the heart.

Looking up at Mount Rushmore today, we could see a guilty and conflicted, maybe even selfish slaveholder who did not completely transcend his time. But we might also see a diplomat, architect, scientist, and idealist who believed in religious freedom and educational opportunity. We might also see the man who wrote the imperishable words that became the basis for a democratic movement that is still sweeping the world today.

Abraham Lincoln

Borglum read and reread Abraham Lincoln's letters and speeches. He had already sculpted a gigantic bust of Lincoln from a six-ton block of marble that President Theodore Roosevelt displayed in the White House in 1908.

On Good Friday, April 14, 1865, John Wilkes Booth shot and killed the president who had preserved the Union and freed the slaves. Just seven months before he was shot, Lincoln feared he might not be reelected in 1864. His enemies called him uncouth and indecisive, bloodthirsty, a dictator, a buffoon. Now, as his funeral train of eight black coaches moved slowly from Washington, D.C., to Springfield, Illinois, grieving citizens filed past his dead body in every major city, and Americans in the North mourned their dead leader.

During the next one hundred years, veneration for Lincoln expanded. Statues of him appeared all over America, the Gettysburg Address was etched in stone and memorized by schoolchildren, and his melancholy face appeared on U.S. currency, in city halls and state capitols, and above the desks of teachers in thousands of classrooms. Lincoln would become the wise statesman, the visionary war leader, the great emancipator, celebrated for his speeches and remembered for his kindness, humor, and sadness. Jane Addams recalled that her father kept the day of Lincoln's death as a holy day. When, in 1931, poet Edgar Lee Masters wrote a harsh biography of Lincoln, Congress debated whether the Postal Service should be permitted to send it through the mail.

Lincoln appeared on the national stage for only six years, a far shorter time than Washington or Jefferson. Only during his last year as president did Americans appreciate him; only after his death did his reputation soar.

Why is Lincoln still so venerated? He really was born in a log cabin and through unremitting effort turned himself into a skilled lawyer. His mother died when he was young, he lost his first love, and he struggled with melancholy. In a time of national crisis, he took office and grew as a leader. Of course he won the war, freed the slaves, and died a martyr. Unlike presidents today, he wrote his own speeches. But what makes Lincoln preeminent among our heroes is that he was a crafty politician who had greatness of soul. He placated office seekers, guided a divided cabinet throughout the war, and choreographed his reelection. Simultaneously, when his son died and his generals failed, he retained an internal compass and unshakable integrity. Of all our presidents, he is the most likable, the most human. He sees deeply, like a poet or a philosopher. And he is mysterious.

Lincoln turned to the men next to him on Mount Rushmore for inspiration. As a boy he read Weems's *Life of Washington*. He considered Jefferson a great politician and regularly quoted from the Declaration of Independence in his condemnations of slavery.

Lincoln was not perfect. He agonized over his relations with women, his long courtship of Mary Todd plunged him into melancholy, and his marriage to her was not idyllic. David Donald, Lincoln's most recent biographer, considers him a fatalist and describes him as fiercely ambitious, even as he admires him. Lincoln is sometimes portrayed as a racist by unfriendly critics who dwell on his statements about racial inferiority and reduce the Emancipation Proclamation to a military tactic rather than a gesture of idealism. Though Lincoln was not an abolitionist, he staked his 1860 campaign on combating the evils of slavery. As president of a divided and racist nation, he moved gradually and cautiously, but it is Lincoln who made eliminating slavery a war aim, who approved the use of African American troops, who fought for the Thirteenth Amendment, and who welcomed Frederick Douglass to the White House.

I am endlessly intrigued by Lincoln. When beaten down, I read about his struggles. Faced with difficult decisions, I ask, "What would Lincoln have done?" His enemies criticized him without restraint. Subjected to more stress than any other American president, he held on, endured, and became tougher, wiser, kinder. That is why historians regularly choose Lincoln as our greatest president, and more books have been written about him than about any other. If George Washington is the father of our nation, Lincoln is its savior. Both are the closest we have to national heroes.

Theodore Roosevelt

Borglum and his South Dakota patrons agreed that Mount Rushmore must include Washington, Jefferson, and Lincoln, but who would stand next to these three giants? Some Americans lobbied for Woodrow Wilson, who had guided America through a World War; some suggested Susan B. Anthony, who had crusaded for women's rights. Borglum decided on his friend, Theodore Roosevelt, who, like him, was outspoken, combative, larger than life, patriotic, and idealistic.

At the end of the nineteenth century, Americans had turned to this new hero, one who was born privileged but who wished to put capitalists in their place. Roosevelt became a New York State assemblyman, assistant secretary of the Navy, a reforming governor of New York, and vice president. When William McKinley was shot, Roosevelt became president.

Roosevelt believed in heroes. He idolized his father, a prominent humanitarian, and Abraham Lincoln. In *Hero Tales from American History,* he celebrated soldiers he admired, such as Admiral Farragut and John Paul Jones.

Roosevelt wanted to be a hero. Through a vigorous combination of boxing and horseback riding, he conquered asthma. Through incessant activity, he coped with the premature deaths of his parents and his first wife. When the Spanish-American War broke out, he charged up San Juan Hill in front of his men, with soldiers dropping on either side. While campaigning in Wisconsin in 1912, he was shot in the chest by a fanatic and continued speaking for an hour as if nothing had happened before seeking medical attention. Late in his life, he canoed in the jungles of Brazil, contracted malaria, and almost died.

Roosevelt was the perfect leader for a proud, confident, aggressive America—one that watched its industrial might surpass that of Great Britain—and the perfect leader for the Progressive Era of an America worried about concentration of wealth and eager for reform. Roosevelt had many opponents. He wrote, "If a man has a decided character, has a strongly accentuated career, it is normally the case of course that he makes ardent friends and bitter enemies." Even historians who admire Roosevelt—David McCullough and Edmund Morris—find him incorrigibly vain. After World War I, Roosevelt's celebration of military glory rings hollow. In an era of gender equality, his praise of masculinity claims few followers. And he was sometimes bombastic, often self-righteous.

Still, I find him very appealing. Roosevelt was more than an adventurer and a soldier. He was a respected scholar, an idealistic reformer, and a gifted speaker. Where we are skeptical, he was enthusiastic and optimistic, abounding with physical and mental energy. Where we have irony, he had certainty. In our age of disintegrating families, he was faithful to his wife, devoted to his children. And in a famous speech in Chicago he offered his credo: "I wish to preach not the doctrine of ignoble ease but the doctrine of the strenuous life." Unlike many contemporary politicians, he did not hire pollsters and speechwriters or spend time with lobbyists.

Our greatest heroes are larger than life. Roosevelt seemed omnipresent in his era, giving speeches, writing books, traveling abroad, playing with his children on the White House lawn, hunting lions in Africa, negotiating a peace treaty to end the Russo-Japanese War, and building the Panama Canal. He became a model for ordinary citizens. Every day of his presidency, Americans sent hundreds of letters to the White House, soliciting his advice. "Men in hope of finding their better selves attached themselves to him," wrote the early-twentieth-century historian Etling Morison. Warrior and reformer, preacher, conservationist, and devoted father, Roosevelt captured the imagination of turn-of-the-century America as no other president had since George Washington.

Chief Crazy Horse

Not far from Mount Rushmore a gigantic monument of Chief Crazy Horse is slowly taking shape on Thunderhead Mountain. The most famous Lakota warrior, respected by his own people as well as by his enemies, Crazy Horse fought George Custer at the Battle of the Little Bighorn and was later killed by American soldiers when he resisted imprisonment. We know comparatively little about this Native American hero because he died young (about thirty-five years old), and the Lakotas kept no written records. Oral histories taken after his death claimed that when he appeared on the battlefield "All Lakotas became brave." According to his most recent biographer, Larry McMurtry, Crazy Horse had moral authority and was valued by his people as much for his charity as for his courage, feeding the poor and helpless members of his tribe in times of scarcity.

Sculptor Korczak Ziolkowski trained under Borglum, working on the carving of Theodore Roosevelt. Living in South Dakota during the year he worked on Mount Rushmore, Ziolkowski became obsessed with the injustices visited on Native Americans and became convinced that they deserved a tribute to their bravery. From 1947 until his death in 1982 at age seventy-four, Ziolkowski worked on Thunderhead Mountain without salary, drilling and chiseling the outlines of the head and outstretched arm of Crazy Horse—just a small part of what will be eventually be a gigantic imposing figure of this Native American warrior on horseback. The work goes on, continued by Ziolkowski's widow, children, great-grandchildren, and extended family. About Crazy Horse, Ziolkowski wrote, "One of the many great and patriotic Indian heroes, Crazy Horse's tenacity of purpose, his modest life, his unfailing courage, his tragic death set him apart and above the others."

Our pluralistic democracy now praises local heroes and honors the contributions and sufferings of women, Native Americans, African Americans, and immigrants. But in expanding the pantheon of our heroes, do we need to demonize our past leaders? In honoring Chief Crazy Horse, do we need to chip away at the presidents on Mount Rushmore? In challenging our past, do we need to repudiate it?

Eight

ASHAMED OF OUR PAST

This I hold to be the chief office of history, to rescue virtuous actions from oblivion.

— Tacitus, circa A.D. 115

Let us remember, when we are told that history is the Newgate Calendar of nations, that it is also the record of a thousand forms of heroism and nobility.

— Will Durant, 1965

On July 4, 1826, the fiftieth anniversary of the Declaration of Independence, a twenty-six-year-old teacher stepped up to a lectern in the meetinghouse of Northampton, Massachusetts, and delivered his first public oration. His speech was celebratory; his subject, the advantages of American democracy. He described cultivated fields and busy wharves, talked about the importance of immigration and equality, and praised a free press, religious liberty, George Washington, and Benjamin Franklin.

As he spoke in the afternoon heat, George Bancroft did not know that two of his heroes, Thomas Jefferson and John Adams, had died within a few hours of each other. That our second and third presidents should die on the fiftieth anniversary of the declaration they had both signed struck most Americans at the time as evidence of a divine plan for the young nation. Later Bancroft, too, was to see the hand of God guiding that July day.

George Bancroft left teaching and eventually became the preeminent historian of the nineteenth century. He founded the Naval Academy and served as secretary of the Navy and minister to Great Britain. When Abraham Lincoln died, it was Bancroft who delivered the main eulogy before a grieving Congress. In 1891, when Bancroft died, President Benjamin Harrison ordered flags to be flown at half mast. From his Mathew Brady photograph, Bancroft stares out at us—slender, vital, serene, and confident—from another age, one that believed in progress, patriotism, and heroes.

Bancroft was a nineteenth-century triumphalist, seeing American history as a march toward goodness and greatness and believing in growth and material progress. The triumphalists also believed that great people make a difference. In the ten volumes of the *History of the Colonization of the United States,* starting with the discovery of America and concluding with the ratification of the Constitution, Bancroft demonstrated that equality was spreading and wealth increasing. In his opening volume, published in 1834, he states that "a favoring Providence . . . has conducted the country to its present happiness and glory." With pride he mentions canals, factories, steamships, railroads, the navy, and a growing population, with immigrants coming from every country. He praises our free press and our aloofness from foreign wars and calls the seven men killed at Lexington "village heroes . . . of a race divine." George Bancroft believed that out of a wasteland, America had created a garden.

Contemporary historian Howard Zinn is convinced that America, once a garden, has become a wasteland. In his 1994 autobiography, *You Can't Be Neutral on a Moving Train,* Zinn describes growing up poor in the tenements of Brooklyn, repairing ships on the docks, working his way through New York University, witnessing the bombing of German cities as an aviator in World War II, and teaching at Spelman College in the 1960s—key experiences, he says, in shaping his approach to history. Zinn went on to became an activist professor, a courageous civil rights leader, and an ardent foe of the Vietnam War. He also became a leading twentieth-century radical revisionist historian.

As he scans the shelves in his therapist's office in the 1997 movie *Good Will Hunting,* the title character says, "You want to read a real history book, read Howard Zinn's *A People's History of the United States*. That book will f- - -ing knock you on your ass." In the opening chapter of *A People's History of the United States*, which Zinn proudly calls "skeptical of governments," he introduces Columbus not as a bold explorer but as an ethnocentric killer. America, says Zinn, was invaded, not discovered, and its history commenced in "conquest, slavery, death." More heroic than Columbus are abolitionists, suffragists, labor organizers, Native Americans, and Vietnam War protesters. The high points of our nation's past are Shays's Rebellion, the draft riots, the Homestead strike, and the rise of the International Workers of the World. The villains are the Puritans, the founding fathers, and all entrepreneurs. Since its publication in 1980, Zinn's *History* has sold over 500,000 copies.

Dismissive of material progress and skeptical of the idea of individual genius, the radical revisionist historian celebrates workers, protesters, and the exploited. History is driven forward not by great men and women but by geography, chance, and greed. Not all revisionists are as radical as Zinn, who repudiates our government, our economic system, and our wars, but the revisionist message to millions of Americans is not that as a nation we are imperfect but that we are deeply flawed, not that our past heroes were human but that they were merely ordinary.

Revisionists do look for new heroes. But educational critic Gilbert Sewall, who has analyzed dozens of history books, notes that in their search, revisionists elevate people who played minor roles. Molly Pitcher may have been brave to take water to fainting soldiers at the Battle of Monmouth in 1778, but, asks Sewall, should she receive almost as much attention as Abraham Lincoln? In her history of school textbooks, *America Revised*, Frances Fitzgerald concludes, "No single president really stands out as a hero."

America would have been better today, say the revisionists, if Washington had been more democratic, Lincoln less racist, Theodore Roosevelt more peaceful, Woodrow Wilson less moralistic, Franklin Roosevelt less devious. Magnified are the sins and shortcomings of American history and its heroes. Revisionism is most interested in mistakes and failures, indifferent to religion, and suspicious of greatness. And the revisionist mentality has become pervasive in our culture and dominant in our schools.

In the first episode of the 2000 History Channel series *Founding Fathers*, John Hancock drinks and smuggles. Vain and hungry for money, he becomes a patriot because the Stamp Act hurts his business. A historian notes that John Adams should have been on Prozac and that Paul Revere's etching of the Boston Massacre would have made "spin doctors proud."

On a recent tour I took of Boston's Freedom Trail, which runs from the site of the Boston Massacre to Paul Revere's house, with stops along the way at various spots associated with the American Revolution, a young ranger from the National Park Service began unofficially at a new memorial to the victims of the Irish potato famine and, after praising the memorial, moved to the site of the Boston Massacre, arguing that the colonists provoked it. At Faneuil Hall, we gathered around a statue of Samuel Adams that stands at the entrance, and he read the inscription aloud, STATESMAN, INCORRUPTIBLE AND FEARLESS. After acknowledging that today we all think of Sam Adams as a beer, he laughed and added, "No one is fearless, no one incorruptible. Sam Adams must have been afraid of British soldiers. He probably cheated at cards."

Later I checked on Sam Adams and discovered that he was not perfect. In 1740, Harvard College disciplined him for oversleeping and missing morning prayers. His family complained that he mismanaged money, and some historians argue that Adams was an agitator, skilled at tearing down governments, clumsy at building them up. But no critic I came across called Adams a coward, considering that in 1775 the British promised to pardon all rebels *except* John Hancock and Samuel Adams. As for cheating, the last Loyalist governor of Massachusetts, Thomas Hutchinson, hated Adams. He noted, however, that Adams was incorruptible.

In a high school history class in a small town outside of Madison, Wisconsin, a student asked, "So what do you think of the founding fathers?" The class had been reading about Charles Beard, who in 1913 wrote one of the first revisionist accounts of the revolutionary period, *An Economic Interpretation of the Constitution*. Beard argued that the founding fathers favored a strong central government and ratified the proposed constitution so that the money they and their friends had loaned to the Continental Congress would be paid back in full.

English citizens at the time of course believed the founding fathers to be traitors, as did the many American loyalists. And since 1913, other revisionist historians have criticized the founding fathers for not freeing slaves, not giving equal rights to women, and not being sufficiently egalitarian. To me the founding fathers were brilliant, visionary, and courageous. By signing the Declaration of Independence, they risked their lives for a war whose outcome was far from certain (an objective observer would have predicted a British victory). By winning the war against the world's superpower, they demonstrated perseverance and bravery. And by writing a Constitution that still governs us today, they exhibited extraordinary foresight. Did the founding fathers have mixed motives? Of course. Could they have been more egalitarian? Perhaps, although it is presumptuous of us to insist that the values of Colonial America be identical to those of contemporary America. Did they create a prosperous, powerful country offering equality of opportunity, orderly government, and accomplishment unmatched by any nation in history? Yes. What do I think of the founding fathers? They were heroes.

An example of the ways radical revisionism takes hold in the classroom recently came to my attention in a suburban school outside Pittsburgh. A student teacher told the class that because Andrew Jackson forced Native Americans to move west, she does not rate him much higher than Hitler. What we now call the Trail of Tears, the route the Cherokee Indians were forced to travel from their villages in Georgia and other southeastern states across the Mississippi to a reservation on barren land in Oklahoma in 1838, does tarnish Jackson. Even Robert Remini, a biographer usually favorable to Jackson, condemns him for pushing through a removal treaty that only a minority of tribesmen signed. In hindsight, Jackson was ethnocentric and paternalistic, his plan egregiously unjust and disastrously executed. Still, I find the student teacher's comparison to Hitler unfair. Jackson did believe that in Oklahoma the Cherokees would have a fresh start and a chance to retain their traditional way of life. Most significantly, neither Jackson nor the most reactionary congressman of the day contemplated placing Cherokees in slave labor camps and shooting them. The Trail of Tears is an aberration of American history, not its essence.

TRIUMPHALISM AND REVISIONISM compete for our allegiance. Triumphalism appeals to our national pride and our tendency to simplify the past. Revisionism allows us to be self-critical and to show sympathy for the underdog. The triumphalist believes that exceptional individuals can alter history but glides over exploitation, unjust wars, and violence. The revisionist limits the pantheon of heroes to victims and protesters and believes that no one person alters history. Triumphalists claim too much for too few, revisionists too little for too many.

In a revisionist age, what might George Bancroft find to celebrate about America today? As a boy, Bancroft hacked all day at the hard soil on his parents' farm in Worcester, Massachusetts. Today he would celebrate supermarkets, fast food, and the few million farmers who now feed an entire nation as well as hungry people around the world. Bancroft watched his young wife and two-year-old daughter die; like many Americans at the time, he was familiar with cholera, dysentery, and childbed fever. He would celebrate today's antibiotics, uneventful pregnancies and births, and longer lives.

One hundred years after the Declaration of Independence, when America displayed its technological potential at the Philadelphia Centennial Exposition of 1876, Bancroft was there. The gigantic steam engines and primitive telephones seemed revolutionary to him. Today he would be stunned by an array of American inventions: automobiles, airplanes, radios, televisions, air conditioners, computers. And he would discover that American engineers set the pace in technology.

Like Adams and Jefferson, Bancroft was a man of learning. He would be fascinated by DNA, the neutrino, the human genome, and the mapping of the universe. The son of a congregational minister, Bancroft would be interested in seeing that, with all our possessions, we retain our work ethic; that despite the increase in scientific knowledge, most Americans remain religious. He would find we are still a nation of opportunity—that we encourage entrepreneurs, respect achievement, and reward excellence.

Beneath our rhetoric of a flawed America, Bancroft also would find thousands of good Samaritans, local heroes quietly serving their communities, and countless voluntary associations and foundations that dispense billions of dollars. He would discover that while many want to immigrate to America, few wish to leave.

Bancroft lived in a century of reform. He would celebrate our diversity and increased tolerance and find progress in equality for women, African Americans, Native Americans, and the disabled. Early in his Northampton speech, he talked about the importance of an educated citizenry. In 1826, few Americans attended high school. With pride he would point to these figures: Today, more than 52 million Americans are enrolled in K-12 schools, and more than a quarter of our population graduates from college.

As a triumphalist, Bancroft felt that America had much to celebrate, but he was not naive. Having lived through the carnage of the Civil War and the acrimony over Reconstruction and witnessed hostility to immigrants, he was familiar with selfishness and greed. He would find flaws in contemporary America. He would be upset about increasing economic inequality, shocked by popular culture, and distressed by our disintegrating families. Still, he would be puzzled by our cynicism and our casual denigration of past and present heroes. With all our comfort and leisure, he would wonder why we are not content and would remind us, as he did in his 1826 speech, that America has been favored.

PERHAPS SOME CONTEMPORARY American historians are too utopian to appreciate their own country. "I love America." This is the opening and closing sentence of *Fields of Battle,* John Keegan's 1996 magisterial history of forts and warfare in North America. Keegan is an accomplished contemporary British historian, and his book is a rebuke to radical revisionists.

What does Keegan love about America? Our landscape, friendliness, energy; the work ethic, optimism, and equality; a can-do spirit, courteous bureaucrats, and high-minded public servants. He respects at the same time the chivalry of the South and the progress America has made in civil rights. He dares to suggest that the Sioux were as cruel and perhaps more warlike than the American cavalry. He makes heroes of movie stars like Gary Cooper, leaders like Dwight Eisenhower, and inventors like the Wright brothers. He reads Ernest Hemingway and Willa Cather. Sixty years ago America rescued England, and Keegan has not forgotten. He respects Americans for disliking war but being good at it. "I go there," says Keegan, "in a mood of exploration and wonder."

Revisionist historians remind us that many immigrants do not prosper, that capitalism does not benefit everybody, that violence has been part of our past, that our presidents are not perfect. Howard Zinn is a courageous activist, and protest movements have helped make America exceptional. But is the *essence* of American history exploitation, injustice, and greed? Do our history books mislead, as Howard Zinn argues? I taught American history for many years and from many different books. There is much in these texts now about income inequality, environmental degradation, the horrors of immigration, and the hardships of the Western frontier. Strikes, massacres, and lynchings are vividly described. Contemporary history books cover in detail the Vietnam War and our shameful mistreatment of Native Americans.

Little mention is made in them, however, of genius or heroism. Omitted is all drama and majesty. From many of our textbooks, one would not know that in the span of human history, the United States has stood for peace, wealth, and accomplishment and has made possible millions of quiet and contented lives.

FORGOTTEN MONUMENTS

*We have moved from an age in which monuments were filled . . . with
meanings . . . to an age in which monuments and memorials stand
mute.*

—Nathan Glazer, 1996
"Monuments in an Age Without Heroes"

Across America, in cities and small towns, I have discovered
memorials to men and women once thought heroes, to people who
in the light of history have become heroes, to forgotten warriors, and
to local heroes who founded cities and hospitals and schools.

Near City Hall in Haverhill, Massachusetts, stands Puritan housewife
Hannah Duston, a hatchet in her hand. Duston is the first Colonial
woman I found to be publicly praised a hero in her own time. In 1697,
Abnaki Indians swept down on the village of Haverhill and captured
Duston. They smashed her newborn baby against a tree and marched
her toward Canada, telling her that once they arrived she would be
stripped and forced to run the gauntlet. Duston retaliated by hacking
nine of her sleeping captors to death in the middle of the night, stealing
a canoe, and returning to Boston with their scalps. The General Court
paid her twenty pounds. Cotton Mather praised her as a heroine. Today
Dustin is considered by many to be more vengeful than heroic.

Outside the Quaker Information Center in Philadelphia sits Mary
Dyer on a bench, wearing a bonnet, her hands folded as in a meeting

for worship. Dyer was hanged by the Puritans in 1660 for repeatedly returning to the Massachusetts Bay Colony and demanding that Quakers be allowed to practice their religion. The Puritans believed each state should have just one religion, that competing sects would incite anarchy, and that Dyer was a fanatic. Today Dyer is celebrated as a hero because she met her death with composure and sacrificed her life for the cause of religious toleration—a belief once radical but now accepted in all democracies.

Not far from Dyer, on the dome of Philadelphia's City Hall, is Alexander Calder's 1894 statue of another famous Quaker, William Penn, holding Pennsylvania's charter in his hand. In addition to welcoming all religions and starting schools, Penn signed a treaty with Native Americans, and when he died, they sent his widow, Hannah, a cloak made of the skins of wild animals. According to one of the travel books I read, the purpose of the gift was "to protect her while passing through the thorny wilderness without her guide."

On Yale's campus in New Haven, Connecticut, stands Nathan Hale, Connecticut's state hero. Statues of Hale can also be found in the capitol rotunda in Hartford; in New London, where he grew up, taught school, and championed women's education before joining the Colonial army; in Alexandria, Virginia, at the entrance to the CIA; and in New York City near the spot where he was hanged.

I first became interested in Hale when I discovered in my travels that this patriot of the American Revolution, once a household name, was no longer familiar to most high school students. In September 1776, George Washington, trapped in upper Manhattan, desperately needed information about British positions on Long Island. Disguised as a loyalist schoolmaster, Hale walked all over Long Island, gathering information and sketching forts. Just as he was about to return to Washington's headquarters, the British captured him and ordered him hanged the next day. When he calmly mounted the scaffold, he echoed the words of the Roman general Cato: "I regret that I have but one life to give for my country."

Due to the efforts of a group of middle-school girls, Connecticut now has another official state hero, Prudence Crandall. Raised a Quaker,

Crandall opened a school for young women in 1831 in Canterbury, Connecticut. Influenced by abolitionist William Lloyd Garrison, she decided to admit Sarah Harris, daughter of a prosperous African American farmer. Parents threatened to withdraw their daughters. When Crandall refused to back down, a mob broke school windows, polluted the well, and tried to set the building on fire. The state legislature retaliated against Crandall by making it illegal for anyone to set up schools for "colored people," and under this law she was arrested and imprisoned in 1833. Crandall later moved to Illinois, where she opened another school and crusaded for temperance and women's suffrage.

Not far from Rome, Georgia, is Oak Hill, a museum that celebrates Martha Berry. On the grounds of the museum is a small log cabin built for Berry after the Civil War by her father, a wealthy cotton planter. In this cabin, Berry first told Bible stories to poor mountain children who couldn't read or write. When attendance swelled, she moved her school to Possum Trot, several miles down the road, where she drew not only poor mountain children but their friends and relatives of all ages. Despite a warning from her lawyer that she was squandering her inheritance, Berry transformed her Bible school into a series of day schools known as the Berry Schools and eventually founded a boarding school, The Boys Industrial School. Berry intended to give her high school students vocational training, religious instruction, and college preparation. To pay for tuition and learn a skill, the students worked on farms, planted trees and gardens, and built dormitories. Berry's schools grew with the help of northern benefactors she zealously cultivated. She persuaded Theodore Roosevelt to visit and Andrew Carnegie to give a $50,000 matching gift. In the 1920s, Henry Ford replaced the simple frame structures built by students in the early years with magnificent Gothic buildings.

Berry College stands today as a memorial to the work of Martha Berry, whose educational complex offered thousands of poor Georgians education and job skills. As the pamphlet at Oak Hill—today the home of Berry College—notes, "She chose to forgo security for the sake of a vision."

Nine

TALKING TO STUDENTS
ABOUT HEROES

Men's evil manners live in brass; their virtues
We write in water.

—Shakespeare,
King Henry VIII

Who'ere excels in what we prize,
Appears a hero in our eyes.

—Jonathan Swift, 1726

As I travel around the country making the case for heroism, I urge
students to look for heroes but not to succumb to hero worship,
to cast their nets wide, to look beyond the athletic field, the movie
screen, and the recording studio, and to let some sort of grandeur be a
factor in their selection. The trick, I suggest, is to be amused by popular culture but not seduced, to know the difference between heroes and
charlatans, to pick worthy heroes. If they have trouble believing in
heroes, I ask them to find heroic qualities in different people and to
celebrate heroic moments.

I offer examples of heroic qualities. Heroes set the bar high. In the
1950s we were told that no one could ever run a four-minute mile. Yet
Roger Bannister trained in secret, ran up and down the hills of Wales,

TALKING TO STUDENTS ABOUT HEROES

and proved the world wrong. Heroes take risks. In June of 1940, Charles de Gaulle saw France vanquished by Adolf Hitler. His colleagues prudently surrendered; de Gaulle refused. Like Winston Churchill, he fought when there seemed no hope. Heroes are altruistic. Albert Schweitzer could have comfortably remained an organist and scholar. Instead, in his thirties, he remade himself into a missionary doctor. Heroes act on their deepest convictions. Eleanor Roosevelt and Florence Nightingale were born privileged and told to stay home. Yet they defied convention and became tough-minded humanitarians.

In mounting my defense of the hero, I stress that great men and women have shaped America as much as social forces and that ideals have been as influential in our history as economic self-interest.

While I describe signs of the times, my message is not that we are declining and decadent, like Rome in the fifth century C.E. I am patriotic and ardently believe in democracy and capitalism. We so love to criticize that we forget what we do well. We do have idealistic politicians, balanced biographers and journalists, and conscientious moviemakers, but their numbers have dwindled and their influence has waned significantly.

My message is not to turn back the clock and embrace the heroes of the nineteenth century—heroes who tended to be white, male, and privileged. Nor do I advocate the 1950s, when John Wayne sat tall in his saddle, Mickey Mantle sped around the bases, Ozzie and Harriet Nelson smiled on television, and we did not debate whether Columbus was an explorer or a killer. The 1950s tolerated a fair amount of hypocrisy and injustice in the middle of affluence. I believe in information, choices, and honesty. The heart of my message to students is that they learn to detect greatness in the midst of all their choices and information.

After my remarks, the questions are always vigorous and wide-ranging. Students in San Francisco and New York City tend to be more combative, students in Atlanta and New Orleans more courtly. But always hands are in the air.

Certain questions surface all the time: "What's your definition of a hero?" "Who are your heroes?" "Why do we need heroes?"

Others are original: "Do you think if women were in control of countries, there would be fewer wars?" "Can you be a happy hero?" "The

Aztecs were defeated by Cortez because they thought he was a god. Isn't it dangerous to be too believing?"

Some questions are disturbing: "What's wrong with hedonism?" "Why is it good that Andrew Carnegie gave his money away? He should have kept it. He earned it."

Students, as well as adults I talk to, always want proof that we are living in more antiheroic times. After questions about definition, this topic comes up in nearly every audience: "Didn't you live in a society that had a lot of facades?" "Were the fifties that much different?"

To counter the image of the 1950s as stuffy and boring, some textbooks are now highlighting rebels like James Dean, who anticipated the more iconoclastic youth of the late 1960s. Students have frequently cited Dean, the Beatniks, and the youth culture of the 1960s as evidence that things have always been this way.

Have Things Changed?

Of course, each generation and each decade mixes the heroic and the antiheroic. During the 1920s, the Hall of Fame for Great Americans inducted Patrick Henry and John Paul Jones, President William Howard Taft dedicated the Lincoln Memorial in Washington, D.C., and Gutzon Borglum began carving the faces on Mount Rushmore. At the same time, the 1920s injected new attitudes into American life that persist today and are hard on heroes: intense devotion to athletes and celebrities, skepticism about soldiers as heroic, repudiation of the nineteenth-century belief in progress, glorification of consumption, and adulation of millionaires.

In the 1950s, teachers wondered whether they could compete with Hopalong Cassidy. Parents worried that teenagers who watched James Dean in *Rebel Without a Cause* would become juvenile delinquents. And everyone worried that rock and roll would corrupt American youth. But there are differences.

Consider the two westerns *High Noon* and *Unforgiven*. In 1952, Gary Cooper won the Academy Award for Best Actor for his portrayal of a U.S. marshal in *High Noon*. Forty years later, *Unforgiven* won four Academy Awards, including Best Picture. *High Noon* opens in the morning sunshine with a wedding; *Unforgiven* opens in the night rain in a brothel. *High Noon* starts with a kiss, *Unforgiven* with the slashing of a prostitute. Will Kane, the hero of *High Noon*, is a U.S. marshal; Will Munny, the hero of *Unforgiven*, is a reformed killer and alcoholic reduced to pig farming. *High Noon* is set in the town of Hadleyville, *Unforgiven* in a town called Big Whiskey whose sheriff, Little Bill, is a sadist. *High Noon* ends with order restored. *Unforgiven* ends essentially as it opens—in the dark and rain, in sorrow and violence, with anarchy ascendant.

High Noon was about physical bravery and moral courage, about overcoming fear and fatigue, about doing the right thing no matter what the cost. *Unforgiven* was about weakness and revenge. The America of *High Noon* was far from perfect, and forty years later *Unforgiven* revealed in many ways a better America—mistrustful of gunfighters, suspicious of myths, open about sex, sensitive to victims— but *Unforgiven* also revealed a more cynical America, with no heroes, no one to admire.

In the entertainment industry, the dark side has become dangerously ascendant. The *Journal of Popular Culture* reported that by 1988 super villains had outnumbered superheroes in movies and television. Michael Medved reported in *Hollywood vs. America* in 1992 that fourth-graders knew more about Freddy Krueger, the slasher in the *Nightmare on Elm Street* movies, than they knew about Abraham Lincoln.

Marilyn Manson, the rock star idolized by the Littleton shooters, named himself after a celebrity and a mass murderer: Marilyn Monroe and Charles Manson. Manson dedicated his autobiography, *the long hard road out of hell*, to his parents: MAY GOD FORGIVE THEM FOR BRINGING ME INTO THIS WORLD.

Silence of the Lambs, a movie starring a cannibal and featuring a serial killer who likes to skin his female victims, swept the Academy Awards in 1991. Eight years later Lecter returned, first in a book called *Hannibal*, which appeared on *The New York Times* Best Sellers list for eleven months, then was back at the box office in a sequel to the first movie advertised on the front page of *TV Guide* as "Hannibal's New Feast." At a school in New Jersey, a girl followed me around between classes, arguing that I had maligned her hero, Hannibal Lecter. "He was clever and bold," she said "Don't you know that he became a cannibal because he came from a dysfunctional family?"

In the 1950s, *The Adventures of Ozzie and Harriet* presented a sentimental and unrealistic portrait of the American family. In 1999 the movie *American Beauty* eviscerated the American family and won five Academy Awards. *American Beauty* opens with Lester Burnham masturbating in the shower. His wife, Carolyn, has an affair. Their daughter, Jane, is an exhibitionist; her friend Angela purports to be an expert on penises; and her boyfriend, Ricky Fitts, is a drug dealer and voyeur. In the Fitts family, the mother is depressed and catatonic; the ex-marine father is homophobic, repressed, and violent.

At a school in Atlanta, students asked: "Should it be censored?" "Wasn't it clever?" "Didn't it represent the American family?" In Pittsburgh, a boy stood up and defended Burnham. "Lester Burnham is honest. Isn't that heroic?"

Isn't there more to heroism than just being honest? How much narcissism is mixed into Burnham's honesty? The student's point, however, was relevant. When Americans are asked to identify the most important quality of a hero, they frequently pick honesty over other qualities.

Students often insist that the movies and television shows they watch do not affect them; they are just a form of mindless entertainment. At the same time, some are concerned about the effects of negative images on younger siblings. In Cleveland, Ohio, a sophomore girl took me aside and confided that super villains were turning her eight-year-old brother into an aggressive brat. I argue that the music we listen to and the movies and television shows we watch wash over us in ways we do not always understand and that a steady diet of antiheroic messages informs the way we interpret the world.

In Georgia, I asked a veteran teacher whether he agrees that students have become more cynical. Before class he had told me about two of his heroes, poets Anne Bradstreet and Phyllis Wheatley, and showed me an article by Adrienne Rich about Bradstreet with this sentence underlined: "It is worth observing that Anne Bradstreet happened to be one of the first American women inhabiting a time and place in which heroism was a necessity of life." Bradstreet, a Puritan housewife, was sick most of her life, bore eight children, lost two grandchildren, yet still wrote poetry that praised God and nature. The teacher told me he had recently read a letter from George Washington to Phyllis Wheatley to his seventh-grade history class in which Washington praises Wheatley's poetry. One of the girls in the class speculated: "Maybe they were having an affair."

In Pennsylvania, I mentioned to a class that I had noticed Daniel Chester French's famous statue of Ulysses S. Grant on my way to school. People, I suggested, can have heroic moments. Grant was a lackluster soldier before the Civil War, an ineffectual president afterward, but a great general during the war itself. "Didn't he beat his wife?" asked a student. He always said his best decision was marrying Julia Dent, who stood by him in his darkest moments. In fact, Grant probably had one of the best marriages of all our presidents.

A perceptive question about the decline of heroism came from a student in a Wisconsin high school: "What about declining literacy? Does that connect to the loss of heroes?" To have historical heroes, one has to read. To make Abraham Lincoln a model, one has to be familiar with his speeches and letters. A society that receives most of its information from television and movies is probably a society with fewer historical heroes. A teacher from Utah told me that his school district carted away and shredded all its Dickens novels because the sentences were too hard and the books too long.

Is This a Hero?

Students like to toss out a name and test it against my definition of *hero*. "Is Michael Jordan a hero?" "What about Bob Dylan?" "Lenny Bruce?" "Are you against humor? Doesn't humor keep us sane?" Iconoclastic students bring up people like Charles Manson. "Why can't Charles Manson be a hero?"

After one assembly, a girl showed me a copy of Ayn Rand's essays and asked about whether Rand believed in heroes. Rand's name has come up in several schools, and she has a following among students who are cerebral and a little rebellious. In another school, a student asked, "Doesn't Ayn Rand believe in both heroes and selfishness?"

Rand, who was born in Russia and fled the Bolshevik revolution, has become synonymous with individualism and free-market capitalism. Rand was a believer in excellence and, in that sense, comfortable with the heroic. But she was also a militant atheist and believed that self-interest governs all behavior, an idea that makes it hard to believe in heroes. *The Fountainhead*, one of Rand's most famous books, was supposed to be based on architect Frank Lloyd Wright, who was a genius but not exactly a nice man.

In individual English and history classes, students tend to bring up whomever they are studying at the time. "Why did Americans think of Woodrow Wilson as a hero?" Wilson spoke with a moral fervor and eloquence that appealed to pre–World War I audiences. When he was president of Princeton, he tried to abolish its elite social clubs. As governor of New Jersey, he defied political bosses. Wilson's hero—I always add—was English Prime Minister William Gladstone, whose life suggested to him that a political leader could be ethical.

Sigmund Freud wrote a psychological study of Wilson in the late 1920s that branded Wilson as self-righteous, inflexible, and prudish. An A&E *Biography* implied that Wilson might have been an adulterer, citing as evidence passionate, flowery letters he had written to a married woman. Today Wilson is associated with a catastrophic war, the Versailles Peace Treaty, and a reactionary civil rights policy. Instead of being cut down by an assassin or facing a hero-making death, he suffered a stroke and lingered on incapacitated, his wife running the White House with his aides. But there is hope for Wilson. In reaction to Henry Kissinger's notion that in foreign policy self-interest rules, some historians now praise Wilson's idealism and commitment to human rights.

"Why do you say polio made FDR a hero?" Up to the age of forty, Roosevelt led a charmed life: doting parents, good looks, wealth, elite schools, the right social clubs, a politically powerful family, connections to the White House. His possibilities seemed endless. He had never been pushed, never had any life-changing reversals, until one day, while vacationing with his family on Campobello Island, New Brunswick— off the coast of Maine—he came down with a high fever and discovered he could not move the lower half of his body. Polio temporarily forced Roosevelt off the political stage, gave him ample doses of pain and despair, and made him more reflective, much braver, more compassionate. Every day he had to drag himself out of bed into his wheelchair. He kept up a good front, fought self-pity, and made a successful return to politics.

When we scratch the surface of even the most comfortable life, we find more suffering than we realized. We all put up good fronts. Even our most upbeat, optimistic president, Ronald Reagan, had his trials. In his recent biography, *Dutch,* Edmund Morris points out that in a two-year span Reagan almost died of viral pneumonia, lost his infant daughter, was divorced from his first wife, and could not land acting jobs. When his life seemed darkest, he started traveling the country, encouraged by Nancy Reagan, giving speeches for *General Electric Theater,* a journey that transformed him from actor to politician. Nor was Reagan's life thereafter an easy ascent. General Electric canceled his contract, he lost the presidential nomination to Gerald Ford, was nearly killed by an assassin's bullet, and fought prostate cancer.

"What about Oskar Schindler as a hero?" It is interesting that Schindler did not personally suffer but transformed himself after seeing the suffering of others. Though he didn't think of himself as heroic and did not want to be a hero, he could not turn away from the barbarism he saw in Nazi-occupied Poland, so he spent his money and risked his life to make his enamel factory a refuge for Jewish workers. A hedonist and member of the Nazi party before the war and a failure afterward, Schindler is a mysterious hero, a hero for the moment, who saved the lives of hundreds of people.

A more consistently heroic man throughout his life would be Dietrich Bonhoeffer, a German Protestant minister. Early in his career he spoke out against the Nazis, and during the war he joined in the plot to kill Hitler. Before he was hanged at the age of thirty-nine, Bonhoeffer wrote *Letters From Prison,* which describes the responsibility of a Christian to defy evil. An SS guard who witnessed his execution said he had never seen a man face death so calmly, so resigned to God's will.

"What made Sir Thomas More a hero?" In classes where students were studying *Utopia,* I volunteered that Sir Thomas More is one of my heroes and recommended they see the movie *A Man for All Seasons,* which won Academy Awards for Best Picture, Actor, and Director in 1966. More was a wise diplomat, brilliant scholar, clever lawyer, good husband, and kind father. As lord chancellor, he corresponded with Erasmus. By following his conscience and refusing to agree to Henry VIII's divorce, he was stripped of his power and thrown into the tower, where he wrote some of his most moving letters as he waited for death. Professor Richard Marius praised More's brave death and told me in an interview he wept when he wrote the last chapter of his 1984 biography, *Thomas More.* Marius also insisted that we recognize More's humanity: his sexual repression, his terror of death, his hunger for office, his cruelty to Protestants.

"Would you call Shakespeare a hero?" a teacher asked in a freshman literature class. Maybe *genius* is a better word for Shakespeare. My favorite Shakespearean characters are Brutus, Cordelia, Hamlet, Horatio, and Prince Hal, and I hope this mysterious genius combined them all. A student chimed in: "I heard someone in a barroom fight wrote Shakespeare's plays." Scholars, I suggested, do not credit that person, Christopher Marlowe, with writing the plays, but there are skeptics who claim that only a person with a university education, which Shakespeare did not have, could combine such beautiful language with philosophical depth.

"What if you have more than one person responsible for heroic action?" In one class a teacher pointed out that we need to honor the brave anonymous followers of Martin Luther King Jr., who marched in Memphis and sat at lunch counters. I agreed that credit should go to many people. King himself warned against hero worship. But without King's vision, the South might have erupted in a violent race war.

QUESTIONS FROM STUDENTS about group heroism have come up in different contexts, such as Habitat for Humanity and Doctors Without Borders. Women more than men, Japanese more than Americans, and Quakers seem to like to share credit. The Nobel Peace Prize in 1947 was awarded to the American Friends Service Committee and the British Friends Service Council, groups that distribute food and clothing to those in need around the world, and in 1999 to Doctors Without Borders.

Though relatively small in number, Quakers have supplied America with a disproportionate number of reformers, including William Penn, Lucretia Mott, early abolitionist John Woolman, Susan B. Anthony, and underground railroad president Levi Coffin. For most of history, men have expressed their heroic impulse through war. The quintessential Quaker is a humanitarian.

While speaking at schools in Philadelphia, I visited the Quaker Information Center, where a guide summarized the Friends' beliefs: that each of us has within us a God-given inner light that should direct our lives; before God all are equal; human beings should live simply; faith is manifested in good deeds. In the traditional Quaker meetinghouse, there are no Bibles, crucifixes, stained-glass windows, or organs—nothing that might distract the worshiper from concentrating on God. No minister here leads services or gives sermons. In silence, Quakers try to forget worldly concerns and concentrate on that of God within us all, sitting quietly for forty-five minutes, speaking only when they feel moved. Sometimes, the guide told me, egocentric, talkative worshippers can ruin a meeting and need to be counseled by a committee.

At a Quaker school before assembly, we sat without talking for ten minutes, a long time even for an adult. I now understand why students at Friends schools say their most lasting memory is of Quaker meeting. To sit still and consider the direction of your life, to concentrate on thinking about something other than sports, friends, homework, and tests, to wait for an inner voice is an unusual experience in a society conditioned by frenetic activity and the omnipresent media. Just as Quakers believe that we all possess an inner light, I told the students, so I believe that in our hearts we all have heroic potential, a better and braver self that can be activated, perhaps by God, but also by studying the lives of great men and women.

Young Heroes

Students always ask me to name *young* people who were heroes, and a recent example is Cassie Bernall. Cassie was one of the girls killed at Columbine, shot after saying she believed in Jesus Christ. Cassie's mother has told her story in *She Said Yes: The Unlikely Martyrdom of Cassie Bernall*. The book, which has sold nearly half a million copies and has been translated into many languages, tells of Cassie's parents' spiritual battle with their daughter's suicide threats and her dangerous friends. It further describes her transformation from a hostile alienated teenager to a loving daughter through her conversion to Christianity. The Bernall Web site has been flooded with prayers, poems, songs, and letters from teenagers calling Bernall a hero and role model and saying that they have turned their lives around and converted to Christianity because of her example.

I often recommend a German movie, *The White Rose*, about five students who decided in 1943 that Adolf Hitler was ruining their country and the war must end. They posted 10,000 leaflets in Munich and Berlin condemning Hitler. On the walls of apartment buildings and state offices they painted the words FREEDOM and DOWN WITH HITLER. The SS discovered the students and executed them. Today many schools in Germany are named after members of the White Rose. (There may be a downside to my emphasis on suffering and calamities as producers of heroes. One a student wryly observed: "You don't offer a very appealing job description.")

Another young hero was Joan of Arc. Joan was illiterate, only nineteen when she died. In Mary Gordon's 2000 biography, *Joan of Arc,* she describes Joan as a person of "remarkable sureness" and "superhuman courage." She says that people who met Joan felt transformed by her. Convinced she heard voices from God, Joan, a poor peasant girl, turned herself into a natural leader and courageous soldier. "We need her," says Gordon, "as the heroine for our better selves."

Probably the most famous teenage hero of the twentieth century is Anne Frank, the youngest person included by *Time* magazine in its list of the century's most influential people. Anne's diary is still a staple of many schools' reading lists, preserved by chance when the Franks were betrayed in 1944 and the Germans looted their apartment. At first no publishing house cared to print it. Today there are 25 million copies of the diary in circulation, it has been translated into 67 languages, and every year hundreds of thousands of people visit the secret annex in Amsterdam. Among those uplifted by Anne's diary was Nelson Mandela, who said it helped sustain him during his twenty-eight years on Robben Island.

Anne was very human, I remind students: bossy, quarrelsome, moody, constantly fighting with her mother, preoccupied with romance and sex. She plastered her bedroom walls with pictures of Greta Garbo and Ray Milland, even as she read *A Tale of Two Cities.* Taken to the Bergen-Belsen concentration camp, Anne died of typhus three months before her sixteenth birthday. Anne is a hero not just because she was a victim of great evil but because she became deeper and more thoughtful when forced into isolation. Aware of the hatred outside her apartment, she forced herself to be optimistic and brave.

After my talk at a school in suburban Pennsylvania, the principal, Michael Pladus, brought sixteen-year-old Becky Dewar in her wheelchair to the front of the auditorium to meet me. Becky is a quadriplegic who was paralyzed ten years earlier in a car accident. As he introduced Becky to me, Michael held her hand and said, "This is *my* hero." We left the auditorium with Becky in her chair and walked down the hall, where Michael stopped at a glass case. On display were watercolor landscapes of sun and ocean and children running along the beach. Becky had taught herself to paint, using a brush attached to a stick in her mouth.

Looking at Becky's paintings, I thought of Miep Gies, hero of the award-winning documentary *Anne Frank Remembered,* which I had seen a few days before. The Frank family's only link to the outside world, this Dutch woman smuggled food into the secret annex for two years. In the documentary, Gies says that before the Nazis entered Holland, she believed the comfortable myth that in this life people get what they deserve, but that Hitler had opened her eyes. It crossed my mind that perhaps the highest form of heroism is being brave in the face of unfair catastrophe, painting a picture with your mouth from a wheelchair you know you will never escape, and smiling at a stranger who is lucky enough to walk.

Myths, Flaws, and the Whole Truth

Many students are familiar with the episode of *The Simpsons* called "Lisa, the Iconoclast." Shortly before a parade celebrating the town's founder, Lisa discovers a letter that reveals a terrible truth about him: He was a pirate who once tried to kill George Washington. She writes an essay for history class, "Jebediah Springfield: Super Fraud." Her teacher gives the paper an *F* and Lisa goes on a crusade, drawing pirate posters and placing them in store windows all over town. One man rips them up, saying, "Your hero phobia sickens me." From the reviewing stand on the day of the parade, Lisa resolves to tell the truth; but as she sees the faces of her friends and neighbors, she realizes the myth of Jebediah has "brought out the good in everyone" and decides to keep quiet.

I often ask students to consider whether myths have any role in a democracy, whether myths can survive in an information society. For most of history, nations have promulgated myths to make them strong and confident and to build up their heroes. Was Abraham Lincoln worse off for reading Mason Locke Weems's hagiography of George Washington? Should Norman Rockwell's 324 *Saturday Evening Post* covers idealizing American life be dismissed because some American families are dysfunctional?

At a public high school in New York City where students are admitted by competitive exam, the ninth-grade humanities class had just read *The Prince* and *The Divine Comedy*. One of the teachers asked whether I thought Machiavelli encourages heroism. No, I argued. Since Machiavelli assumes that men are motivated by fear and hate, he does not encourage heroism, at least not in *The Prince*. The students debated whether it is better to have ideals or to face reality and whether one can do both. "Isn't it dangerous to be innocent and naive like Billy Budd?" "Are information and reality bad for us?" I threw out this quotation by Matthew Arnold: "The world is forwarded by having its attention fixed on the best things." A quick-witted student shot back, "Machiavelli says we should see the world as it is, not as it ought to be."

On the board I wrote *No man is a hero to his valet* and then summarized a book I had just read, *The Private Life of Chairman Mao*, written by Li Zhisui, Mao's doctor for twenty-two years, and banned in China. In 638 pages, Li Zhisui describes Mao's rotting teeth, devious wife, dependence on barbiturates, dalliances with young women, and genital herpes. Li Zhisui blames the 1959 famine on Mao's contempt for experts and the cultural revolution on his lust for power. A young Chinese friend of mine was raised on Mao and refuses to read the book.

Is it right, I asked the students, for China to try to ban the book in order to keep Mao a hero? They wanted to know about the doctor's motives and the accuracy of his account. Mao did lose his temper with the doctor and twice sent him into peasant villages to work with his hands and be reeducated. And Dr. Li did not attend party meetings where key decisions were made, so he had an incomplete view of his patient. Even so, they concluded, although it is too bad that China has lost a hero, China should not ban the book.

I asked the students whether they think we need to examine a leader's private life in order to understand his policies. Can any leader survive such scrutiny? We discussed the need to be patriotic and the importance of myths. To my surprise, they admitted they would not like to see George Washington savaged.

I also wrote on the board the title of George Stephanopoulos's memoir of his five years with President Clinton, *All Too Human.* Stephanopoulos was Clinton's top aide until he resigned to become a commentator for *ABC News* and to write his book, a riveting and honest account of presidential decision-making and life in the White House. Stephanopoulos begins by saying the American people want their president to be majestic, larger than life, and then spends over four hundred pages making Clinton very human. *All Too Human,* I suggested, is the perfect title for an age that has eliminated privacy and obliterated the mystique upon which heroes have depended. A student commented that Clinton gave his aide some good material.

IN A CLASS at a private school in Connecticut, the students were eager to pick my brain because they had just been given an assignment to write a paper on a hero. One girl planned to write about her father. "Do I have to include his flaws?" Even John McCain, I suggested, a war hero and candidate for the Republican nomination at the time, said, "I am a man of many faults."

"Do you think part of the reason we don't have heroes is jealousy?" another girl asked. I asked the class for some answers as to why we tear people down. "Flaws are interesting." "It makes you feel better." "People are envious."

Jonathan Swift wrote, "'Tis eminence makes envy rise/As fairest fruit attracts the flies." Envy is listed as one of the seven deadly sins. We all have people in our lives who cannot be pleased, who perpetually find fault. When someone else is successful, they are annoyed. Incapable of admiration, they question everyone's motives, detect lapses and inconsistencies, and pounce on weakness. Envy is allowed more expression today because we are inundated with intimate information and feel less guilty about gossip and slander.

Sometimes I feel uneasy: I criticize the contemporary focus on the personal life, yet I report it. At a high school in Cambridge, a girl asked, "Isn't it hypocritical of you to say we know too much about the personal lives and then reveal little-known facts?" After a speech on Martin Luther

King Day in a Westchester County, New York, high school, some students were concerned that I had maligned their hero by mentioning his flaws. Still, my goal is to make heroes credible and relevant by acknowledging their failings. Not all people agree with my realistic approach. Some cannot simultaneously commend ideals and contemplate weakness. My challenge to these students is to be able to embrace complexity yet still be able to look up and admire.

Of course, King's promiscuity was not irrelevant. It clashed with the Ten Commandments he preached, upset his close associates, and gave J. Edgar Hoover ammunition with which to blackmail him. In an interview, Harvard professor Henry Louis Gates suggested to me that the punishing guilt it created may have driven King harder, made him bolder, more inclined to take risks.

"Do we need to know the whole truth about our heroes?" The whole truth is elusive. It changes with available information and often depends on a person's interpretation. We should give our public heroes some zone of privacy, particularly in their sexual lives. For a president the zone is less, especially when it comes to medical histories. We had a right to know that FDR had heart disease when he was running for a fourth term and that John F. Kennedy took medicine to control Addison's disease.

The problem today is that the "truth" about heroes tends to be about sexual indiscretions rather than significant achievements. And we are self-righteous. What is more significant about Thomas Jefferson, that he had a slave mistress or that he wrote the Declaration of Independence and the Virginia Statute of Religious Freedom? What should a fourth-grader be told? It might not be the same information that is presented to older students.

AT A SUBURBAN SCHOOL outside Philadelphia, a student who had read reviews of *Forced Into Glory: Abraham Lincoln's White Dream,* Lerone Bennett's new book that portrays Lincoln as a racist, announced to the class, "The Emancipation Proclamation did nothing."

At a private school in New York City known for having a high percentage of celebrity children, students in an American history class were studying the Civil War. I put my definition of *hero* on the blackboard: a person of extraordinary achievement, courage, and greatness of soul. "How can you argue that Lincoln was great-souled?" "Abraham Lincoln was a racist." "Why was Lincoln a hero rather just an ordinary politician?"

Suffering from melancholy, Lincoln forced himself out of gloom with humor and hard work. When the Mexican War started, he protested, fully knowing it was political suicide. And when the majority of Americans were willing to extend slavery into the western territories, he denounced the plan as evil. With consummate political skill, Lincoln maneuvered the South into firing the first shot in the Civil War and kept a divided cabinet and fragmented Union from splitting apart. Aware that a president in a democracy cannot be too far ahead of the voters who put him in office, he insisted that the primary purpose of the war must be the preservation of the Union. He listened to abolitionists like Frederick Douglass and Ralph Waldo Emerson and—I believe—sympathized with them. When the moment was right, he made the war against the southern rebellion into a war for human freedom, working behind the scenes to assure the passage of an amendment that would free the slaves.

"Do you know," I always ask students, "that Lincoln commuted the death sentences of hundreds of deserters and Native Americans sentenced to be hanged by a Minnesota court? Have you read the Second Inaugural Address or his letter to Mrs. Bixby, who lost two of her sons in battle?" I try to explain that in their eagerness to find reality and expose hypocrisy, they have exchanged the myth of Lincoln the Saint for the myth of Lincoln the Racist.

Fictional Heroes and Antiheroes

Many students ask about heroes of fiction. How important are fictional heroes? Theodore Roosevelt called his father Greatheart after a character in *The Pilgrim's Progress*. Many women report modeling their lives on Jo March, the heroine of *Little Women;* some studies have claimed that Scarlett O'Hara, the feisty Southerner in *Gone With the Wind,* has made more women independent and confident than have Eleanor Roosevelt or Gloria Steinem. People travel from all over the world to visit Prince Edward Island to pay homage to Anne of Green Gables, a spirited orphan girl who transformed lives.

Students frequently ask me, "Who were *your* fictional heroes?" The Hardy Boys. Tom Swift. In high school, reciting speeches by Brutus made me want to be a Stoic. I still remember the last words of Charles Dickens's *A Tale of Two Cities,* where Sydney Carton says, as he climbs the steps to the guillotine to redeem his life and save the woman he loves, "It is a far, far better thing that I do, than I have ever done; it is a far, far better rest that I go to, than I have ever known."

Students keep asking my opinion of *The Catcher in the Rye,* wondering whether Holden Caulfield is a hero or an antihero. In one school a teacher reminded me that toward the end of the book Holden Caulfield talks about heroes with one of his teachers, who says, "The mark of the immature man is that he wants to die nobly for a cause, while the mark of the mature man is that he wants to live humbly for one." Holden looks down on his parents, teachers, and friends, as well as ministers, lawyers, and soldiers. Except for his dead brother, his ten-year-old sister, and his friend, Jane, everyone else is a phony. Holden's indictment of life is witty, honest, and complex, and he has moments of tenderness and compassion. I can see why the novel endures and why some students will call him a hero. He is no fool. He sees deeply. But the trick is to see deeply and somehow still keep moving—not end up, like Holden, depressed and disillusioned.

Of course, antiheroes come up all the time. By questioning convention and exposing hypocrisy, some antiheroes can be appealing and even useful. They test our ideals to make sure they are not shallow. By understanding Falstaff's mockery of military honor, we come to a more realistic definition of courage. After finishing Albert Camus's *The Stranger,* we understand the allure of Mersault's detached nihilism and can even conclude that human beings *need* connection and purpose. Antiheroes permit us to explore our dark side safely. But

antiheroes can be dangerous when, instead of seeing them as characters to be wary of, as examples of behavior we should try to transcend, we are seduced by them.

What I Have Found

In a culture in which many politicians in the news no longer put the
interests of their country above their own, students rarely mention politicians as heroes, even if some occasionally defend the division between
public and private lives. At the same time, many blame the media for
focusing on personal and sexual lives. "In the news everything you see
is negative." "Adults give us the images we consume."

Students are reluctant to invest in public heroes, fearful that they
will be let down by some media revelation. I was in Ohio just after John
Glenn had rocketed back into space. One student asked, "Are we going
to embrace John Glenn or are we going to find out he had a liaison
twenty-five years ago that we don't want to know about?"

I have found a fair amount of sexual gossip and misinformation
about historical figures. "Did you know that George Washington died
of syphilis?" "I heard that Franklin Roosevelt's mother slept between
him and Eleanor." "Wasn't Ben Franklin an alcoholic?"

Students rarely mention soldiers as heroes. In one school I put the
words *bravery* and *courage* next to *hero* on the blackboard. "Were the
soldiers who fought for Hitler heroes?" "Aren't heroes the soldiers on
the winning side?" "How can anyone who kills be a hero?"

Even after September 11, many students remain skeptical about the
notion of soldiers as heroes. Immediately following the terrorist attacks,
I visited several high schools in Missouri. Students acknowledged that
before September 11, we had taken soldiers (as well as firefighters and
police) for granted. But they wondered how long our patriotism would
last, why death makes heroes, and whether you become a hero by per-
forming one brave deed. One girl asked, "Have we used the word too
casually since September 11?" Five months later, the questions were
tougher. "Were the marines who crashed into the mountain in Paki-

stan heroes?" "Doesn't being a hero depend on what country you live in?" "Does America use propaganda to make heroes?"

When selecting public heroes, students tend to pick humanitarians. Interestingly enough, they rarely mention scientists or mathematicians. I have corresponded with a teacher in Philadelphia who has built his curriculum around scientist heroes. He believes great scientists should be as venerated as baseball players. Without radar and code breakers, he reminded me, America could have lost to Hitler.

I have found that many students are inclined to moral and aesthetic relativism. They do not want to be thought judgmental. As one teacher put it, many think one action is as good as another. Reflecting a culture that questions authority in all forms, they want to define *hero* in their own way—as anyone they admire. They name their heroes and ask me to name mine. "Who is to say Mozart is any better than Marilyn Manson?" "How can you say Shakespeare is better than Danielle Steel? Everything is interpretation." Several students have referred to my condemnation of Adolf Hitler as "just an opinion."

Discussing the dangers of celebrity worship in one assembly, I told the story of three young Canadians who in 1994 killed themselves in imitation of rock star Kurt Cobain. After driving from Quebec City to British Columbia, they climbed into a storage locker and died, inhaling the exhaust fumes from the car while listening to Cobain's music. A young teacher raised his hand, said that Ernest Hemingway was "an alcoholic, a womanizer, and blew his head off with a shotgun," and asked, "Why is he more of a hero than Kurt Cobain?"

Hemingway of course is less idealized today, criticized as a poseur and womanizer. Still, he was up with the sun every morning, writing. Hemingway's novels will probably outlast Cobain's music and he shot himself at the end of his life, when his body and mind were breaking down and he could no longer write.

Students frequently raise the issue of a hero's motives. "Is there a connection between psychological knowledge and disappearing heroes?" Psychology makes us introspective and focuses on what we are, not on what we might become. Before Sigmund Freud, it was probably easier to have heroes. If we believe we are controlled by our libido and our subconscious, we are perpetually uncertain about our motives. It is interesting that Freud believed that heroes were projections of our infantile needs and fantasies, reflecting our yearning for an all-powerful father figure. At the same time, Freud kept on his desk a bust of Moses.

In a school in San Francisco, students were studying behavioral psychologist B. F. Skinner, prompting a long discussion about heroes and altruism. Skinner stresses that we are powerfully molded by our environment and thus have little free will, that we are conditioned like rats and pigeons. Only with the belief that human beings have free will and the capacity for generous impulses does heroism become possible.

At an all girls' school in Connecticut, a student asked me whether I had read Albert Camus's *The Fall.* Camus, she volunteered, believes that all people are selfish. She had been wondering as she listened to the list of great deeds in my talk whether at bottom all heroes weren't just selfish. Undoubtedly, their motives are mixed and human beings are very complicated, but, I asked, could selfishness have driven Harriet Tubman into Maryland to rescue slaves she did not know?

Students will often name a hero and link that person to one trait they admire. "Dennis Rodman is my hero. He brought himself up from nothing." "Athletes are worth the money they make, worthy of being heroes." "Why can't Adolf Hitler be a a hero? He had a following." "Can't Marilyn Manson be considered a hero because he defied society, like Tom Paine and Martin Luther King Jr.?"

These one-dimensional definitions surface frequently. I ask these students to consider a more complex definition. What else does a man who has brought himself up from nothing do with his life? Of course athletes can be heroes, but shouldn't they have something more than extraordinary skill to qualify? Is defying society *always* the right thing to do?

Students and teachers frequently point out that protest movements have made America great. "We need to be very critical. Wasn't this country founded on protest and criticism?" "Is irreverence and disrespect for authority necessarily a bad thing? Didn't civil rights advance history?" "Isn't it healthy to challenge our heroes?"

The founding fathers, the nineteenth-century reformers, and the civil rights protesters were all rebels in their time. Should we challenge our heroes? Of course. A healthy skepticism is necessary for a healthy society. Irreverence among the young is inevitable and in some ways desirable. But, I argue, irreverence, skepticism, and mockery permeate our scholarship and culture to such a degree that it is difficult for young people to have public heroes.

Students today know more. They are more open, honest, tolerant, and realistic. But their realism easily turns to cynicism. After I described the heroics of a man in Boston who had died trying to rescue a boy from an icy pond, one student coolly commented, "Maybe he wanted to be on television."

Students can also be practical: "What can heroes do for me, get me into college?" "How is having heroes going to affect our lives?" And narcissistic: "I am my own hero."

IT WOULD BE misleading to suggest that all the students I talk to are cynical or confrontational, slaves to celebrities or devotees of antiheroes. One of the most poignant things I have found is the number of students who come up to me after my talk and shyly confide in me their hero: Felix Mendelsohn, Burmese dissident Aung San Suu Kyi, General William Tecumseh Sherman, the Dalai Lama, Alvin York.

"Even though Rigoberta Menchu is controversial, she is my hero," a student in a suburban high school announced in assembly. In Menchu's best-selling autobiography, *I, Rigoberta Menchu,* she describes how the Guatemalan government tortured and killed her family in her country's long civil war and how she fled to Mexico, joined the revolution, and risked her life to fight for the rights of indigenous peoples throughout the Americas. Menchu is controversial because in a 1999 book, *Rigoberta Menchu and the Story of All Poor Guatemalans,* anthropologist David Stoll questions the accuracy of Menchu's autobiography. Stoll believes that Menchu was more opportunistic than brave, a tool of Communist propagandists, and creator of personal myth.

In front of 800 students in an assembly combining high school and middle school students in Georgia, a seventh-grader stood up and said, "I still look up to George Washington and Abraham Lincoln."

In a class on American history, a ninth-grader volunteered that if we knew the private lives of all past presidents, they would be no better than Bill Clinton. In a rare moment, a classmate vehemently disagreed and talked about the integrity and courage of George Washington, adding that Andrew Jackson was a gritty frontiersman and a gentleman "who really loved his wife."

At a high school in Connecticut, a boy announced, "Jesus Christ is my hero."

One student came up to me after my talk and said, "All my heroes are from the nineteenth century." "Like whom?" I asked. "Winston Churchill. He really belonged to the nineteenth century."

You never know what students will latch on to in a speech. After hearing me praise Aleksandr Solzhenitsyn, a ninth-grader told me he went to the library and started reading *The Gulag Archipelago*. A senior girl who was on her way to Belgium the following week to visit her father asked me where she could find Käthe Kollwitz's sculpture *Mourning Parents*.

At a nearly all African American elementary school outside of Philadelphia, one hundred fifth-graders filed into a cafeteria. "Good afternoon, Dr. Gibbon," they said in unison. Their teachers had told them all to pick a hero. I asked them whom they had picked. Hands shot up all over the room: Jackie Robinson, Harriet Tubman, Sojourner Truth, Frederick Douglass, Ruby Bridges, Malcolm X, Ida B. Wells, Phyllis Wheatley, Matthew Henson, Thurgood Marshall, Rosa Parks. What did they do? I asked. I tried to embellish their accounts with any information that might click with ten-year-olds. I described how Sojourner Truth couldn't read but traveled all over America talking about equal rights for African Americans and women, how Jackie Robinson and Thurgood Marshall kept their composure even after receiving death threats, how Ida B. Wells saw three friends lynched in Tennessee and decided she had to act, how Malcolm X went into a prison a petty criminal but emerged a leader. Heroes, I added, change and grow.

What made Rosa Parks refuse to move to the back of the bus, even though she knew she could be beaten? How could Ruby Bridges keep her head up and walk to Franz Elementary School in New Orleans when a screaming mob told her to go home? Heroes, I added, are fascinating to study. I was amazed at the range of their heroes, at how much they knew at their age, at how eager they were.

TEACHERS FREQUENTLY TELL me about heroes they have discovered. Teacher Douglas Keith asked me if I knew about his hero, Pablo Casals, and told me that German novelist Thomas Mann once wrote, "In a brutalized age, Pablo Casals provides an example of proud, utterly incorruptible integrity." When threatened by Franco, Casals moved to France, where he gave concerts to help refugees. He refused to play in Franco's Spain, Mussolini's Italy, or Hitler's Germany. I remember when Casals played at the White House for John F. Kennedy in the 1960s. In his autobiography, *Joys and Sorrows,* Casals describes how he strives for simplicity, tenderness, and beauty of tone in his music. Every day, Casals wrote, "I go to the piano and I play two preludes and fugues of Bach. . . . I cannot think of doing otherwise. It is a sort of benediction on the house."

Another teacher, Deb Coughton, wrote to me about her hero, Kurt Hahn, the founder of Outward Bound. She concluded after hearing my talk that my mission was similar to Hahn's. In 1935, after storm troopers trampled a young Communist to death in front of his mother, Hahn, then a headmaster of Salem, a well-known German school, wrote to the school's alumni, insisting that they break either with Hitler or with Salem. The Nazis arrested Hahn and he spent a year in a German prison camp before escaping to England. Penniless and dispirited, he remembered his personal credo: "Your disability is your opportunity." In Scotland, he founded the Gordonstoun School, whose motto is *Plus est en vous* (There is more in you than you think).

Outward Bound believes that young people should be educated by physical challenges as much as by books, that through solving problems in the wilderness they can become braver, better, more independent.

Perhaps my mission is similar to Hahn's. We both believe that human beings have untapped potential that is brought forth by challenge and adversity. My advice is to read the biographies of great men and women. Hahn's is to climb mountains. We both agree that schools spend too much time making students smart and too little time making them good.

At a Catholic school in New Jersey, Father Bill Worman told me his heroes are boxer Joe Louis, Lieutenant Colonel Matthew Urban, and Father Jean de Brébeuf. Urban was eventually awarded the Congressional Medal of Honor for leading his men against the Nazis; he was wounded seven times, sent home after being shot in the throat, and went AWOL so he could return to his men. Brébeuf, an obscure seventeenth-century missionary, had his life ended at the stake. The Iroquois poured boiling water over him, imitating baptism, and then ate his heart, hoping to acquire the bravery he had showed facing death.

An English teacher came up to me after an assembly at a school in Connecticut and asked if I knew a poem by Emily Dickinson on heroism, which I did not. He recited it on the spot:

> We never know how high we are
> Till we are called to rise;
> And then, if we are true to plan,
> Our statures touch the skies.
> The heroism we recite
> Would be a daily thing,
> Did not ourselves the cubits warp
> For fear to be a king.

Teachers often ask me what schools can do to encourage a belief in heroism. To teach about exemplary lives was a goal of American education for hundreds of years. Schools automatically offered young people heroes. How else to combat the ambiguities and temptations of adult life? Where else to find the good to be imitated and the evil to be avoided? And so young people read Plutarch's *Lives* and were saturated with the pious maxims of their McGuffey's "Readers" and inculcated with the triumphs of Washington, Jefferson, and Lincoln.

The tradition of education by exemplary lives has ended and in its place we now offer lives that are seriously flawed, juvenile novels that emphasize "reality," and a history that is uncertain and blemished. In an information-rich world, we need to guide our young people to a more realistic definition of *hero* and bring balance to the way past heroes are evaluated.

To counteract radical revisionist history, a moderate triumphalism would highlight America's humanitarianism, our genius at invention and production, and our fundamental and ever-increasing commitment to equality. A moderate triumphalism would admit the mistakes America has made but insist that America learns from its mistakes and takes corrective action. From Wounded Knee, we learned. From the Homestead strike and the Triangle Shirt Waist fire, we learned. From the Treaty of Versailles and Vietnam. A moderate triumphalism would honor heroes like Chief Joseph, the brilliant strategist and magnanimous leader of the Nez Perce; would look into all corners of America's population for heroes; and would expand the pantheon beyond explorers, soldiers, and generals. But it would not automatically denigrate heroes of the past because they were privileged or powerful, because they fought and explored, or because they did not surmount every prejudice of their era.

I admit to having an old-fashioned view of the kind of novel to assign in high school English classes: I like to teach novels that not only mirror reality but also uplift in some way. The genre of the realistic juvenile novel romanticizes antisocial behavior and, I believe, should have only a minor role in the English curriculum. I am not a big fan of the book *A Hero Ain't Nothing but a Sandwich,* about a thirteen-year-old drug addict; or *The Outsiders,* about alienated adolescents who find solace in gangs. Instead of Ernest Hemingway's *The Sun Also Rises,* which offers cynical expatriates, I would recommend *For Whom the Bell Tolls,* about Robert Jordan, a brave soldier fighting in the Spanish Civil War.

Books for English classes could be realistic without being nihilistic. After reading George Eliot's novel *Adam Bede,* the British philosopher Herbert Spenser commented, "I feel greatly the better for having read it." Might this not be a reasonable test for at least some of the books on our reading lists?

Socratic dialogue need not mean there is no truth and that adults never have answers. Teachers should think of themselves as more than facilitators, more than "guides on the side."

A genius of teaching, Jaime Escalante, the mathematics teacher portrayed in the movie *Stand and Deliver,* refused to go to department meetings or do his paperwork, expelled students from his class who didn't do their homework, and wasn't always kind to colleagues or deferential to principals. Yet this cantankerous high school teacher in East L.A. cajoled and inspired dozens of Hispanic students to excel at college-level calculus, a course most American students avoid.

A former colleague of mine, Arthur Naething, taught senior English to generations of Hackley School students in Tarrytown, New York. The paper on tragedy they had to produce before commencement became a rite of passage, and many—now in their fifties—still talk about it. I cannot fully explain the Naething effect. He was a teacher, not a facilitator, certainly not a pal. Students warned their younger brothers and sisters to expect hard work and low grades. He was above all else a man they did not want to disappoint. In Naething's class they did their best and then some. Most of us can recall at least one teacher like this who, by setting high standards and transmitting a love of subject— whether calculus or the plays of Shakespeare—forged a vision of greatness in the classroom.

Critical inquiry, the reigning goal of contemporary American education, is only *one* goal; for much of American history, encouraging virtue was considered more important. Horace Mann advised teachers to make their students smart *and* good.

At the Seventh National Forum for the Character Education Partnership, the executive director presented awards to National Schools of Character. Almost all the awards were to elementary schools. We seem to give up on ethical instruction in high school.

One of the presentations at the Forum centered on peace heroes inspired by Raoul Wallenberg, a Swedish aristocrat who in 1944 rescued Hungarian Jews from the Germans and then disappeared into Stalin's gulag, never to be seen again. Wallenberg distributed food and clothing to Jews in the Budapest ghetto, provided protective passports that allowed them to escape from Adolf Eichmann, sheltered them in buildings that flew the Swedish flag, and bribed Nazi officials and Budapest police. He stood on the tops of trains headed for death camps and demanded that guards release Jews into his custody.

The Raoul Wallenberg Committee of the United States has created an elementary- and middle-school curriculum revolving around nonviolent men and women, like Gandhi, Martin Luther King Jr., and Mother Teresa. Its larger purpose is to inspire students "to discover their inner strengths, compassion for others, a sense of right and wrong . . . and the realization that every individual has the power to make a positive difference in the lives of others."

The U.S. Congress granted honorary citizenship to Wallenberg in 1981, the only person so honored after the Marquis de Lafayette and Winston Churchill. A bust honoring Wallenberg stands in the Capitol Rotunda, and the U.S. Postal Service issued a stamp in 1997 to honor him. I once read a letter Wallenberg wrote to his mother, saying that his rescue operation was the most exciting and interesting period of his life. It occurred to me that Wallenberg was transformed and galvanized by having a purpose other than maintaining the comfort of his prosperous life as a businessman. In my reading about heroes, I have discovered that altruism makes people happy.

MOST OF THE students I talk to have no trouble finding local heroes. Already conditioned by revisionist history to distrust the American past, many are reluctant to invest in public ones. They invariably talk about someone they know and can trust: a parent, a teacher, a friend. Many tell poignant stories: a teacher with cancer, a single parent holding the family together, a pregnant classmate. When asked to describe a hero, many describe victims.

Perhaps most importantly, I have found that students are intensely interested in heroes. They pepper me with questions, and teachers tell me that discussions often continue for weeks. Heroes are connected to questions they have about celebrities and popular culture, athletes and soldiers, the sexual revolution and the information revolution. Heroes are related to the literature they are reading, to the history they are studying, and to their search for meaning and mentors. Heroes also prompt significant questions about the meaning of life. Are human beings selfish or altruistic? Do we need to imitate and admire? Can individuals influence history? As I travel around the country, I have found a yearning among many students for something nobler than what our culture is currently offering. I have found that many are still searching for heroes.

Ten

WHY HEROES?

Heroes enhance life; the world expands and becomes less menacing and more hopeful by their very existence.

—Noel Annan, 1980

I first began to make the case for heroes to students on an afternoon in June after reading about three women of extraordinary courage. Quite by accident, I had picked off from the same shelf of my local library the letters of American missionary Eva Jane Price and the diary of German artist Käthe Kollwitz. In my Russian literature course, I had always taught *Journey into the Whirlwind*, Eugenia Ginzburg's memoir of her years in the infamous Gulag Archipelago, a memoir as powerful as anything written by Aleksandr Solzhenitsyn. Price, Kollwitz, and Ginzburg became the subject of my commencement speech and the genesis of my journey around the country to talk to students about heroes.

Eva Jane Price

Reading Eva Jane Price's letters, I was immediately caught up in the drama of an idealistic young nineteenth-century woman marooned in the middle of a feudal, decaying China fifteen thousand miles from home, trying to make a difference. Except for her evangelical beliefs,

Price was, in some ways, an ordinary middle-class nineteenth-century wife and mother, putting husband and children first, concerned with cleanliness and respectability. She embodied typical nineteenth-century feminine virtues: warmth, uncomplaining hard work, and a capacity for loyalty and self-sacrifice. Her ordinariness lends a poignancy and fascination to her story, for Price was thrust into the most trying circumstances and met an unfair and terrible end.

Eva and her husband, Charles, were trained as missionaries at Oberlin College. With their two small sons, they volunteered to serve the small Christian mission in Shansi, deep in central China. The Prices would have been obscure except for the bad luck of the Boxer Rebellion and the good luck that Eva's letters were preserved and published by Oberlin College. Through dozens of these letters, sent back to her family in America, we learn about her life in China.

To get to Shansi in the nineteenth century, you had to travel by slow train to San Francisco, be seasick on the Pacific for weeks, and then be borne by boat, donkey, and litter to the interior of China. Once in Shansi, you confronted dirt, monotony, isolation, unremitting work— and misunderstanding. Never does Price become accustomed to being constantly stared at, to opium addiction, bound feet, and famine. "What can a few Christians do to evangelize such a vast, vast country?" she wonders.

A skillful reporter, Price brings alive her ordinary days in nineteenth-century China, and that is one of the fascinations of her letters:

> We often see men whose faces have been terribly torn at some time in their lives by these big ugly wolves that come even into the city sometimes. Yesterday, I saw the worst-looking one I have ever seen. There really did not seem to be a bit of flesh left on the man's face—just the scarred skin drawn over the bones, the eyes set back in the sockets, the teeth all exposed, the nose gone, the flesh of the cheeks gone, no lips. It was simply dreadful to look at him. So many have sores or are blind or crippled.

But the letters sent to America are not just a catalog of horrors. While tending her own family, she makes time for addicts, maimed women, and a steady stream of sufferers. There are flashes of appreciation for the beauty of China—and always pity for the suffering around her.

I like Price's honesty. I like her grit and inner toughness, her capacity for work, and her endurance. Her unwavering religious belief does not degenerate into narrow hypocrisy or preclude a sense of social justice.

Halfway through their first tour, the Prices' own three-year-old son wastes away from diphtheria; then their twelve-year-old boy is afflicted with kidney failure. They return home on leave. Only unwavering religious belief could have impelled the Prices to forsake the comfort of America and return for a second tour of duty, and it is then that they meet their unfair and terrible end and become a small footnote in history.

The Chinese did not necessarily appreciate missionaries. There were those who scorned the foreigners' queer ways and those who coveted their goods. Some converted and then recanted; and, of course, Europeans and Americans made many enemies by carving up China and encouraging the sale of opium. The Shansi mission was replete with failures.

In 1900, young Chinese men hostile to foreigners for a variety of causes organized and began to extirpate Americans and Europeans in what would become known in history as the Boxer Rebellion. Called "Boxers" because of their unusual rituals and hand movements, the men were motivated by rumor, ignorance, national shame, poverty, idealism, and greed. After terrorizing the rest of Shansi province, the Boxers slowly closed in on the Price mission.

In her last letter, Price writes:

Thirty-three of our friends, most of whom we know personally and including the two older children of Mr. Atwater of our mission who were in Shou Yang in school, were beheaded in the presence of the Governor on July 8. Among the thirty-three lives were those of twelve children and two pregnant women soon expecting confinement.

I don't think it occurred to this devout woman, even at the end, that saving souls may have been foolish or that their missionary efforts were misguided. Typically, Price struggles to preserve normalcy while the news is terrible and the noose is slowly tightening.

The Boxers arrived at the mission and permitted the Prices and their followers to leave their compound and walk twenty miles to the village of Nan-an Shih. Temporarily their spirits were uplifted. Little did they know that they were safe only because the leaders of outlying villages of Shansi had bribed the Boxers not to massacre the Price party on their territory.

In Nan-an Shih, the leaders of the village did not come up with enough blood money to ransom the missionaries. Intent on wiping out all foreigners and restoring China's honor, the Boxers waited for them, cut them down with sword and pistol, stripped the corpses of their clothing, and tossed the Price family into a roadside ditch.

Käthe Kollwitz

German artist Käthe Kollwitz is less obscure than Price—at least in artistic circles. She is a more modern woman. She has a career and an identity of her own, an assertiveness that often comes into conflict with her family life. Born into a pre–World War I culture, Kollwitz lives through the Great War, Nazism, and World War II. She believes the important thing is to endure and do your work, and fills her diaries with injunctions to honor one's talent.

In the midst of a disintegrating Europe and family tragedy, only artistic production is consoling; yet she lives through long stretches empty of inspiration, unable to sculpt or draw. "Ever so many times come when sadness weighs me down like lead. I must fight my way out of this gray despair and find purpose and calm in the daylight of work." This pursuit of artistic achievement in the midst of long periods of sterility is one manifestation of Kollwitz's heroism.

In her early twenties, Kollwitz comes to believe that art should expose injustice and improve the world. She marries an idealistic doctor and finds beauty in the poor patients that crowd his clinic. In 1898 she creates her first masterpiece, *The Weavers,* a series of seven etchings in which she tells the story of the hungry linen workers of Silesia who in June of 1844 revolted against factory owners and were crushed by Prussian troops. Kaiser Wilhelm II called *The Weavers* "gutter art."

In the first year of World War I, her oldest son, Peter, is killed in Flanders. Paralyzed by grief, Kollwitz dreams about him constantly and transcends her grief by chiseling out of blue-gray granite *Mourning Parents*, a mammoth, brooding piece of work that overlooks the military cemetery near Roggevelde, Belgium.

There is a Chinese curse, "May you live in interesting times." Kollwitz was raised in a secure, prosperous, idealistic bourgeois home. She talks about "the old civilized atmosphere" of her grandparents' home, "the inner dignity, the peculiar composure, the definiteness and courtesy that prevailed there . . . and loftiness." It was Kollwitz's fate to be thrust out of this civilized atmosphere into interesting times—to the carnage of two world wars and the nihilism of the Nazis.

Haunted by "frightful insanity"—the youth of Europe hurling themselves at one another—Kollwitz curses the war, yet she still reads Goethe and Tolstoy and listens to Beethoven. In the middle of war, family tragedy, and social disintegration, she maintains the ideals she revered in her grandparents.

Because she opposes Hitler in 1933, Kollwitz is forced to resign from the Prussian Academy of Arts and forbidden to teach. Her etchings are removed from museums throughout Germany, confiscated, and sold abroad. She worries that the Nazis may destroy *Mourning Parents*. Interrogated by the Gestapo, she carries a vial of poison in case she is sent to prison.

When her husband slowly dies in 1940, she sculpts a small bronze masterpiece, *Farewell,* of a woman vainly trying to embrace a man whose arms fall slack as he slips from life. Her house is bombed, many of her works destroyed. In Russia, her grandson, also named Peter, is killed. She records in her diary, *Everywhere the same boundless misery.* Kollwitz's last work is a lithograph of a mother embracing and protecting three frightened children.

Weary and sick of war, Kollwitz dreams of death. Still, she writes her children and grandchildren a valedictory: *I bless my life, which has given me such an infinitude of good along with all the hardships. Nor have I wasted it; I have used what strength I had to the best of my ability.* Dreaming of peace, she dies quietly in 1945 at age seventy-eight—maternal, melancholy, tough, idealistic, obsessed with artistic perfection.

Eugenia Ginzburg

It is 1935. Eugenia Ginzburg is a teacher, writer, mother, and Communist, proud and idealistic, a believer in truth and justice. It is a bad year to be proud and idealistic, a bad year to be a believer in truth and justice. The Great Purge has begun. Joseph Stalin is determined to rid Russia of the proud and independent.

Over the next four years Stalin will murder political rivals, decimate the Communist party, execute generals, purge his own secret police, and send to prison camps poets, artists, historians, priests, peasants, and countless citizens who happen to live next door to a jealous neighbor or to have the wrong friend. To convince the world that the Soviet Union is threatened by a massive conspiracy, he will stage and film sham trials and distribute them to newsreels in Europe and America.

Because her professor is a Trotskyite and she refuses to denounce him, Ginzburg becomes suspect and loses her teaching position and party card. She repeatedly returns to Moscow to protest. Her grandmother urges her to hide in the country, her doctor counsels her to fabricate her own death or run away with the Gypsies. In 1937 she is called to party headquarters, turned over to the secret police, accused of belonging to a terrorist organization, and thrown into the Russian prison system—the gulag. She will not be released until 1955. During her eighteen years in the gulag, as Stalin goes berserk and the secret police fill their quota of enemies, her husband will disappear and her youngest son will die of starvation in Leningrad.

Ginzburg goes from Kazan's Black Lake prison to Yaroslavl. To ward off despair, she taps out messages to other prisoners through thick stone walls, talks out loud, and thinks of everything she has ever read. Insisting that solitary confinement can make one "kinder, more intelligent and perceptive," she struggles for serenity. Finally out of solitary confinement, she is transported by boxcar from Vladivostok on the Pacific Ocean and ferried to the Elgen labor camp in eastern Siberia. There she endures night blindness, a diet of putrid fish, scurvy, frostbite, lice, malaria, attacks by criminals, threats of rape. Once in the middle of the night the prison camp commandant pulls her out of her cold barracks and takes her to a greenhouse, where she is forced to identify her friend hanging from the ceiling. Ginzburg is tempted to suicide, fears for her sanity, and collapses from dysentery.

How does Ginzburg survive? Through friendship. As she is being transferred out of Black Lake prison, a man taps through the wall, "I wish you courage and pride." When she can't stop thinking about her dead son and collapses in despair, her cell mate strokes her head and recites passages from the book of Job. Near death after the sea voyage from Vladivostok, Ginzburg is rescued by a woman doctor who picks her up from a streetcar on the beach and nurses her back to health. "There are no more fervent friendships that those made in prison," Ginzburg writes.

She survives through poetry. In a cold punishment cell, as rats scuttle past her, she recites Blok, Nekrasov, and Pasternak and writes poems, "Silence" and "The Punishment Cell." In a crowded boxcar in the middle of Siberia, she recites poetry by the hour to divert her fellow prisoners who are dying from thirst. The guards hear her and are furious because they think someone has smuggled books into the boxcar. They stop the train and search for books, then demand proof of Ginzburg's amazing memory, insisting that she recite *Eugene Onegin* and promising to give the women water if she can perform. For three hours Ginzburg recites Pushkin.

Refusing to denounce other party members, Ginzburg survives by having a clear conscience. She survives by refusing to think about her children, by escaping physical torture, by luck. Ginzburg also survives through insatiable curiosity: "My intense curiosity about life in all its manifestations—even in its debasement, cruelty, and madness—sometimes made me forget my troubles." Working on a dairy farm, she finds time to talk about "the great riddles of the universe and the inexhaustibility of human genius." And she survives through defiant optimism. In a tragic world, she convinces herself that suffering offers insight. Despite suffering, tedium, and outrageous injustice, she refuses to become morally or spiritually dead—as were her captors and many of her fellow prisoners. Like Eva Jane Price and Käthe Kollwitz, she is possessed of unflinching honesty. She almost succumbs to despair but always pulls back. Ginzburg is indignant, but at the same time she possesses an unusual gift of appreciation—whether of a park glimpsed through a prison window, a sunset, or prison camp children.

Why did I celebrate these women on a hot afternoon in June? It is not pleasant to be caught up in the Boxer Rebellion, not easy to watch your country ruined by fascism, not an enviable fate to disappear into the gulag. Yet these misfortunes brought forth nobility, and these women had a vision of greatness that sustained them in crisis: Price her Christianity, Kollwitz her grandparents' prewar European culture, and Ginzburg her Russian literary giants.

Renewing America's Vision of Greatness

Our society is uneasy with greatness. Reluctantly, we find virtue. Easily, we detect flaws. Where the nineteenth century was predisposed to affirm and believe, we distrust and mock. Today public heroes are hard to find and difficult to defend.

Heroes make our lives more interesting. With heroes, we confront crisis and experience terror. We discover new lands and help the sick. We write memorable poems and compose stirring symphonies. With heroes, we experience the extraordinary and expand our notion of what it means to be human. With heroes, we escape the mundane.

We hear Winston Churchill defy Adolf Hitler and Franklin Roosevelt denounce Japan in 1941. We voyage with Captain Cook to Tahiti; with Florence Nightingale, we sail to the Crimea. We watch Mother Teresa comfort the dying. We are in prison with Aleksandr Solzhenitsyn and Dietrich Bonhoeffer. Like Sir Isaac Newton, we explain the universe.

Growing deaf, we compose the *Ninth Symphony;* on our backs we paint Adam on the ceiling of the Sistine Chapel.

Heroes are fascinating and puzzling. What made Abraham Lincoln rise from poverty and obscurity to become a successful lawyer? How could a successful, ambitious lawyer afflicted with doubt and depression become a wise, cunning, and compassionate president? How could he write such memorable prose with no formal education? How could he carry on in the middle of the Civil War when his son died and his generals failed?

In love with life and books and conversation, what made Sir Thomas More defy Henry VIII and die for the Catholic Church? Why did Jane Addams found Hull House and help the poor instead of going to health spas or succumbing to depression? Why did the villagers of Le Chambon risk their lives and hide Jews from the Germans? Heroes make us interested in the mystery of bravery and goodness.

Heroes instruct us in greatness. When Nelson Mandela leaves his South African cell without rancor and invites his guards to his inauguration, we are instructed in magnanimity. By not quitting after the winter at Valley Forge, George Washington teaches us perseverance and endurance. When Mother Teresa leaves her comfortable convent school and moves to Calcutta, we learn about compassion. Hearing that James Stockdale spent eight years in a North Vietnamese prison and is not broken, we understand bravery. Exiled and in despair, Dante writes *The Divine Comedy.* In isolation, Einstein rethinks the universe. Impoverished, Rembrandt paints profound portraits.

Heroes encourage us to search for our better selves. Shrewdly, George Orwell wrote, "There is one part of you that wants to be a hero or a saint, but another part of you is a little fat man who sees very clearly the advantages of staying alive with a whole skin." When in 1936 he fought fascism in Spain, Orwell repudiated smallness and safety.

Heroes encourage us to look up and admire. Of Joseph Lister, the discoverer of antiseptic surgery, Sherwin Nuland observed, "His opponents admired him. He seemed the embodiment of high purpose; an emanation of goodness radiated from him." Even Lister's enemies conceded his courage and goodwill. Heroes overcome our predisposition to envy, our temptation to scorn.

Heroes not only encourage us to search for our better selves, they remind us of our braver selves. Ernest Becker writes, "We admire most the courage to face death; we give such valor our highest and most constant adoration." Thus we draw sustenance from the suicide of Socrates and the martyrdom of Joan of Arc. We venerate Stonewall Jackson, who died in front of his troops at Chancellorsville. We remember the words of the patriot Nathan Hale when the noose was around his neck and those of Commander John Paul Jones—"I've just begun to fight"—when his ship, *The Bonhomme Richard,* was on fire. We recite Martin Luther King Jr.'s defiant speech when racists were closing in.

For Mary Dyer, hanged for her Quaker beliefs in 1660, there is now a statue in Philadelphia and Boston. For the African American soldiers of the 54th Massachusetts regiment, who in 1863 fell in front of the concrete walls of Fort Wagner, Augustus Saint-Gaudens carved a memorial on Boston Common. And to those who are neither martyrs nor soldiers, to the civilian heroes who descend into burning mines and dive into flooded rivers, who risk and sometimes sacrifice their lives to save a stranger in trouble, we award the Carnegie Medal of Honor.

Bravery comes in other forms as well as standing fast in battle, rescuing a stranger in trouble, facing death without flinching. Robert Kennedy noted, "Few men are willing to brave the disapproval of their fellows, the censure of their colleagues, the wrath of their society. Moral courage is a rarer comodity than bravery in battle or great intelligence." Heroes teach us about moral bravery as well as physical courage.

When in the 1840s Dorothea Dix told America that the mentally ill belonged in hospitals, not prisons, most citizens scoffed. At the Seneca Falls Convention in 1848, Elizabeth Cady Stanton and Lucretia Mott insisted that females be given the right to vote; not many American women or men understood why. Few Americans in the 1840s supported Elizabeth Blackwell in her attempt to attend medical school or, later, in her effort to find a hospital post. Nor in 1915 did many Americans applaud when Margaret Sanger argued in favor of birth control.

Early in the nineteenth century, English reformer and politician

Henry Brougham observed, "The true test of a great man—that, at least, which must secure his place among the highest order of great men—is having been in advance of his age." Moral heroes often see farther. They persist and cannot be budged. They teach us to transcend our time and to defy common opinion. They teach us to listen to our conscience, to do what is right, and to stand fast.

But heroes are not perfect. "The one cruel fact about heroes," comments La Rochefoucauld, "is that they are made of flesh and blood." We should search for greatness but not be surprised by flaws. King David fought Goliath but lusted after Bathsheba. Sir Thomas More sacrificed his life for the Catholic Church but authorized the burning of Protestants. About Adolf Hitler, Churchill was prophetic; holding on to the colonies, he was reactionary. Eleanor Roosevelt fought injustice all over America but was far from an ideal mother.

Aware of flaws, we can still admire. Clara Barton may have been arrogant, but she single-handedly founded the Red Cross. Admittedly ethnocentric, Albert Schweitzer cured thousands of sick Africans. Even his friends thought Oskar Schindler selfish, yet he saved thousands of Jews from Nazi death camps.

Heroes have splendid moments, but they are familiar with doubt and depression. When audiences didn't respond to the *Eroica* symphony, Beethoven was stunned. At age sixty-five, John Quincy Adams wrote that his "whole life had been a succession of disappointments." At first an indifferent student, Woodrow Wilson concluded, "I am nothing as far as intellect goes." After he was driven from power, Churchill was often melancholy. Working his way through medical school, Schweitzer was always fatigued. "It is not all pleasure, this exploration," noted David Livingstone, sick and alone in the middle of Africa.

Heroes triumph but often fail. Before the Civil War, Ulysses S. Grant was an alcoholic, William Sherman chronically depressed. Before 1860, Abraham Lincoln lost two Senate races and was turned out of Congress after serving one term. Twice, Ferdinand and Isabella turned down Christopher Columbus. Many times, Orville and Wilbur Wright watched their gliders crash. It took years for Pierre and Marie Curie to separate radium from pitchblende; months before Ann Sullivan could communicate with

Helen Keller; nearly a century before Herman Melville received praise for *Moby-Dick*. From experience he wrote, "He who has never failed somewhere, that man cannot be great. Failure is the test of greatness." Heroes soar, but always they suffer. "All supreme spirits have come out of great tribulation," noted preacher Harry Emerson Fosdick. John Bunyan produced *The Pilgrim's Progress* while in the Bedford jail, and Cervantes conceived *Don Quixote* in the Crown Jail of Seville. Beethoven composed his finest quartets while completely deaf. Anton Chekhov created *The Cherry Orchard* while dying from tuberculosis. From the slaughter of the Western Front came Wilfred Owen's poems and the sculpture of Käthe Kollwitz. Anne Frank started her diary after the Nazis forced her into hiding. After Auschwitz, Viktor Frankl wrote *Man's Search for Meaning.*

As diamonds are made by pressure and pearls formed by irritation, so greatness is forged by adversity. Blind Louis Braille invented a code for all who could not see. Ulysses S. Grant wrote his magisterial memoirs while he was dying from throat cancer. When John Stuart Mill's maid accidentally burned the first draft of *The French Revolution,* Carlyle started over.

Crippled by migraines and emotionally paralyzed by the death of his wife, Thomas Jefferson returned to Philadelphia in 1783 to help his country. Theodore Roosevelt's first wife *and* his mother died on the same day. In his diary, he recorded, *The light has gone out of my life* and returned to Albany to fight for bills that would uplift the poor. Devastated by his wife's death, Henry Wadsworth Longfellow forced himself to translate *The Divine Comedy.* The serenity of Ralph Waldo Emerson was tested when he watched his young wife and older brother die from tuberculosis. Ann Lee founded the Shakers after watching her four children die in infancy. Impoverished by the death of her husband and devastated by the death of her young children, Mary Harris (Mother) Jones became one of America's best-known labor leaders.

Without polio, Franklin Roosevelt might not have been as compassionate. Without chronic pain, John F. Kennedy might have remained a mere playboy. If her husband had not been unfaithful, Eleanor Roosevelt might not have become a crusader. Slavery made Frederick

Douglass indignant and Harriet Tubman courageous. Driven from his ancestral home, Chief Joseph fought brilliantly. Before they became reformers, Dorothea Dix and Clara Barton suffered breakdowns.

Heroes instruct us in greatness when they triumph. Idealistic, they ask us to be better. Courageous, they urge us to be braver. Visionary, they show us how to transcend our time. But they also instruct us when they are imperfect and in doubt, when they suffer and fail. Human beings become extraordinary when they surmount adversity and fight despair. Human beings become heroic when, against all odds, they persist; when, despite their flaws, they achieve.

Heroes may be sent from God, as Thomas Carlyle argued, but they do not stand alone. They are fortified by the examples of others who are extraordinary, brave, or noble. Edwin Armstrong, the inventor of the radio, wanted to be like Thomas Edison. Emerson preached self-reliance but depended on Goethe; Goethe worshiped Shakespeare. Melville read *King Lear* while he wrote *Moby-Dick*. Without Pushkin, Eugenia Ginzburg could not have endured solitary confinement. Without the Stoic philosopher Epictetus, James Stockdale might have given into torture.

Until Elizabeth Cady Stanton met Lucretia Mott, she floundered. After listening to Theodore Parker preach, Stanton wrote, "He finds my soul—he speaks to me." Before Susan B. Anthony knew Elizabeth Cady Stanton, she had scant interest in feminism. Over Woodrow Wilson's desk hung a picture of William Gladstone. Thomas Jefferson declared that the three greatest men who ever lived were Francis Bacon, Isaac Newton, and John Locke. Imitating them, he revered reason, order, and equality.

John F. Kennedy was moved by the courage of John Quincy Adams. For guidance, Martin Luther King Jr. looked to Gandhi; Gandhi looked to Tolstoy; Tolstoy read Thoreau. In all serious endeavors, we depend on exemplary lives and link ourselves to loftiness. We are fortified by examples of resolution and high achievement and bravery.

Still, in America today, it is not easy to make a case for heroes. Most of us would rather read about heroes than be heroic. Heroes are found in prisons and among the poor; are forged by disaster and battle, by sickness and suffering. They are created by crisis and know terror and danger. Heroes think new thoughts, which are often frightening, and they do not live serenely.

We don't want to go to prison or be poor. We don't want to be sick or to suffer. We are not eager to experience despair, even if it leads to insight. Not for us Puritan introspection or the rocky New England soil. Not for us Valley Forge. Not for us chasing whales and madness. Not for us the deprivation of the western frontier. Not for us the war to end wars, the fight against fascism, or the gulag and Auschwitz. Not for us plague and famine and Mother Teresa's untouchables.

Yet we will all in our lives experience injustice, reversals, and pain. We could all be more awake, kinder, braver, not succumbing to fatigue and pettiness, more clear-minded and lofty and less self-pitying. And we all need to be fortified and raised, to search for our higher selves.

I cannot imagine a world without heroes, a world without genius and nobility, without exalted enterprise, high purpose, and transcendent courage, without risk and suffering. It would be gray and flat and dull. Who would show us the way or set the mark? Who would inspire us and console us? Who would energize us and keep us from the darkness?

AFTERWORD

MORE: *But, Richard, in office they offer you all sorts of things. I was once offered a whole village, with a mill, and a manor house, and heaven knows what else—a coat of arms, I shouldn't be surprised. Why not be a teacher? You'd be a fine teacher. Perhaps even a great one.*

RICHARD: *And if I was, who would know it?*

MORE: *You, your pupils, your friend, God. Not a bad public that. . . . Oh, and a quiet life.*

—Robert Bolt, 1960
A Man for All Seasons

When I am asked how I became interested in heroes, I mention my commencement speech on three women of courage, the *Newsweek* piece, my research, my visits to schools. Looking back, however, I think this book has been slumbering in me for a long time.

Growing up in Shaker Heights, Ohio, in the 1950s, I read incessantly. In Landmark biographies, I traveled across the Atlantic with Columbus in his tiny ships and up the Missouri River with Lewis and Clark. I was with George Washington when he conquered the British at Yorktown. In high school, my tenth-grade history book was called the *Triumph of the American Past.* In English class we studied *Julius Cae-*

sar and memorized Mark Antony's eulogy on Brutus: "This was the noblest Roman of them all."

In the Freshmen Union, where I ate my meals at Harvard College in 1960, I sat under a portrait of Theodore Roosevelt. At the Fogg Art Museum, I studied self-portraits by Rembrandt and van Gogh and a large bust of Henry Wadsworth Longfellow. In Sanders Theater, I heard my first live performance of a Beethoven symphony. Widener Library, where I studied, was built to honor Harry Widener, collector of rare books and a member of the class of 1907. Widener was one of the men who remained on the deck of the *Titanic,* allowing women and children to get to lifeboats and safety. Memorial Church was built to honor students who died in the Great War. Long plaques listing the names of those lost to war hang on the walls, and in the front hallway is this inscription: WHILE A BRIGHT FUTURE BECKONED THEY FREELY GAVE THEIR LIVES AND FONDEST HOPES FOR US AND OUR ALLIES THAT WE MIGHT LEARN FROM THEM COURAGE IN PEACE TO SPEND OUR LIVES MAKING A BETTER WORLD FOR OTHERS.

All around us in 1960 was a sense of the heroic. It was before Vietnam and Watergate, Watts and Woodstock, and the assassinations of the Kennedy brothers and Martin Luther King Jr. John F. Kennedy had just been elected president. I remember standing on the steps of Widener Library, shivering in my brown sports coat and khaki pants, during Kennedy's visit to Harvard Yard in January 1961, shortly before his inauguration. The Yard was packed with students as Kennedy stopped to greet us on his way up the steps of University Hall next to his old freshman dormitory. Smiling in a blue pinstriped suit and no coat, he told us that he had come to check our grades and raid our professors.

Kennedy was charismatic, witty, urbane, irreverent. By 1963 he had cast a wide net among students, probably the last American president so many young people of my generation believed in. With his clipped Boston accent, he spoke to us in heroic language. I remember I was knotting my tie in front of my mirror in Adams House when someone came running down the hall yelling, "Kennedy has been shot!"

I was not political, but Kennedy's recruiting of professors to the White House had made him more appealing to me. Along with my high

school teachers, Jack Pickering and Burton Randall—who instilled in
me a love of literature, forced me to read critically, and suggested by
their example that teaching could be an important, even exalted, activity—my earliest heroes were some of my professors. I studied Puritanism with Perry Miller and was mesmerized by the first chapter of
his book *The New England Mind.* Occasionally I would see Miller
hunched over coffee at Tommy's Lunch and wonder how one brain
could summarize so much information in such majestic sentences. My
class with theologian Paul Tillich was in a large lecture room in a building named after Ralph Waldo Emerson. I can still see Tillich at the
podium in 1962—his craggy face and full head of white hair, his ram-
rod posture—and hear his German accent as he led us from St. Augus-
tine to Sigmund Freud, from Raphael to Picasso. I once saw Tillich in
the Harvard Trust Bank on Massachusetts Avenue and was stunned to
think he ever encountered money. From I. Bernard Cohen, who taught
the history of physics, I learned that scientists could be as heroic as poets.

My lifelong interest in Samuel Johnson began in biographer W. Jackson Bate's classroom, and I interviewed Professor Bate for this book just
before he died in 1999. I met him in his office at the top of Widener Library. I had not seen him since I took his course, *The Age of Johnson,*
forty years ago. His face was lined, his hair white. He still had the same
melancholy, kind expression. He coughed when he talked and told me
he had to spend most of the year in Florida because of his emphysema.
I immediately blurted out how much his course had meant to me. I am
sure he had heard this many times. I told him I still read Samuel Johnson
and guided my life by a line I remembered from his course—"Be not solitary . . . be not idle." He told me he still read Johnson, even as his life
was winding down, but he didn't think he would write any more books.
(For his biographies of John Keats and Samuel Johnson, Bate won two
Pulitzer Prizes.) He asked me whether high school students read Johnson. Johnson's ornate sentences are a stretch, I replied, and Boswell's
biography of Johnson is too long, but when teaching eighteenth-century
English history, I would have students look up Samuel Johnson in
Bartlett's *Familiar Quotations* and write down the five entries they found
most interesting. I asked Bate about heroes. He replied that he agreed

with everything in my *Newsweek* article and recommended Longinus' essay "On the Sublime." I thanked him for his time and his memorable course. My voice quavered, because I knew I would never see him again.

I walked over to Sever Hall and stood in the room where I had taken *The Age of Johnson* and recalled Bate's riveting lectures. On cold December mornings, he would describe how Johnson left Oxford because he had no shoes, how he triumphed over disease and poverty, how he kept terror and depression at bay, how he kept his wit, was loyal to his friends, and single-handedly created a dictionary. Bate convinced me there was a heroic world beyond the suburbs, and one could do worse than spend one's life reading great thinkers. I remembered being nineteen and leaving Sever Hall exalted.

Not long after my interview with Bate, he died. I wish I had told him more: how once during difficult times I reread his biography of Johnson to give me courage. Lodged in my brain and guiding this book is Johnson's phrase that it is "much easier to find reasons for rejecting than embracing." I wish I could tell him that I looked up Longinus in the index of his Johnson biography and found this description: "Longinus speaks of the influence of great models in enabling us to become our best selves."

Reading the Memorial Minute written by five of Bate's colleagues and published in the *Harvard Gazette* after his death, I discovered that Bate was influenced by Alfred North Whitehead, whose commentary linking education with a vision of greatness had influenced my thinking in writing this book. I learned that Bate's biography of Johnson was on lists of the top hundred books of the century in the 1970s, that he made an appearance in *People* magazine, and that more books had been dedicated to him than to any other "American humanist of the past century."

And I found in the tribute to Bate a statement summarizing the heroic sensibility. "He gave his students what he said Johnson had given so many, the greatest gift that any human can give another, the gift of hope: that human nature can overcome its frailties and follies and, in the face of ignorance and illness, can through courage still carve out something lasting and worthwhile, even something astonishing, something that will act as a support and friend to succeeding generations."

Notes

xxiv   *"Go with mean people ..."* Quoted in Edmund Grindlay Berry, *Emerson's Plutarch.* Harvard University Press, 1961, p. 2.

xxiv   *"with the great ..."* Ralph Waldo Emerson, *Representative Men.* Marsilio Publishers, 1995, p. 18.

xxiv   *"Times of terror ..."* Ralph Waldo Emerson, *Selected Essays.* Penguin Books, 1982, p. 259.

xxiv   *"Moral education ..."* Alfred North Whitehead, *The Aims of Education and Other Essays.* The Free Press, 1967, p. 69.

xxv   *"The search after the great ..."* Ralph Waldo Emerson, *Representative Men,* p. 3.

1   *"Let me tell you they are out there ..."* James Bond Stockdale, *Thoughts of a Philosophical Fighter Pilot.* Hoover Institution Press, 1995, p. 101.

1   *"It's a tricky word ..."* Lance Armstrong, *Fox News,* September 22, 2001.

1   *"He who conquers his evil inclinations ..."* Quoted in Norman Podhoretz, "Heroism in a Politically Correct Age," *National Review,* January 26, 1998, p. 45.

1   *"He who hangs on ..."* Quoted in Bergen Evans, *Dictionary of Quotations.* Delacorte Press, 1968, p. 314.

2   *"A true American hero ..."* Quoted in "Mother Hale's Lasting Gift," *The New York Times,* December 24, 1992.

2   *"My boat sank."* Quoted in Arthur M. Schlesinger Jr., *A Thousand Days:*

John F. Kennedy in the White House. Houghton Mifflin, 1965, p. 114.

2 *"Our definition . . ."* Author interview. March 1997.

2 *"A hero is usually smug . . ."* Author interview. July 27, 1996.

3 *"Many heroic actions . . ."* Quoted in John Mack Faragher, *Daniel Boone: The Life and Legend of an American Pioneer.* Henry Holt, 1992, p. 302.

3 *George A. Custer died a hero.* Marshall Fishwick is particularly effective in describing the role of publicists. See Fishwick, *American Heroes: Myth and Reality.* Public Affairs Press, 1954. Fishwick's book is the definitive treatment of the history of heroism in America.

4 *"The main thing to do . . ."* Will Rogers, Donald Day, ed. *The Autobiography of Will Rogers.* Houghton Mifflin Company, 1949, p. 183.

4 *Modern dictionaries . . . Bloomsbury Dictionary of Word Origins* reminds us, "It was not until the late 16th century that the extended and more general sense 'brave or otherwise admirable man' began to emerge." See John Ayto, *Bloomsbury Dictionary of Word Origins.* Bloomsbury Publishing, 1991, pp. 280–281.

5 *The moral component . . . Webster's Dictionary of Synonyms* has an excellent definition: "Heroism implies superlative, often transcendent, courage or bravery, not only as exhibited by deeds or daring in the presence of danger . . . but in carrying through without submitting or yielding an eminently arduous but exalted enterprise, such as exploration, or in the same spirit fulfilling a superhumanly high purpose where the odds are against one, such as the conquest of self or the institution of a great moral reform." *Webster's Dictionary of Synonyms.* G. & C. Merriam Co., Publishers, 1951. The same passage quotes Jeremy Bentham: "Acts of heroism are in the very essence of them but rare, for if they were common, they would not be acts of *heroism.*"

5 *"King-becoming graces . . ."* William Shakespeare, *Macbeth* (4.3.91–94).

6 *Plutarch's biographies . . .* Plutarch offered the following justification for his *Lives:* "to habituate my memory to receive and retain images of the best and worthiest characters . . . I am thus enabled to free myself from any ignoble, base, or vicious impressions contracted from the contagion of ill company." See Edmund Grindlay Berry, *Emerson's Plutarch,* Harvard University Press, 1961, p. 86.

7 *mistreating his slaves . . .* See Plutarch, *Makers of Rome: Nine Lives of Plutarch.* Penguin Books, 1965, p. 125: "We ought never to treat living crea-

tures like shoes or kitchen utensils." Samuel Johnson noted that "the sacred writers related the vicious as well as the virtuous actions of men; which had this moral effect, that it kept mankind from *despair*." See W. Jackson Bate, *Samuel Johnson*. Harcourt Brace Jovanovich, 1977, p. xix.

7   *In America today* . . . Mark Edmundson trenchantly notes: "We have a right to know the worst about anyone, immediately." Mark Edmundson, *Nightmare on Main Street: Angels, Sadomasochism, and the Culture of the Gothic*. Harvard University Press, 1997, p. 66.

7   *"not a list of the noblest characters."* Michael H. Hart, *The 100: A Ranking of the Most Influential Persons in History*. Hart Publishing Co., 1978, p. 81.

7   *"on the whole, heroes in history* . . ." Hook goes on to add that he does not believe we can connect hero to ethics or morality: "We must rule out as irrelevant the conception of the hero as a morally worthy man, not because ethical judgments are illegitimate in history, but because so much of it has been made by the wicked." Sidney Hook, *The Hero in History: A Study in Limitation and Possibility*. Beacon Press, 1955, p. 230.

9   *In a fact-based* . . . Alan Edelstein, in his book exploring the disappearance of heroes, notes that with so much reality we have lost the "romantic embellishment and, therefore, illusion, a critical part of the creation of heroes." See Alan Edelstein, *Everybody Is Sitting on the Curb: How and Why America's Heroes Disappeared*. Praeger, 1996, p. 204.

9   *Idolatry implies* . . . Edward O. Wilson reminds us: "True to their primate heritage, people are easily seduced by confident, charismatic leaders, especially males. That predisposition is strongest in religious organizations. Cults form around such leaders." Edward O. Wilson, *Consilience: The Unity of Knowledge*. Alfred A. Knopf, 1998, p. 260.

9   *"Women should have heroines* . . ." Author interview. June 30, 1999. See also Joseph Epstein, "Say No to Role Models," *The New York Times,* April 23, 1991.

10   *"quiet role models working* . . ." Author interview. June 1999.

11   ". . . *admiration, terror, and awe."* A. C. Bradley, *Shakespearean Tragedy: Lectures on Hamlet, Othello, King Lear, Macbeth*. Macmillan, 1956, pp. 19–20.

11   *"I believe that the common man* . . ." Arthur Miller, "Tragedy and the Common Man," in *The Theatre Essays of Arthur Miller*. The Viking Press, 1978, p. 3.

11   "*I don't say he's a great man . . .*" Arthur Miller, *Death of a Salesman.* The
      Viking Press, 1958, p. 57.

12   "*I vote for everyone.*" John Updike, *Picked-Up Pieces.* Alfred A. Knopf, 1976,
      p. 518.

12   "*small victories . . .*" John Kasich, *Courage Is Contagious: Ordinary People
      Doing Extraordinary Things to Change the Face of America.* Doubleday,
      1998, p. 12.

12   *. . . second half of the twentieth century.* In an issue of *culture front,* Joyce
      Carol Oates notes, "The very concept of 'hero'—or 'heroine' has under-
      gone a considerable modification in our time. Where once we might have
      imagined such models of integrity and performance to be larger than life,
      now we know them to be merely human like ourselves. . . ." Oates goes
      on to mention her parents as heroes. See Joyce Carol Oates, *culture front,*
      Summer 1998. Bill Berkowitz has written an entire book asserting that "A
      new heroic model for our time . . . is the local hero working at a commu-
      nity level." See Bill Berkowitz, *Local Heroes.* Lexington Books, 1987,
      p. x. I have worked with Dr. Irving Fradkin, a resident of Fall River, Mas-
      sachusetts, and founder of Dollars for Scholars, who has honored living
      heroes in local communities in an attempt to motivate young people. After
      surveying the attitudes of young Americans, Robert J. Pamplin concluded
      that "their heroes are found among family members, friends, teachers, and
      others they can trust." Pamplin believes there is a shortage of heroes but
      that heroes should be found "among us instead of above us." See Robert
      J. Pamplin, *American Heroes: Their Lives, Their Values, Their Beliefs.*
      Master Media, 1995, p. xxi.

15–17 Author interviews with Ralph Rourke, director of the the Hall of Fame
      for Great Americans, author visits to the Hall of Fame, and books listed in
      the bibliography. I am grateful to Paul Dickson for introducing me to the
      Hall of Fame for Great Americans.

18   "*The faculty of love . . .*" Thomas Carlyle, "Essay on Voltaire," in G. M.
      Trevelyan, ed. *Carlyle: An Anthology.* Longmans, Green and Co., 1953,
      p.139.

18   "*The interests of a client . . .*" Quoted in B. A. Hinsdale, *Horace Mann and
      the Common School Revival in the United States.* Charles Scribner, 1913,
      p. 114.

18   "*an extravagant worship . . .*" James Anthony Froude, *The Hundred Greatest
      Men,* Volume VII. Sampson, Low, Marston, Searle, and Rivington, 1880, p. v.

18   *"Lives of great men . . ."* Henry Wadsworth Longfellow, "A Psalm of Life." Lewis Untermeyer, ed. *The Poems of Henry Wadsworth Longfellow.* The Heritage Press, 1943, p. 141. Longfellow first read this poem to his Harvard students at the close of a lecture on Goethe.

19   *. . . once familiar to generations of Americans.* The financier John Templeton remembers: "In my teenage years . . . I memorized Longfellow's 'A Psalm of Life.' It has encouraged me to use to the limit any gifts God may have given me." John Templeton with James Ellison, eds., *Riches for the Mind and Spirit.* HarperSanFrancisco, 1990, p. 163.

19   *"No sadder proof . . ."* Thomas Carlyle, *On Heroes, Hero-Worship, and the Heroic in History.* Houghton Mifflin, 1907, p. 18.

19   *Americans also named cities . . .* See Page Smith, *The Shaping of America: A People's History of the Young Republic.* McGraw-Hill, 1980, p. 391.

20   *. . . emotional reunions with John Adams and Thomas Jefferson.* See Smith, *The Shaping of America: A People's History of the Young Republic,* pp. 802–814.

20   Known as *"the Hero . . ."* According to biographer Robert Remini, "Andrew Jackson was one of the few genuine heroes to grace the presidency. He was courageous and strong. And he was indomitable. The American people always believed that as long as General Andrew Jackson lived, the democracy was safe." Robert V. Remini, *The Life of Andrew Jackson.* Penguin Books, 1990, p. 326.

20   *"our destiny and duty."* Quoted in Blanche Linden-Ward, *Silent City on a Hill: Landscapes of Memory and Boston's Mount Auburn Cemetery.* Ohio State University Press, 1989. I have made many visits to the Mount Auburn Cemetery and Linden-Ward's excellent book has helped me to understand the cemetery's history.

21   *Francis Bellamy wrote . . .* In his book, *The Mystic Chords of Memory,* Michael Kammen notes that "flag worship was a prevalent phenomenon between 1885 and 1915" and that "patriotism and hero worship enjoyed a very broad appeal that cut across class lines." See Michael Kammen, *The Mystic Chords of Memory: The Transformation of Tradition in American Culture.* Vintage Books, 1991, pp. 204–205.

22   *"Of many races . . ."* Brian Burrell, *The Words We Live By: The Creeds, Mottoes, and Pledges that Have Shaped America.* The Free Press, 1997,

p. 309. I am indebted to Burrell for making me more analytical about inscriptions.

22   "... *to know a good man* ..." William James, *Memories and Studies.* Longmans Green and Co., 1911, p. 309. Professors may be skeptical, but many laud the life of James and call him a hero. Linda Simon, James's most recent biographer, claims: "It was impossible not to be morally elevated by the smallest contact with William James." See Linda Simon, *Genuine Reality: A Life of William James.* Harcourt Brace, 1998, p. xv.

23   "*You must not think* ..." Quoted in John A. Garraty and Marc C. Carnes, eds., *American National Biography: Volume 11.* Oxford University Press, 1999, p. 342.

23   "*Peace hath higher tests* ..." John Greenleaf Whittier, "The Hero," in *The Complete Poetical Works of John Greenleaf Whittier.* Houghton Mifflin, 1894, p. 193.

23   ... *offering new heroes* ... Eakins has always been my favorite American painter. I am indebted to art critic Elizabeth Johns for connecting Eakins to a new vision of heroism. See Elizabeth Johns, *Thomas Eakins, The Heroism of Modern Life.* Princeton University Press, 1983.

23   "*living and breathing men* ..." Quoted in Clyde N. Wilson, ed., *Dictionary of Literary Biography: American Historians, 1607–1865.* Volume 30. Gale Research Company, 1984, p. 124.

23   "*That man is no man* ..." Quoted in Leonard Roy Frank, ed., *Random House Webster's Quotationary.* Random House, 1999, p. 358.

24   *The dominant voice of the century* ... A keen interest in heroes was not confined to America. The literary critic Walter Edwards Houghton noted, "In the fifty years after 1830, the worship of the hero was a major factor in English culture." Many American intellectuals, including Longfellow, visited England and were influenced by Matthew Arnold; Alfred, Lord Tennyson; and John Stuart Mill—who all emphasized the need for heroes. In an acute observation, Houghton noted that the Victorians had an "innate desire to affirm and conform rather than to reject or question." See Walter Edwards Houghton, *The Victorian Frame of Mind, 1830–1870.* Yale University Press, 1985, pp. 310, 394. It is risky to generalize about a century, but in *The Proud Tower,* Barbara W. Tuchman offers what seems to me a reasonable assessment of the European-American world at the end of the nineteenth century: "Its inhabitants lived, as compared to a later time, with more self-reliance, more confidence, more hope; greater magnificence, extravagance and elegance; more carelessness, more gaiety, more pleasure

in each other's company and conversation, more injustice and hypocrisy, more misery and want, more sentiment including false sentiment, less sufferance of mediocrity, more dignity in work, more delight in nature, more zest." Barbara W. Tuchman, *The Proud Tower: A Portrait of the World Before the War, 1890–1914.* Macmillan, 1966, p. 436.

24 *... it is the scornful ...* William K. Kilpatrick observes: "Whereas earlier ages engaged in unabashed hero worship, ours prefers to cut them down to size. Instead of pointing to the noble qualities of public figures, we feel compelled to point out their feet of clay. This is an age that feels more comfortable with the confessional mode than the heroic one." William K. Kilpatrick, *Why Johnny Can't Tell Right from Wrong.* Simon & Schuster, 1992, p. 106.

24 *"We must endeavor to hide ..."* James Anthony Froude, *Thomas Carlyle: A History of his Life in London 1834–1881.* Harper & Brothers, 1885, p. 13. James Froude wrote the first biography of Carlyle. He intended it to be honest and admiring, while alluding to tensions within Carlyle's marriage. A number of readers at the time denounced Froude as a Judas and a muckracker. Today the biography seems reverential, but Victorian readers resisted any discussion of Carlyle's intimate life. For an analysis, see Rochelle Gurstein, "The Case of Thomas Carlyle: Published Letters, Private Life, and the Limits of Knowledge." *American Scholar,* Summer 2001. Gertrude Himmelfarb notes, "The Victorians humanize their heroes, reveal their private vices without denying their public virtues. The new biographers [Strachey] reveal their vices (or more often follies) to dishonor them—to make antiheroes of them." See Gertrude Himmelfarb, *On Looking into the Abyss: Untimely Thoughts on Culture and Society.* Alfred A. Knopf, 1994, p. 34. In a trenchant phrase, Himmelfarb warns that today, "the presumption against greatness goes deep," p. 40.

25 *"All souls feel ..."* Thomas Carlyle, *On Heroes, Hero-Worship, and the Heroic in History,* p. 2. It is interesting that Carlyle believed he lived in an anti-heroic age, "an age that as it were denies the existence of great men, denies the desirableness of great men." Carlyle, pp. 16–17.

25 *"the history of the world ..."* Thomas Carlyle, *On Heroes, Hero-Worship, and the Heroic in History,* p. 18.

25 *"The battle of belief ..."* Thomas Carlyle, *On Heroes, Hero-Worship, and the Heroic in History,* p. 239.

25 *"Do the duty ..."* Quoted in Frederick William Roe, *Victorian Prose.* The Ronald Press Company, 1947, p. 31.

26   "*A silent, great soul* . . ." Thomas Carlyle, *On Heroes, Hero-Worship, and the Heroic in History,* p. 75.

26   "*a deep, great, genuine sincerity.*" Thomas Carlyle, *On Heroes, Hero-Worship, and the Heroic in History,* p. 62.

27   *searching for greatness* . . . Typical of Emerson's fervor is this statement: "I cannot even hear of personal vigor of any kind, great power of performance, without fresh resolution." Ralph Waldo Emerson, *Representative Men,* p. 10.

27   "*the biography of a few stout* . . ." Ralph Waldo Emerson, *The Selected Writings of Ralph Waldo Emerson.* Random House, 1940, p. 154. Even in the nineteenth century there were dissenters. In *Les Miserables,* Victor Hugo noted: "Life, misfortunes, isolation, abandonment, poverty, are battlefields which have their heroes; obscure heroes, sometimes greater than the illustrious heroes." Quoted in Ralph L. Woods, *World Treasury of Religious Quotations.* Hawthorn Books, 1966, p. 436.

27   "*All men have wandering* . . ." Ralph Waldo Emerson, *The Selected Writings of Ralph Waldo Emerson,* p. 258.

27   "*Heroism feels and never reasons* . . ." Ralph Waldo Emerson, *The Selected Writings of Ralph Waldo Emerson,* p. 253.

27   "*Always do what you are* . . ." Quoted in Robert D. Richardson Jr., *Emerson: The Mind on Fire: A Biography.* University of California Press, 1995, p. 25.

28   "*hero-worship always retained* . . ." Quoted in Edmund Grindlay Berry, *Emerson's Plutarch,* p. 98.

28   *Carlyle's heroes seem unapproachable.* Carlyle believed that there were certain men in whom divine energy seemed to flow abundantly, but he was not entirely an elitist. His veneration for genius was coupled with compassion for ordinary people, who could become heroic. "If Hero means *sincere man,* why may not every one of us be a hero?" he asked his London audience. Thomas Carlyle, *On Heroes, Hero-Worship, and the Heroic in History,* p. 178.

29   "*We are proud of him* . . ." Quoted in Eugen Kuehnemann, *Charles W. Eliot: President of Harvard University, May 19, 1869–May 19, 1909.* Houghton Mifflin Company, 1909, p. 82. The portrait of Eliot is based on biographies by Kuehnemann and Henry James and the file on Eliot in the Harvard University archives.

29   "*fifteen minutes a day* . . ." Henry James, *Charles W. Eliot, President of Harvard University, 1869–1909.* Vol. II, p. 194.

30   "*Anyone who stops* . . ." Burrell goes on to note that Eliot assumed that

"there is a core of knowledge rooted in the Western tradition that expresses universal truths, and forms the proper basis of an enlightened education." Traditional creeds, he adds, started to disappear in the 1960s. See Brian Burrell, *The Words We Live By: The Creeds, Mottoes, and Pledges that Have Shaped America*, p. 210.

30   *"He was our great . . ."* Quoted in *Boston Evening Transcript*, August 26, 1926.

30   *"Industry or diligence became . . ."* Quoted in Jonathan Messerli, *Horace Mann: A Biography*. Alfred A. Knopf, 1972, p. 9. I am indebted to Messerli's splendid biography for parts of this portrait.

31   *"of splendid composition . . ."* Quoted in Messerli, *Horace Mann: A Biography*, p. 84.

31   *"All my boyish castles . . ."* Quoted in Lawrence A. Cremin, ed., *The Republic and the School: Horace Mann on the Education of Free Men*. Teachers College Press, 1957, p. 4.

32   *"The path of usefulness . . ."* Joy E. Morgan, *Horace Mann: His Ideas and Ideals*. The National Home Library Foundation, 1936, p. 13.

32   *"Train up a child . . ."* Quoted in Cremin, *The Republic and the School: Horace Mann on the Education of Free Men*, p. 100.

32   *"Never will wisdom preside . . ."* Quoted in Cremin, *The Republic and the School: Horace Mann on The Education of Free Men*, p. 7.

33   *"biography, especially the biography of the great . . ."* Quoted in Raymond Benjamin Culver, *Horace Mann and Religion in the Massachusetts Public Schools*. Arno Press and *The New York Times*, 1969, p. 170.

33   *"Sages imbue him . . ."* Quoted in Raymond Benjamin Culver, *Horace Mann and Religion in the Massachusetts Public Schools*, p. 170.

33   *"Teaching is the most difficult . . ."* Quoted in Cremin, *The Republic and the School: Horace Mann on the Education of Free Men*, p. 21.

33   *"The molding of minds . . ."* Quoted in Messerli, *Horace Mann: A Biography*, p. 134.

34   *"Take egotism out . . ."* Quoted in Messerli, *Horace Mann: A Biography*, p. 339.

35   *"I beseech you . . ."* Quoted in Messerli, *Horace Mann: A Biography*, p. 584.

37   *. . . stands John Bridge . . .* Information about John Bridge came from the file on John Bridge in the Cambridge Historical Society.

38 *one purpose of monuments* . . . In a brilliant essay, the sociologist Nathan Glazer argues that monuments no longer serve that purpose. Today, he argues, we "detect in these extravagant enterprises the symbols of imperialist arrogance, Western cultural hegemony, male chauvinism, homophobia, and on and on." Glazer goes on to say, "We no longer know clearly who our heroes are, because none of them come to us without a crippling ambiguity." Nathan Glazer, "Monuments in an Age Without Heroes." *The Public Interest,* Spring 1996.

40 *"On my arrival* . . ." Alexis de Tocqueville, *Democracy in America.* Translated by Harvey C. Mansfield and Delba Winthrop. The University of Chicago Press, 2000, p. 282.

40 *"It is one of my favorite thoughts* . . ." Quoted in Tyron Edwards, ed., *The New Dictionary of Thoughts.* Standard Book Company, 1961, p. 236.

40 Sent to Groton . . . For Peabody's influence, see Joseph P. Lash, *Eleanor and Franklin: The Story of Their Relationship Based on Eleanor Roosevelt's Private Papers.* New American Library, 1971, p. 171. Eleanor Roosevelt's favorite song was the Sunday school hymn, "Brighten the Corner Where You Are." See Peter Gomes, *Yet More Sundays at Harvard: Sermons for an Academic Year.* President and Fellows of Harvard College, 1997, p. 108.

41 *Many of our most influential* . . . Abraham Lincoln wrote, "I have been driven many times to my knees by the overwhelming conviction that I had nowhere else to go. My own wisdom, and that of all about me, seemed insufficient for the day." Quoted in Tyron Edwards, ed., *The New Dictionary of Thoughts.* p. 504. Merrill Peterson notes that out of the 722 words of the Second Inaugural Address, 266 of them came from the Bible. Merrill D. Peterson, *Lincoln in American Memory.* Oxford University Press, 1994.

41 *So have some of our* . . . Phyllis Theroux notes that Henry David Thoreau "thought that without religion or devotion of some kind, nothing great was ever accomplished." See Theroux, *The Book of Eulogies: A Collection of Memorial Tributes, Poetry, Essays, and Letters of Condolence.* Scribner, 1997, pp. 94–95.

41 *"That great and benevolent Being* . . ." Quoted in Harlow Giles Unger, *Noah Webster: The Life and Times of an American Patriot.* John Wiley & Sons, 1998, p. 303.

41 *"He who dies rich* . . ." Andrew Carnegie, *The Gospel of Wealth and Other Timely Essays.* Belknap Press of Harvard University Press, 1962, p. 49.

41 *revolved around the Bible* ... Dick Keyes writes about heroism from the perspective of a Christian. He argues that celebrity and cynicism have cast down heroes and that contemporary society is infatuated with evil and anti-heroes. Keyes argues that true heroism is moral heroism, which can be achieved by imitating Jesus Christ. See Dick Keyes, *True Heroism in a World of Celebrity Counterfeits.* NavPress, 1995.

42 *"Whatsoever thy hand ..."* Ecclesiastes 9:10. Authorized King James Version.

43 *"Finally, brothers, whatever is true ..."* Philippians 4:8. *New American Bible.*

45 *"bound with chains ..."* Quoted in John A. Garraty and Marc Carnes, eds., *American National Biography,* Volume 6. Oxford University Press, 1999, p. 636.

46 *... a Declaration of Sentiments ...* Quoted in Edward T. James, ed., *Notable American Women 1607–1950,* Volume 3. Belknap Press of Harvard University Press, 1971, p. 343.

46 *"I shall in the future ..."* Quoted in Elisabeth Griffith, *In Her Own Right: The Life of Elizabeth Cady Stanton.* Oxford University Press, 1985, p. 175.

47 *"I have received ..."* Quoted in William S. McFeely, *Frederick Douglass.* W. W. Norton, 1991, p. 263.

47 *"You would laugh to see ..."* Quoted in Griffith, *In Her Own Right: The Life of Elizabeth Cady Stanton,* p. 163.

49 *"an African Prince."* Quoted in William S. McFeely, *Frederick Douglass,* p. 383.

49 *"there was a right side ..."* Quoted in David W. Blight, *Frederick Douglass' Civil War: Keeping Faith in Jubilee.* Louisiana State University Press, 1989, p. 235. My view of Douglass was shaped by reading his speeches, letters, and autobiography, but David Blight's excellent books and an author interview were also influential.

50 *"If there is no struggle ..."* Quoted in John Bartlett and Justin Kaplan, eds., *Familiar Quotations.* Little, Brown, 1992, p. 480.

51 *"Something about our time ..."* Quoted in Marc Pachter, ed., *Telling Lives: The Biographer's Art.* New Republic Books, 1979, p. 139.

56 *"If there be one principle ..."* Available on *www.dromo.com/fusionano maly/.* November 14, 2001.

Notes

56   *"All the great masterful races ..."* Available on *www.theodore-roosevelt. com/trspeeches.html-uk.* November 20, 2001.

56   *"Isn't it time we destroyed ..."* Quoted in Michael Kimmel, *Manhood in America: A Cultural History.* The Free Press, 1996, p. 293.

57   *"the greatest thing accomplished ..."* Quoted in Garraty and Carnes, *American National Biography,* Volume 24, p. 832. In explaining his appeal, David D. Lee emphasizes York's character and modesty and the fact that "biographies offer the public an archetypical American frontiersman called to be a soldier of the Lord in the war to end all wars." David D. Lee, *Sergeant York: An American Hero.* University Press of Kentucky, 1985, p. 93.

58   *"In heroism, we feel ..."* William James, "The Moral Equivalent of War," in *Writings: 1902–1910.* The Library of America, 1987, p. 1292.

58   The portrait of Carnegie is based on Joseph Frazier Wall's excellent biography, Carnegie's autobiography, and materials from the Carnegie Hero Fund Commission.

58   *"the foulest fiend ..."* Quoted in Joseph Frazier Wall, *Andrew Carnegie.* Oxford University Press, 1970, p. 916. Wall notes: "There was a strong predilection on Carnegie's part to engage in hero worship, and to have implicit faith in the cult of personality. He was always looking for *the man.*" Wall, p. 914.

59   *"I can't get the women and children ..."* Available on *www.carnegiehero. org/.* November 7, 2001.

60   *"preserve and rescue ..."* Available on *www.carnegiehero.org/.* November 7, 2001.

61   *"embarrassed by the words ..."* See Ernest Hemingway, *A Farewell to Arms.* Simon & Schuster, Inc., 1995, p 184. In *The Great War and Modern Memory,* Paul Fussell also describes the disappearance of heroic language after World War I.

61   *"The world will never be again ..."* Quoted in Ann Douglas, *Terrible Honesty: Mongrel Manhattan in the 1920's.* Farrar, Straus and Giroux, 1995, p. 157.

62   *... and turns him away.* This movie is described in Michael Kimmel's excellent history, *Manhood in America: A Cultural History,* The Free Press, 1996, pp. 191–192.

63   *The few heroes to emerge ...* Nell Boyce, "Hugh Thompson," *U.S. News & World Report,* August 20–27, 2001, pp. 33–34.

Notes

65   *In an interview* ... Available on *www.writes.org/conversations/conver-4. html.* November 14, 2001.

65   *"I don't know what a hero is ..."* Robert Cormier, *Heroes.* Delacorte Press, 1998, p. 131. In a *Washington Post* article on March 11, 2001, Linton Weeks noted about young-adult fiction: "Lust, hatred, horror, darkness, dysfunction, drugs, disease and gruesome death permeate young adult literature."

65   *"that America could do nothing ..."* Quoted in A. D. Horne, ed., *The Wounded Generation: America After Vietnam.* Prentice-Hall, 1981, p. 210.

66   *"Men see that the Compulsive Warrior ..."* John C. Robinson, *Death of a Hero, Birth of the Soul: Answering the Call of Midlife.* Tzedakah Publications, 1995, p. 168.

67   *"the great virile virtues..."* Quoted in Michael Kimmel, *Manhood in America: A Cultural History,* p. 426.

68   *An article* ... Jack Hitt, "Battlefield: Space," *The New York Times Magazine,* August 5, 2001.

71   I discovered the Sports Bay on one of my many tours of the cathedral. Information on the bay comes from the archives of the Cathedral Church of St. John the Divine.

71   *"What could be happier ..."* Quoted in Julian S. Myrick, "Address at the Dedication of the Sports Bay and Chapel, Cathedral of St. John the Divine," Sunday, October 21, 1951, p. 6.

72   *"stand against hate ..."* Grantland Rice, fundraising booklet. The Committee for Completing the Cathedral of St. John the Divine, circa 1926.

73   *"the value of courage and self-sacrifice ..."* Julian S. Myrick, "Address at the Dedication of the Sports Bay and Chapel, Cathedral of St. John the Divine."

73   *"the highest ideals ..."* Julian S. Myrick, "Address at the Dedication of the Sports Bay and Chapel, Cathedral of St. John the Divine," p. 2.

74   *"I don't give a rat's turd ..."* Brian Bosworth with Rick Reilly, *The Boz: Confessions of a Modern Anti-Hero.* Doubleday, 1988, p. 125.

74   *"a spectacle more brutalizing,"* Quoted in *Harvard University Annual Report,* March 3, 1906.

75   *"No games so tries the temper ..."* Quoted in Harford Powel Jr., *Walter Camp, The Father of American Football, An Authorized Biography.* Little, Brown, 1926, p. 99.

76   "*If baseball will hold . . .*" Quoted in Ray Robinson, *Matty: An American Hero: Christy Mathewson of the New York Giants.* Oxford University Press, 1993, p. 217. Robinson's excellent book argues that Mathewson, with his exemplary character, was America's "first authentic sports hero." Robinson notes, "Today it is difficult for personalities in any sport to be regarded as heroes or role models. The relentless, often prurient eye of TV and other brands of the media . . . tend to reduce current sports stars into ordinary human beings." See Robinson, p. 8.

77   "*You handle your machine . . .*" Quoted in John Dunn Davies, *The Legend of Hobey Baker.* Little, Brown, 1966, p. 96.

77   "*He was a sort of legendary hero . . .*" Quoted in John Dunn Davies, *The Legend of Hobey Baker,* p. 114.

79   When "*The Star Spangled Banner*" played . . . Jim Bouton, *Ball Four.* Twentieth Anniversary Edition. Edited by Leonard Schecter. Macmillan, 1990, p 38.

79   "*I think we are all better off . . .*" Jim Bouton, *Ball Four,* p. xi.

79   "*take pep pills . . .*" Jim Bouton, *Ball Four,* p. x.

79   "*There are no great men . . .*" Quoted in Jim Bouton, *Ball Four,* p. xi.

79   "*It was not our purpose . . .*" Quoted in Jim Bouton, *Ball Four,* p. xiv.

79   Pete Rose screamed . . . Jim Bouton, *Ball Four,* p. x.

80   "*raunchy stories.*" Jim Bouton, *Ball Four,* p. xii.

81   "*A star player . . .*" Ron Fimrite, "A Flame that Burned Too Brightly," *Sports Illustrated,* March 18, 1991, p. 80.

81   "*Nurtured on Frank Merriwell stories . . .*" Benjamin G. Rader, *American Sports from the Age of Folk Games to the Age of Spectators.* Prentice-Hall, 1983, p. 225.

82   "*Where are your whiskers?*" Quoted in Susan E. Cayleff, *Babe: The Life and Legend of Babe Didrikson Zaharias.* University of Illinois Press, 1995, p. 108.

82   "*She didn't know the meaning . . .*" Quoted in Susan E. Cayleff, *Babe: The Life and Legend of Babe Didrikson Zaharias,* p. 239.

82   "*illegal subsidies for players . . .*" Quoted in Robert Lipsyte and Peter Levine, *Idols of the Game: A Sporting History of the American Century.* Turner Pub., 1995, p. 89.

82   *"many top stars ..."* Bob Cousy (as told to Al Hirshberg), *Basketball Is My Life.* Prentice-Hall, 1958, p. 97.

84   *"Will you not give back ..."* Quoted in Robert W. Creamer, *Babe: The Legend Comes to Life.* Simon & Schuster, 1992, pp. 274–275.

84   *"Boys worship the muscle hero."* Marshall Smelser, *The Life that Ruth Built, A Biography.* University of Nebraska Press, 1975, p. 190.

84   *"[Lombardi's] bronze bust ..."* David Maraniss, *When Pride Still Mattered: A Life of Vince Lombardi.* Simon & Schuster, 1999, p. 14.

85   *"There is always some kid ..."* Quoted in Dick Johnson and Glenn Stout, *DiMaggio: An Illustrated Life.* Walker & Company, 1995, p. 119.

85   *"I am not paid ..."* Quoted in *USA Today,* April 30, 1993, p. 16. Barkley repeats the sentiment of his ad in his autobiography: "I'll start at the beginning, and I'll only say this once: Professional athletes should not be role models." Charles Barkley and Roy S. Johnson, *Outrageous!: The Fine Life and Flagrant Good Times of Basketball's Irresistible Force.* Simon & Schuster, 1992, p. 305.

87   *"The Washington is nearly done ..."* Quoted in John A. Garraty and Marc C. Carnes, eds., *American National Biography,* Volume 9, p. 546.

90   *"You no sooner set ..."* Available on *www.online-literature.com/dickens/ american notes/ul/.* November 20, 2001.

90   *"The men with the muck-rakes ..."* Quoted in Brian MacArthur, ed., *The Penguin Book of Twentieth-Century Speeches.* The Viking Press, 1992, p. 8.

90   *"Let us not make a god ..."* Quoted in Barry Schwartz, *George Washington: The Making of an American Symbol.* The Free Press, 1987, p. 42.

90   *"Beware of great men."* In his analysis of the American Revolution, Gordon Wood notes how "equality tore through American society and culture with awesome power." Wood goes on to state that "the power of genius and great-souled men no longer seemed to matter." Gordon S. Wood, *The Radicalism of the American Revolution.* Alfred A. Knopf, 1992, p. 232, 359.

91   *"the worst form ..."* Angela Partington, ed., *The Oxford Dictionary of Quotations.* Revised Fourth Edition. Oxford University Press, 1996, p. 202.

92   *"Strength, Hardiness, Activity ..."* Letter to Mercy Warren. Available at *http://press.pubs.UChicago.edu/founders/documents/.* November 14, 2001.

92   *"back toward himself alone ..."* Alexis de Tocqueville, *Democracy in America*, p. 484. De Toqueville worried about a democratic America eliminating a veneration for greatness and genius.

92   *He did not enjoy reading* . . . Quoted in Barry Schwartz, *George Washington: The Making of an American Symbol*, p. 89.

93   *"The reporter used to gain status ..."* Quoted in John F. Thornton and Katharine Washburn, eds., *Dumbing Down: Essays on the Strip Mining of American Culture*. W. W. Norton, 1996, p. 29.

94   *we have gone too far* . . . Author interview. May 3, 1996.

94   *"the way we used to gossip ..."* Ellen Goodman, "Politics: Up Close and Too Personal," 8th Annual John S. Knight Lecture, Stanford University, February 26, 1996.

94   *rogues "more loathsome ..."* James Fallows, *Breaking the News: How the Media Undermine American Democracy*. Pantheon Books, 1996, p, 44.

94   *"If one were searching ..."* Quoted in Miriam Allott and Robert H. Super, eds., *Matthew Arnold*. Oxford University Press, 1986, p. 498.

94   *"No man ever quite believes ..."* H. L. Mencken, *The Vintage Mencken*. Vintage Books, 1990, p. 78.

94   *"Talk of virtue ..."* Walter Winchell, *Winchell Exclusive*. Prentice-Hall, 1975, p. 18. Winchell's present-day counterpart is Matt Drudge, who described his job this way: "I go where the stink is." In a *Wall Street Journal* interview, Drudge noted: "We have entered an era vibrating with the din of small voices. I envision a future where there will be 300 million reporters where anyone from anywhere can report for any reason." *The Wall Street Journal*, July 15, 1999.

95   *... make us cynical.* Paul Starobin argues that there has been a "migration from honest skepticism to rampant cynicism." Paul Starobin, "A Generation of Vipers: Journalists and the New Cynicism," *Columbia Journalism Review*, March–April 1995.

96   *... the death of silent screen star* ... The account of Valentino's funeral is based on the clippings file in the Harvard Theater Collection, Houghton Library.

96   *we had "come to a pretty pass ..."* Thomas L. Masson, "Mortals and Immortals," *Boston Transcript*, October 23, 1926. Masson went on to say, "President Eliot's great work in life was to teach people, not alone to feel,

but to control their feelings. Valentino's work was to make them feel and show it. That is all the difference in the world."

96 *"The idealist gazes . . ."* "Fame and the Movie," *Chicago Tribune,* August 26, 1926. The *Chicago Tribune* then analyzed Valentino's popularity: "The answer is that most of us go to the movies. It is there we escape from ourselves and our troubles and that escape is as essential to living as what wise men call knowledge."

97 *In the 1920s . . .* My view of the 1920s has been influenced by Ann Douglas's excellent book that describes how the realism and hedonism of New York City competed with the optimism and idealism of New England. Ann Douglas, *Terrible Honesty: Mongrel Manhattan in the 1920's.* Emblematic of the 1920s were its most popular songs: "My God, How the Money Rolls In" and "Makin' Whoopee."

98 *Today celebrities are omnipresent . . .* In an article in *Psychology Today,* Jill Neimark notes: "There has been a tremendous increase not only in coverage of celebrities but in the number of celebrities themselves. Thirty years ago the only real celebrities were in the movies. Now they're everywhere." Jill Neimark, "The Culture of Celebrity," *Psychology Today,* May 1995.

99 *"Americans spend 58 percent . . ."* Michael J. Wolf, *The Entertainment Economy: How Mega-Media Forces Are Transforming Our Lives.* Times Books, 1999, p. 203. Neal Gabler notes that "entertainment is the most pervasive, powerful and ineluctable force of our time." See Neal Gabler, *Life, the Movie: How Entertainment Conquered Reality.* Alfred A. Knopf, 1998, p. 9.

99 *"I really believe . . ."* Quoted in *The New Yorker,* November 29, 1999.

100 *"The hero is distinguished . . ."* Daniel J. Boorstin, *The Image: A Guide to Pseudo-Events in America.* Harper & Row, 1964, p. 61.

103 *"If to be venerated . . ."* Quoted in H. W. Brands, *The First American: The Life and Times of Benjamin Franklin.* Doubleday, 2000, p. 709.

103 *"Dr. Franklin lately arrived . . ."* Quoted in Charles Henry Hart and Edward Biddle, *Memoirs of the Life and Works of Jean-Antoine Houdon, the Sculptor of Voltaire and of Washington.* Charles Henry Hart and Edward Biddle, 1911, p. 75.

104 *In a 1780 letter . . .* Letter to Joseph Priestly. Available on *www.parsec. santa.com/words/Ruthmontg.htm.* November 15, 2001.

105 *Cohen said . . .* Author interview. August 1997.

107   *"Formerly we used to . . ."* Quoted in Robert Andrews, ed., *The Columbia Dictionary of Quotations.* Columbia University Press, 1993, p. 92.

107   *"Did anybody ever see . . ."* Quoted in Michael Kammen, *The Mystic Chords of Memory: The Transformation of Tradition in American Culture,* p. 649.

108   *"If a man's public record . . ."* Quoted in Ellen Goodman, "Politics: Up Close and Too Personal," 8th Annual John S. Knight Lecture. February 29, 1996.

108   *"What business has the public . . ."* Quoted in Gertrude Himmelfarb, *On Looking into the Abyss: Untimely Thoughts on Culture and Society,* p. 31.

108   *Or we can claim . . .* Blanche Wiesen Cook is typical. In her biography of Eleanor Roosevelt she criticizes "the failure to consider the nature of passion, lust, and love in a woman's life." Blanche Wiesen Cook, *Eleanor Roosevelt: 1884–1933.* Volume I. Penguin Books, 1993, p. 12.

108   *"is the brilliant triumph . . ."* Quoted in H. L. Mencken, ed., *A New Dictionary of Quotations on Historical Principles from Ancient and Modern Sources.* Alfred A. Knopf, 1989, p. 533.

109   *"hold out images of beauty . . ."* Maynard Solomon, *Beethoven.* Schirmer Books, 1977, p. 310.

110   *"Shame, Despair, Solitude! . . ."* Nathaniel Hawthorne, *The Scarlet Letter.* New American Library, 1959, p. 190.

111   *"I cannot read a book . . ."* Available on *www.cuc.claremont.edu/idbs/struth.htm.* November 13, 2001.

111   *"Frederick, is God dead?"* Quoted in John A. Garraty and Marc C. Carnes, eds., *American National Biography,* Volume 21. Oxford University Press, 1999, p. 881.

112   *. . . no excuses for those . . .* Wilbur R. Jacobs discusses Parkman's heroism and prejudices as well as the "strong backlash by modern critics who seek his decanonization." See Wilbur R. Jacobs, *Francis Parkman, Historian as Hero: The Formative Years.* University of Texas Press, 1991, p. 165.

112   *"Biographers, of all people . . ."* Lyndall Gordon, *T. S. Eliot: An Imperfect Life.* W. W. Norton, 1999, p. 2.

113   *coined the word* pathography . . . Pathography is now in *The American Heritage Dictionary:* "A style of biography that overemphasizes the negative aspects of a person's life and work, such as failure, unhappiness, illness and tragedy."

Notes

113   "*The design of biography* ..." Quoted in Theodore P. Greene, *America's Heroes: The Changing Models of Success in American Magazines.* Oxford University Press, 1970, p. 38.

113   "*Such an act of heroism* ..." Mason Weems, *A History of the Life and Death Virtues and Exploits of General George Washington.* Grosset & Dunlap, 1927, p. 25.

114   "*If I was ever* ..." Stephen E. Ambrose, *Undaunted Courage: Meriwether Lewis, Thomas Jefferson and the Opening of the American West.* Simon & Schuster, 1996, p. 471.

114   *In a telephone interview* ... Author interview, October 1996. In the interview, Ambrose recalled that a young reader of *Undaunted Courage* mentioned to him that "it is far easier to watch *Beavis and Butthead* and to listen to Howard Stern than to believe in something noble."

114   *The need for heroes* ... Author interview, October 1996.

114   "*a figure of world stature* ..." David McCullough, *Truman.* Simon & Schuster, 1992, p. 991.

114   "*at his best*..." William R. Manchester, *American Caesar: Douglas MacArthur.* Little, Brown, 1978, p. 11.

114   "*moral biography.*" Richard Brookhiser, *Founding Father: Rediscovering George Washington.* The Free Press, 1996, p. 11.

115   *mocking Florence Nightingale* ... Strachey seemed iconoclastic at the time and he could be acid, but in this sentence about Nightingale he demonstrates a rare balance: "Certainly, she was heroic. Yet her heroism was not of that simple sort so dear to the readers of novels and the compilers of hagiologies–the romantic sentimental heroism with which mankind loves to invest its chosen darlings: it was made of sterner stuff!" Lytton Strachey, *Eminent Victorians.* Random House, 1918, p. 155. Nevertheless, a number of writers see Strachey's influence as critical. William Zinsser argues that "the Strachean notion that nothing is sacred has been a hallmark of the century ever since." In an insightful comment, he goes on to suggest, "Future historians may characterize the late 20th century by its sense of fragmentation, its lack of confidence in history's progress, its loss of consensus about what an 'exemplary life' might be." William Zinsser, ed., *Extraordinary Lives: The Art and Craft of American Biography.* American Heritage, 1986, pp. 19, 184.

115   *our founding father* ... John Garraty has a nice description of debunking biographies of the 1920s: "They tried to make the intelligent seem stupid,

the dignified foolish, the earnest hypocritical and the humble vain. They dwell upon petty idiosyncrasies, physical ailments, inconsistent or erratic behavior." John Arthur Garraty, *The Nature of Biography*. Alfred A. Knopf, 1957, p. 136.

115 *Might we not recognize* . . . Contemporary academics have also come up with the notion that individuals should not be "privileged." Commenting on this trend, biographer James Atlas wrote in *The New York Times:* "The Great Man used to be one of our cherished myths, but it's gone out of fashion now. The great ideas of our times are thought to be collective products." James Atlas, "Hero Worship: Longing for a New Lone Genius," *The New York Times,* April 28, 1996.

115 *"Do we really have to know* . . ." Barbara W. Tuchman, *Practicing History: Selected Essays.* Alfred A. Knopf, 1981, p. 90.

117 The portraits of the four presidents are based upon primary sources as well as the many biographies and studies listed in the bibliography.

117 *"It is to be lamented* . . ." Letter to Lafayette. Quoted in Stephen Lucas, *The Quotable George Washington.* Madison House, 1999, p. 88.

117 *"None of us* . . ." Quoted in Edwin Morris Betts and James Adam Bear Jr., eds., *The Family Letters of Thomas Jefferson.* University of Missouri Press, 1966, p. 61.

117 *"The author of the life* . . ." Quoted in Albert J. Beveridge, *Abraham Lincoln 1809–1858.* Volume I. Houghton Mifflin, 1928, p. 520. Beveridge is not read today, but his writing is excellent and his portrait of the young Lincoln riveting.

117 *"It is not having been* . . ." Quoted in Elting E. Morison, ed., *The Letters of Theodore Roosevelt.* Harvard University Press, 1951, p. 1024.

118 . . . *offending many* . . . Today Borglum is properly criticized for his membership in the Ku Klux Klan. Robert L. Gale notes: "Controversy swirled about the combative, irascible artist, who had briefly joined the Ku Klux Klan, [and] had also made foolish, inconsistent anti-Semitic remarks." John A. Garraty and Marc Carnes, eds., *American National Biography,* Volume 3. Oxford University Press, 1999, p. 214.

118 *"we believe a nation's memorial* . . ." Available on *www.americanpark network.com/parkinfo/ru.* November 11, 2001.

120 *"I never was in such an unhappy, divided state."* George Washington, *Writings.* The Library of America, 1997, p. 249.

121 *"Integrity and firmness . . ."* Quoted in Samuel Eliot Morison, *The Young Man Washington.* Harvard University Press, 1932, p. 317.

122 *one can improve both mind* . . . Jefferson noted: "Without emulation, we sink into meanness or mediocrity, for nothing great or excellent can be done without it." Quoted in Tyron Edwards, ed., *The New Dictionary of Thoughts,* p. 172.

122 *"Under temptations and difficulties . . ."* Thomas Jefferson, *Writings.* The Library of America, 1984, p. 1194.

123 *"There are . . . even in the happiest life . . ."* Andrew Burstein, *The Inner Jefferson: Portrait of a Grieving Optimist.* University Press of Virginia, 1995, p. 257.

125 *When, in 1931* . . . This anecdote is reported in Merrill D. Peterson, *Lincoln in American Memory,* University Press of Virginia, 1994, p. 286. Peterson's book is excellent and es-sential for understanding the changing face of Lincoln in American history.

125 *. . . greatness of soul.* Dixon Wecter argues that "the major idols of America have been men of good will." This observation is confirmed by my research. Dixon Wecter, *The Hero in America: A Chronicle of Hero-Worship.* Scribner's Sons, 1941, p. v. Wecter's book is a superb survey.

127 *He idolized* . . . See Merrill D. Peterson, *Lincoln in American Memory,* p. 164.

127 *"If a man has a decided character . . ."* Quoted in H. Paul Jeffers, ed., *The Bully Pulpit: A Teddy Roosevelt Book of Quotations.* Taylor Publishing Company, 1998, p. 58.

128 *"I wish to preach . . ."* Quoted in Brian MacArthur, ed., *The Penguin Book of Twentieth-Century Speeches,* p. 5.

128 *"Men in hope . . ."* Quoted in Kathleen Dalton, "Why America Loved Teddy Roosevelt or, Charisma Is in the Eyes of the Beholders," *The Psychohistory Review 8,* no. 3, Winter 1979, p. 274.

128 *According to his most recent* . . . Larry McMurtry, *Crazy Horse.* A Lipper/Viking Book, 1999, p. 3.

129 *"One of the many great . . ."* Quoted in Robb DeWall, *Korczak: Storyteller in Stone.* Korczak's Heritage, 1984, p. 53.

130 *"This I hold . . ."* Quoted in Tyron Edwards, ed., *The New Dictionary of Thoughts,* p. 270.

130   *"Let us remember . . ."* Will and Ariel Durant, *The Age of Voltaire*. Simon and Schuster, 1965, p. 561.

131   *"a favoring Providence . . ."* George Bancroft, *History of the Colonization of the United States,* Volume I. Little, Brown, 1852, p. 4.

131   *"village heroes . . ."* George Bancroft, *The American Revolution,* Volume I. Little, Brown, 1875, pp. 294–295.

132   *"skeptical of governments."* Howard Zinn, *A People's History of the United States.* Harper & Row, 1980, p. 570.

132   *"conquest, slavery, death."* Howard Zinn, *A People's History of the United States,* p. 7.

132   *"No single president . . ."* Frances Fitzgerald, *America Revised: History Schoolbooks in the Twentieth Century.* Little, Brown, 1979, p. 9.

132   *Magnified are the sins and shortcomings . . .* Hardly a triumphalist, Arthur Schlesinger Jr. argues that dismissing the influence of exceptional individuals and seeing history as governed only by social forces leads to a kind of historical fatalism in which citizens feel that nobody controls events, nobody makes a difference. Says Schlesinger, "An age without great men is one which acquiesces in the drift of history." See Arthur M. Schlesinger Jr., "The Decline of Greatness," *Saturday Evening Post,* November 1, 1958.

137   *"I go there . . ."* John Keegan, *Fields of Battle: The Wars for North America.* Alfred A. Knopf, 1996, p. 17.

139   *"We have moved . . .* Nathan Glazer, "Monuments in an Age Without Heroes." *The Public Interest,* Spring 1996.

140   *"I regret that I have . . ."* Quoted in John A. Garraty, John A. and Marc Carnes, eds., *American National Biography,* Volume 9, p. 832.

141   *"She chose to forgo security . . ."* Available at *http://www.berry.edu/oakhill/story.html.* September 4, 2001.

142   *"Men's evil manners . . ."* William Shakespeare, *King Henry VIII* (4.2.45–46).

142   *"Who'ere excels in what we prize . . ."* Quoted in H. L. Mencken, ed., *A New Dictionary of Quotations on Historical Principles from Ancient and Modern Sources,* p. 532.

145   *"May God forgive them . . ."* Marilyn Manson with Neil Strauss, *the long hard road out of hell.* Regan Books, 1998, dedication page.

147 *"it is worth observing . . ."* Quoted in Jeannine Hensley, *The Works of Anne Bradstreet,* in the Foreword by Adrienne Rich. Belknap Press of Harvard University Press, 1967, p. xx.

148 *Sigmund Freud wrote . . .* Barbara Tuchman observes of this study: "Their emphasis is always on the failure, not the achievement." Barbara W. Tuchman, *Practicing History: Selected Essays,* p. 153.

150 *Marius also insisted . . .* Author interview. February 15, 1996.

153 *"remarkable sureness" and "superhuman courage"* Mary Gordon, *Joan of Arc.* Viking Penguin, 2000, p. 18.

153 *"We need her as the heroine for our . . ."* Mary Gordon, *Joan of Arc,* p. xxiii.

154 *. . . decides to keep quiet.* Historian Thomas A. Bailey observes: "In this uncertain world we crave certainties, and if an iconoclast were suddenly to shatter all myths, our social structure would suffer a traumatic shock." Thomas A. Bailey, "The Mythmakers of American History," *Journal of American History,* June 1968, p. 5.

155 *"The world is forwarded. . . ."* Quoted in William J. Bennett, ed., *The Moral Compass: Stories for a Life's Journey.* Simon & Schuster, 1995, p. 671.

156 *"I am a man of many faults."* Quoted in *Time,* November 8, 1999.

156 *"'Tis eminence makes envy rise."* Quoted in Burton Stevenson, *The Home Book of Quotations—Classical and Modern.* Dodd, Mead, and Company, 1967, p. 837.

157 *The punishing guilt . . .* Author interview. February 10, 1997.

159 *Jo March . . .* I recently came across a web site (open books, find heroes) where middle school students wrote essays about heroic characters. One girl wrote, "Jo is a hero because she showed so much fight and wasn't afraid of what other people thought of her. I wish I had more courage to just push away the negative remarks my peers say about me. I wish I could do what I wanted without worrying what other people think."

159 *"It is a far, far better thing . . ."* Charles Dickens, *A Tale of Two Cities.* The Easton Press, 1981, p. 371.

159 *"The mark of the immature man . . ."* J. D. Salinger, *The Catcher in the Rye.* Bantam Books, 1964, p. 188.

162 *Only with the belief . . .* In his book about creativity, Mihaly Csikszentmihalyi

states that "many social scientists in the last hundred years have made it their task to expose the hypocrisy, self-delusion, and self-interest underlying human behavior traits." Mihaly Csikszentmihalyi, *Creativity: Flow and the Psychology of Discovery and Invention.* HarperCollins, 1996, p. 16.

165 *"I go to the piano . . ."* Pablo Casals, *Joys and Sorrows: Reflections.* Simon and Schuster, 1970, p. 17.

165 *In 1935 after . . .* The account of Kurt Hahn is based on Martin Flavin's *Kurt Hahn's Schools and Legacy.* The Middle Atlantic Press, 1996, and on Joshua Miner's *Outward Bound, U.S.A.: Learning Through Experience in Adventure-Based Education.* Morrow, 1981.

167 *America learns from its mistakes . . .* Richard Bernstein observes: "In 1892, Americans rigorously stamped out of public view the moral costs involved in nation building. By 1992, we were able to incorporate them into the picture." Richard Bernstein, *Dictatorship of Virtue: Multiculturalism and the Battle for America's Future.* Alfred A. Knopf, 1994, p. 59.

167 *"I feel greatly the better . . ."* Quoted in Gordon S. Haight. *The George Eliot Letters,* Volume 8, 1840–1870. Yale University Press, 1978, p. 246.

169 *"to discover their inner strengths . . ."* Rachel Oestreicher Bernheim. "A Study of Heroes," The Raoul Wallenberg Committee of the United States, p. 2.

171 *"Heroes enchance life . . ."* Quoted in Isaiah Berlin, *Personal Impressions.* The Viking Press, 1981, p. 18.

172 *"What can a few Christians do . . ."* Eva Jane Price, *China Journal 1889–1900: An American Missionary Family During the Boxer Rebellion.* Charles Scribner's Sons, 1989, p. 53.

172 *"We often see . . ."* Eva Jane Price, *China Journal,* p. 178.

173 *"Thirty-three of our friends . . ."* Eva Jane Price, *China Journal,* p. 235.

174 *"Ever so many times . . ."* Käthe Kollwitz, *The Diaries and Letters of Käthe Kollwitz.* Northwestern University Press, 1988, p. 156.

175 *"the old civilized atmosphere."* Käthe Kollwitz, *The Diaries and Letters of Käthe Kollwitz,* p. 167.

175 *"frightful insanity . . ."* Käthe Kollwitz, *The Diaries and Letters of Käthe Kollwitz,* p. 74.

175 *"Everywhere the same boundless misery . . ."* Käthe Kollwitz, *The Diaries and Letters of Käthe Kollwitz,* p. 182.

175 "*I bless my life . . .*" Käthe Kollwitz, *The Diaries and Letters of Käthe Kollwitz*, p. 187.

176 "*kinder, more intelligent . . .*" Eugenia Semyonovna Ginzburg, *Journey into the Whirlwind*. Harcourt Brace Jovanovich, 1967, p. 206.

177 "*I wish you courage and pride.*" Eugenia Semyonovna Ginzburg, *Journey into the Whirlwind*, p. 99.

177 "*There are no more fervent friendships . . .*" Eugenia Semyonovna Ginzburg, *Journey into the Whirlwind*, p. 99.

177 "*My intense curiosity . . .*" Eugenia Semyonovna Ginzburg, *Journey into the Whirlwind*, p. 107.

177 "*the great riddles of the universe . . .*" Eugenia Semyonovna Ginzburg, *Within the Whirlwind*. Harcourt Brace Jovanovich, 1982, p. 53.

179 "*There is one part of you . . .*" George Orwell, *A Collection of Essays*. Harcourt Brace Jovanovich, 1953, p. 113.

179 "*His opponents admired him . . .*" Sherwin B. Nuland, *Doctors: The Biography of Medicine*. Vintage Books, 1989, p. 350.

180 "*We admire most the courage . . .*" Ernest Becker, *The Denial of Death*. The Free Press, 1973, p. 11.

180 "*Few men are willing . . .*" Quoted in Maxwell Taylor Kennedy, *Make Gentle the Life of the World: The Vision of Robert F. Kennedy*. Harcourt Brace, 1998, p. 134.

181 "*The true test . . .*" Quoted in Tyron Edwards, ed., *The New Dictionary of Thoughts*, p. 249.

181 "*The one cruel fact about heroes . . .*" La Rochefoucauld, *Maxims*. Penguin Books, 1959, Maxim # 24.

181 "*. . . a succession of disappointments.*" John Quincy Adams, Allan Nevins, ed., *The Diary of John Quincy Adams, 1794–1845*. Longmans, Green and Co., 1928, p. 441.

181 "*I am nothing as far as intellect . . .*" Quoted in Henry Wilkinson Bragdon, *Woodrow Wilson: The Academic Years*. Belknap Press of Harvard University Press, 1967, p. 23.

181 "*It is not all pleasure . . .*" Quoted in Antonia Fraser, ed., *Heroes and Heroines*. Weidenfeld & Nicolson, 1980, p. 231.

182   *"He who has never failed . . ."* Quoted in William S. McFeely, *Grant: A Biography.* W. W. Norton, 1981, p. 495.

182   *"All supreme spirits . . ."* Harry Emerson Fosdick, *Riverside Sermons.* Harper & Brothers, 1958, p. 48. Fosdick stresses how many great books have been written in prison.

182   *After Auschwitz . . .* In this book, Frankl notes: "I am grateful that fate has hit me so hard. In my former life I was spoiled and did not take spiritual accomplishment seriously." Viktor Frankl, *Man's Search for Meaning.* Beacon Press, 1992, p. 90.

182   *"The light has gone out of my life."* Quoted in Edmund Morris, *The Rise of Theodore Roosevelt.* Coward, McCann & Geoghegan, 1979, p. 241.

183   *"He finds my soul . . ."* Quoted in Elisabeth Griffith, *In Her Own Right: The Life of Elizabeth Cady Stanton,* p. 45.

185   *"But, Richard, in office . . ."* Robert Bolt, *A Man for All Seasons.* Vintage Books, 1990, pp. 8–9.

187   *"Be not solitary . . ."* Quoted in James Boswell, *The Life of Samuel Johnson.* Doubleday and Company, 1946, p. 886. The line is in a letter Johnson wrote to Boswell in October 1779. Johnson is paraphrasing Robert Burton, author of *Anatomy of Melancholy,* and suggesting a way to combat Boswell's periodic depressions.

187   *He replied that he agreed . . .* Author interview, January 20, 1996.

188   *"much easier to find reasons for rejecting . . ."* Quoted in W. Jackson Bate, *Samuel Johnson,* p. 258.

188   *"Longinus speaks of . . ."* W. Jackson Bate, *Samuel Johnson,* p. 292

188   *"American humanist . . ."* James Engell et al., "Memorial Minute," *Harvard University Gazette,* June 1, 2000, pp. 9–10.

188   *"He gave his students . . ."* James Engell et al., "Memorial Minute," *Harvard University Gazette,* June 1, 2000, p. 10.

Bibliography

Abrams, Ann Uhry. *The Valiant Hero: Benjamin West and Grand-Style History Painting*. Smithsonian Institution Press, 1985.

Ackroyd, Peter. *T. S. Eliot: A Life*. Simon & Schuster, 1984.

Adams, John Quincy. *The Diary of John Quincy Adams, 1794–1845*. Nevins, Allan, ed. Longmans, Green and Co., 1928.

Alan-Williams, Gregory. *A Gathering of Heroes: Reflections on Rage and Responsibility: A Memoir of the Los Angeles Riots*. Academy Chicago Publishers, 1994.

Alden, John R. *George Washington: A Biography*. Louisiana State University Press, 1984.

Alexander, Caroline. *The Endurance: Shackleton's Legendary Antarctic Expedition*. Alfred A. Knopf, 1998.

Alger, Horatio, Jr. *Strive and Succeed*. Horatio Alger Association, 1994.

Allen, Frederick Lewis. *Only Yesterday: An Informal History of the Nineteen-Twenties*. Harper & Brothers, 1931.

———. *Since Yesterday: The Nineteen-Thirties in America, September 3, 1929– September 3, 1939*. Harper & Brothers, 1940.

Allott, Miriam, and Robert H. Super, eds. *Matthew Arnold*. Oxford University Press, 1986.

Ambrose, Stephen E. *Crazy Horse and Custer: The Parallel Lives of Two American Warriors*. Doubleday, 1975.

———. *Eisenhower: Soldier and President*. Simon & Schuster, 1990.

———. *Undaunted Courage: Meriwether Lewis, Thomas Jefferson and the Opening of the American West.* Simon & Schuster, 1996.

Anderson, Jervis A. *Philip Randolph: A Biographical Portrait.* Harcourt Brace Jovanovich, 1973.

Andrews, Robert, ed. *The Columbia Dictionary of Quotations.* Columbia University Press, 1993.

Aristotle. *The Ethics of Aristotle.* Penguin Books, 1953.

Armstrong, Karen. *A History of God: The 4,000-Year Quest of Judaism, Christianity and Islam.* Ballantine Books, 1993.

Armstrong, Lance, with Sally Jenkins. *It's Not About the Bike: My Journey Back to Life.* Berkley Books, 2001.

Arnason, H. H. *The Sculptures of Houdon.* Phaedon Press, 1975.

Ashburn, Frank D. *Peabody of Groton: A Portrait.* Coward McCann, 1944.

Ashe, Arthur R., Jr., *A Hard Road to Glory: A History of the African-American Athlete, 1919–1945.* Warner Books, 1988.

Ashe, Arthur R., Jr., and Arnold Rampersad. *Days of Grace: A Memoir.* Alfred A. Knopf, 1993.

Atlas, James. *The Battle of the Books: The Curriculum Debate in America.* W. W. Norton, 1992.

Aurelius, Marcus. *Meditations.* Henry Regnery, 1956.

Ayto, John. *Bloomsbury Dictionary of Word Origins.* Bloomsbury Publishing, 1991.

Bacon, Margaret Hope. *Valiant Friend: The Life of Lucretia Mott.* Walker, 1980.

Bailyn, Bernard, et al. *Glimpses of the Harvard Past.* Harvard University Press, 1986.

Baker, Carlos. *Ernest Hemingway: A Life Story.* Charles Scribner's Sons, 1969.

Baldwin, Neil. *Edison: Inventing the Century.* Hyperion, 1995.

Bancroft, George. *The American Revolution.* Volume I. Little, Brown, 1875.

———. *History of the Colonization of the United States.* Volume I. Little, Brown, 1852.

Bibliography

Barkley, Charles, and Roy S. Johnson. *Outrageous!: The Fine Life and Flagrant Good Times of Basketball's Irresistible Force*. Simon & Schuster, 1992.

Barnett, Louise. *Touched by Fire: The Life, Death, and Mythic Afterlife of George Armstrong Custer*. Henry Holt, 1996.

Bartlett, John, and Justin Kaplan, eds. *Familiar Quotations*. Little, Brown, 1992.

Barzun, Jacques. *From Dawn to Decadence: 500 Years of Western Cultural Life, 1500 to the Present*. HarperCollins, 2000.

Bate, W. Jackson. *Samuel Johnson*. Harcourt Brace Jovanovich, 1977.

Becker, Ernest. *The Denial of Death*. The Free Press, 1973.

Bell, Vereen M. *Robert Lowell, Nihilist as Hero*. Harvard University Press, 1983.

Benedict, Jeff. *Public Heroes, Private Felons: Athletes and Crimes Against Women*. Northeastern University Press, 1997.

Bennett, Lerone, Jr. *Forced into Glory: Abraham Lincoln's White Dream*. Johnson Publishing, 2000.

Bennett, William J., ed. *The Book of Virtues: A Treasury of Great Moral Stories*. Simon & Schuster, 1993.

———. *The Moral Compass: Stories for a Life's Journey*. Simon & Schuster, 1995.

Bentley, Eric. *A Century of Hero Worship: A Study of the Idea of Heroism in Carlyle and Nietzsche*. Beacon Press, 1957.

Bergin, Thomas G. *The Game: The Harvard-Yale Football Rivalry, 1875–1983*. Yale University Press, 1984.

Berkowitz, Bill. *Local Heroes*. Lexington Books, 1987.

Berlin, Isaiah. *The Hedgehog and the Fox: An Essay on Tolstoy's View of History*. Simon & Schuster, 1953.

———. *Personal Impressions*. The Viking Press, 1981.

Bernall, Misty. *She Said Yes: The Unlikely Martyrdom of Cassie Bernall*. Plough Publishing Company, 1999.

Bernstein, Richard. *Dictatorship of Virtue: Multiculturalism and the Battle for America's Future*. Alfred A. Knopf, 1994.

Berry, Edmund Grindlay. *Emerson's Plutarch*. Harvard University Press, 1961.

Berson, Robin Kadison. *Marching to a Different Drummer: Unrecognized Heroes of American History.* Greenwood Press, 1994.

———. *Young Heroes in World History.* Greenwood Press, 1999.

Bettmann, Otto. *The Good Old Days—They Were Terrible!* Random House, 1974.

Betts, Edwin Morris, and James Adam Bear Jr., eds. *The Family Letters of Thomas Jefferson.* University of Missouri Press, 1966.

Beveridge, Albert J. *Abraham Lincoln 1809–1858.* Houghton Mifflin, 1928.

Biel, Steven. *Down with the Old Canoe: A Cultural History of the Titanic Disaster.* W. W. Norton, 1996.

Bierman, John. *Righteous Gentile: The Story of Raoul Wallenberg, Missing Hero of the Holocaust.* Penguin Books, 1995.

Blight, David W., ed. *The Columbian Orator.* New York University Press, 1998.

———. *Frederick Douglass' Civil War: Keeping Faith in Jubilee.* Louisiana State University Press, 1989.

———. *Race and Reunion: The Civil War in American Memory.* Belknap Press of Harvard University Press, 2001.

Bodo, Peter. *The Courts of Babylon: Tales of Greed and Glory in a Harsh New World of Professional Tennis.* Scribner, 1995.

Bok, Sissela. *Alva Myrdal: A Daughter's Memoir.* Addison-Wesley, 1991.

Bolotin, Norman, and Christine Laing. *The World's Columbian Exposition: The Chicago World's Fair of 1893.* Dover Publications, 1980.

Bolt, Robert. *A Man for All Seasons.* Vintage Books, 1990.

Boorstin, Daniel J. *The Americans: The Democratic Experience.* Vintage Books, 1974.

———. *The Americans: The National Experience.* Vintage Books, 1965.

———. *The Creators: A History of Heroes of the Imagination.* Random House, 1992.

———. *The Image: A Guide to Pseudo-Events in America.* Harper & Row, 1964.

Boswell, James. *The Life of Samuel Johnson.* Doubleday, 1946.

Bosworth, Brian, with Rick Reilly. *The Boz: Confessions of a Modern Anti-Hero.* Doubleday, 1988.

Bibliography

Bouton, Bobbie, and Nancy Marshall. *Home Games: Two Baseball Wives Speak Out.* St. Martin's/Marek, 1983.

Bouton, Jim. *Ball Four,* ed. Leonard Shecter. Twentieth-Anniversary Edition. Macmillan, 1990.

Bowen, Catherine Drinker. *Biography: The Craft and the Calling.* Little, Brown, 1969.

Bowers, John. *Stonewall Jackson: Portrait of a Soldier.* Avon Books, 1989.

Brabazon, James. *Albert Schweitzer: A Biography.* G. P. Putnam, 1975.

Bradley, A. C. *Shakespearean Tragedy: Lectures on Hamlet, Othello, King Lear, Macbeth.* Macmillan, 1956.

Bragdon, Henry Wilkinson. *Woodrow Wilson: The Academic Years.* Belknap Press of Harvard University Press, 1967.

Brands, H. W. *The First American: The Life and Times of Benjamin Franklin.* Doubleday, 2000.

Braudy, Leo. *The Frenzy of Renown: Fame and its History.* Oxford University Press, 1986.

Brinkley, Douglas. *The Magic Bus: An American Odyssey.* Harcourt Brace, 1993.

Brock, Pope. *The Frank Merriwell Mythology.* Thesis, A. B., Harvard University Archives, 1972.

Brodie, Fawn M. *The Devil Drives: A Life of Sir Richard Burton.* W. W. Norton, 1967.

———. *Thomas Jefferson: An Intimate History.* Bantam Books, 1975.

Brookhiser, Richard. *Alexander Hamilton: American.* The Free Press, 1999.

———. *Founding Father: Rediscovering George Washington.* The Free Press, 1996.

Brooks, John. *The Great Leap: The Past 25 Years in America.* Harper & Row, 1966.

Brown, Dee. *The Year of the Century: 1876.* Charles Scribner's Sons, 1966.

Brown, Thomas J. *Dorothea Dix: New England Reformer.* Harvard University Press, 1998.

Browne, Pat, ed. *Heroines of Popular Culture.* Bowling Green State University Popular Press, 1987.

Bibliography

Browne, Ray B., and Marshall W. Fishwick, eds. *The Hero in Transition*. Bowling Green State University Popular Press, 1983.

Brudnoy, David. *Life Is Not a Rehearsal: A Memoir*. Doubleday, 1997.

Bullock, Alan. *Hitler: A Study in Tyranny*. Harper & Row, 1962.

Bunyan, John. *The Pilgrim's Progress*. Penguin Books, 1965.

Burke, Chris, and Jo Beth McDaniel. *A Special Kind of Hero: Chris Burke's Own Story*. Doubleday, 1991.

Burkett, B. G., and Glenna Whitley. *Stolen Valor: How the Vietnam Generation Was Robbed of Its Heroes and Its History*. Verity Press, 1998.

Burnham, Scott. *Beethoven Hero*. Princeton University Press, 1995.

Burnham, Smith. *Hero Tales from History*. The John C. Winston Company, 1922.

Burns, James MacGregor, and Susan Dunn. *The Three Roosevelts: Patrician Leaders Who Transformed America*. Atlantic Monthly Press, 2001.

Burns, Norman T., and Christopher J. Reagan, eds. *Concepts of the Hero in the Middle Ages and Renaissance*. State University of New York Press, 1975.

Burrell, Brian. *The Words We Live By: The Creeds, Mottoes, and Pledges that Have Shaped America*. The Free Press, 1997.

Burstein, Andrew. *The Inner Jefferson: Portrait of a Grieving Optimist*. University Press of Virginia, 1995.

Butler, Bill. *The Myth of the Hero*. Rider, 1979.

Butterfield, L. H., et al., eds. *The Book of Abigail and John: Selected Letters of the Adams Family, 1762–1784*. Harvard University Press, 1975.

Calder, Jenni. *Heroes: From Byron to Guevara*. Hamilton, 1977.

Camp, Walter. *The Daily Dozen*. Reynolds Publishing Company, 1925.

Campbell, Joseph. *The Hero with a Thousand Faces*. MJF Books, 1949.

Carey, Art. *The United States of Incompetence*. Houghton Mifflin, 1991.

Carlyle, Thomas. *On Heroes, Hero-Worship, and the Heroic in History*. Houghton, Mifflin, 1907.

Carnegie, Andrew. *Autobiography of Andrew Carnegie*. Northeastern University Press, 1986.

―――. *The Gospel of Wealth and Other Timely Essays*. Belknap Press of Harvard University Press, 1962.

Carnes, Mark C., et al., eds. *Past Imperfect: History According to the Movies*. Henry Holt, 1995.

Carson, Clayborne, ed. *The Autobiography of Martin Luther King, Jr*. Warner Books, 1998.

Cart, Michael. *From Romance to Realism: 50 Years of Growth and Change in Young Adult Literature*. HarperCollins, 1996.

Carter, Stephen L. *The Culture of Disbelief: How American Law and Politics Trivialize Religious Devotion*. Basic Books, 1993.

Casals, Pablo. *Joys and Sorrows: Reflections*. Simon & Schuster, 1970.

Casey, Robert J., and Mary Borglum. *Give the Man Room: The Story of Gutzon Borglum*. Bobbs-Merrill, 1952.

Cayleff, Susan E. *Babe: The Life and Legend of Babe Didrikson Zaharias*. University of Illinois Press, 1995.

Chamberlain, Wilt. *A View from Above*. Villard Books, 1991.

Chambers, R. W. *Thomas More*. University of Michigan Press, 1958.

Cheney, Lynne V. *Telling the Truth: Why Our Culture and Our Country Have Stopped Making Sense—And What We Can Do About It*. Simon & Schuster, 1995.

Chernow, Ron. *Titan: The Life of John D. Rockefeller, Sr*. Random House, 1998.

Childress, Alice. *A Hero Ain't Nothin' but a Sandwich*. Coward, McCann & Geoghegan, 1973.

Chute, Marchette Gaylord. *Shakespeare of London*. E. P. Dutton, 1949.

Cohen, I. Bernard. *Science and the Founding Fathers: Science in the Political Thought of Jefferson, Franklin, Adams, and Madison*. W. W. Norton, 1995.

Coles, Robert. *Lives of Moral Leadership*. Random House, 2000.

―――. *A Robert Coles Omnibus*. University of Iowa Press, 1988.

Collier, Peter, and David Horowitz. *Deconstructing the Left: From Vietnam to the Persian Gulf*. Second Thoughts Books, 1991.

―――. *Destructive Generation: Second Thoughts About the Sixties*. Summit Books, 1989.

———. *The Roosevelts: An American Saga.* Simon & Schuster, 1994.

Commager, Henry Steele. *The Commonwealth of Learning.* Harper & Row, 1968.

———. *Theodore Parker.* Beacon Press, 1947.

Conn, Peter J. *Pearl S. Buck: A Cultural Biography.* Cambridge University Press, 1996.

Connelly, Thomas Lawrence. *The Marble Man: Robert E. Lee and His Image in American Society.* Alfred A. Knopf, 1977.

Conway, Jill Ker. *The Road From Coorain.* Alfred A. Knopf, 1989.

———. *Written by Herself: Autobiographies of American Women: An Anthology.* Vintage Books, 1992.

Cook, Blanche Wiesen. *Eleanor Roosevelt: 1884–1933.* Vol. I. Penguin Books, 1993.

Cooper, James F. *Knights of the Brush: The Hudson River School and the Moral Landscape.* Hudson Hills Press, 2000.

Cormier, Robert. *The Chocolate War.* Pantheon, 1974.

———. *Heroes.* Delacorte Press, 1998.

Cousineau, Phil, ed. *The Hero's Journey: The World of Joseph Campbell.* Harper & Row, 1990.

Cousy, Bob (as told to Al Hirshberg). *Basketball Is My Life.* Prentice-Hall, 1958.

Cowley, Malcolm. *Exile's Return: A Literary Odyssey of the 1920s.* Penguin Books, 1976.

Craddock, Patricia B. *Edward Gibbon, Luminous Historian 1772–1794.* Johns Hopkins University Press, 1989.

Cramer, Richard Ben. *Joe DiMaggio: The Hero's Life.* Simon & Schuster, 2000.

Craven, Wayne. *Sculpture in America.* Thomas Y. Crowell, 1968.

Creamer, Robert W. *Babe: The Legend Comes to Life.* Simon & Schuster, 1992.

Cremin, Lawrence A. *American Education: The Colonial Experience, 1607–1783.* Harper & Row, 1970.

———. *American Education: The National Experience, 1783–1876.* Harper & Row, 1980.

Cremin, Lawrence A., ed. *The Republic and the School: Horace Mann on the Education of Free Men.* Teachers College Press, 1957.

Cromwell, Otelia. *Lucretia Mott.* Harvard University Press, 1958.

Cronkite, Walter. *A Reporter's Life.* Alfred A. Knopf, 1996.

Csikszentmihalyi, Mihaly. *Creativity: Flow and the Psychology of Discovery and Invention.* HarperCollins, 1996.

Culver, Raymond Benjamin. *Horace Mann and Religion in the Massachusetts Public Schools.* Arno Press and *The New York Times,* 1969.

Cunliffe, Marcus. *George Washington: Man and Monument.* New American Library, 1982.

Curie, Eve. *Madame Curie: A Biography.* Doubleday, Doran & Company, 1937.

Dabbs, James McBride, with Mary Godwin James. *Heroes, Rogues and Lovers: Testosterone and Behavior.* McGraw-Hill, 2000.

Damon, William. *Greater Expectations: Overcoming the Culture of Indulgence in America's Homes and Schools.* The Free Press, 1995.

Davies, John Dunn. *The Legend of Hobey Baker.* Little, Brown, 1966.

Davis, Allen F. *American Heroine: The Life and Legend of Jane Addams.* Oxford University Press, 1973.

Davis, Kenneth Sydney. *The Hero: Charles A. Lindbergh and the American Dream.* Doubleday, 1959.

DeLattre, Edwin J. *Character and Cops: Ethics in Policing.* AEI Press, 1994.

Delbo, Charlotte. *Auschwitz and After.* Yale University Press, 1995.

Denenberg, Dennis Roscoe. *Hooray For Heroes!* The Scarecrow Press, 1994.

Derr, Mark. *The Frontiersman: The Real Life and the Many Legends of Davy Crockett.* William Morrow, 1993.

Desmond, Adrian. *Huxley: From Devil's Disciple to Evolution's High Priest.* Addison-Wesley, 1994.

D'Este, Carlo. *Patton: A Genius for War.* HarperCollins, 1995.

de Tocqueville, Alexis. *Democracy in America.* Translated by Harvey C. Mansfield and Delba Winthrop. University of Chicago Press, 2000.

DeWall, Robb. *Korczak: Storyteller in Stone.* Korczak's Heritage, 1984.

Dickens, Charles. *A Tale of Two Cities*. The Easton Press, 1981.

Dickson, Paul, and Robert Skole. *The Volvo Guide to Halls of Fame*. Living Planet Press, 1995.

Donald, David Herbert. *Lincoln*. Simon & Schuster, 1995.

———. *Lincoln's Herndon*. Alfred A. Knopf, 1948.

Dorson, Richard M. *America in Legend: Folklore from the Colonial Period to the Present*. Pantheon, 1973.

Dostoevsky, Fyodor. *Three Short Novels of Dostoevsky*. Anchor Books, 1960.

Douglas, Ann. *Terrible Honesty: Mongrel Manhattan in the 1920's*. Farrar, Straus and Giroux, 1995.

Dower, John W. *Embracing Defeat: Japan in the Wake of World War II*. W. W. Norton, 1999.

Drury, Roger Wolcott. *Drury and St. Paul's: The Scars of a Schoolmaster*. Little, Brown, 1964.

D'Souza, Dinesh. *Ronald Reagan: How an Ordinary Man Became an Extraordinary Leader*. The Free Press, 1997.

Durant, Will. *Caesar And Christ*. Simon & Schuster, 1944.

———. *The Life of Greece*. Simon & Schuster, 1939.

Durant, Will, and Ariel Durant. *The Age of Voltaire*. Simon & Schuster, 1965.

———. *A Dual Autobiography*. Simon & Schuster, 1977.

Eastman, Max. *Great Companions: Critical Memoirs of Some Famous Friends*. Farrar, Straus and Giroux, 1959.

Edelman, Marian Wright. *The Measure of Our Success: A Letter to My Children and Yours*. Beacon Press, 1992.

———. *Lanterns: A Memoir of Mentors*. Beacon Press, 1999.

Edelstein, Alan. *Everybody Is Sitting on the Curb: How and Why America's Heroes Disappeared*. Praeger, 1996.

Edmundson, Mark. *Nightmare on Main Street: Angels, Sadomasochism, and the Culture of the Gothic*. Harvard University Press, 1997.

Edwards, Tyron, ed. *The New Dictionary of Thoughts*. Standard Book Company, 1961.

Ellis, Joseph J. *American Sphinx: The Character of Thomas Jefferson.* Alfred A. Knopf, 1997.

———. *Passionate Sage: The Character and Legacy of John Adams.* W. W. Norton, 1993.

Emerson, Ralph Waldo. *Essays and Lectures.* The Library of America, 1983.

———. *Representative Men.* Marsilio Publishers, 1995.

———. *Selected Essays.* Penguin Books, 1982.

———. *The Selected Writings of Ralph Waldo Emerson.* Random House, 1940.

Engelmann, Larry. *The Goddess and the American Girl: The Story of Suzanne Lenglen and Helen Wills.* Oxford University Press, 1988.

Epstein, Joseph. *Narcissus Leaves the Pool: Familiar Essays.* Houghton Mifflin, 1999.

———. *With My Trousers Rolled: Familiar Essays.* W. W. Norton, 1995.

Evans, Bergen. *Dictionary of Quotations.* Delacorte Press, 1968.

Evensen, Bruce J. *When Dempsey Fought Tunney: Heroes, Hokum, and Storytelling in the Jazz Age.* University of Tennessee Press, 1996.

Everdell, William R. *The First Moderns: Profiles in the Origins of Twentieth-Century Thought.* Chicago University Press, 1997.

Falkner, David. *The Last Hero: The Life of Mickey Mantle.* Simon & Schuster, 1995.

Fallows, James. *Breaking the News: How the Media Undermine American Democracy.* Pantheon Books, 1996.

Faragher, John Mack. *Daniel Boone: The Life and Legend of an American Pioneer.* Henry Holt, 1992.

Faris, John Thompson. *The Book of Everyday Heroism.* J. P. Lippincott, 1924.

Finn, Chester E., Jr. *We Must Take Charge: Our Schools and Our Future.* The Free Press, 1991.

Fischer, Louis. *Gandhi: His Life and Message for the World.* New American Library, 1954.

Fishwick, Marshall William. *American Heroes: Myth and Reality.* Public Affairs Press, 1954.

——. *A Bibliography of the American Hero.* Bibliographical Society of the University of Virginia, 1950.

——. *The Hero, American Style.* D. McCay, 1969.

Fite, Gilbert Courtland. *Mount Rushmore.* University of Oklahoma Press, 1952.

Fitzgerald, Frances. *America Revised: History Schoolbooks in the Twentieth Century.* Little, Brown, 1979.

Flavin, Martin. *Kurt Hahn's Schools and Legacy.* The Middle Atlantic Press, 1996.

Fleming, Thomas, ed. *Ben Franklin: A Biography in His Own Words.* Newsweek, 1972.

Flexner, James Thomas. *Washington: The Indispensable Man.* Little, Brown, 1974.

Foner, Philip S., ed. *Mother Jones Speaks: Collected Writings and Speeches.* Monad Press, 1983.

Fosdick, Harry Emerson. *Riverside Sermons.* Harper & Brothers, 1958.

Frank, Anne. *The Diary of a Young Girl.* Anchor Books, 1995.

Frank, Leonard Roy, ed. *Random House Webster's Quotationary.* Random House, 1999.

Frankl, Viktor. *Man's Search for Meaning.* Beacon Press, 1992.

Franklin, Benjamin. *Autobiography and Selected Writings.* Holt, Rinehart & Winston, 1961.

——. *The Life and Letters of Benjamin Franklin.* E. M. Hale, 1962.

Fraser, Antonia, ed. *Heroes and Heroines.* Weidenfeld & Nicolson, 1980.

Fredrickson, George M. *The Inner Civil War: Northern Intellectuals and the Crisis of the Union.* Illini Books, 1993.

Freedman, James O. *Idealism and Liberal Education.* University of Michigan Press, 1996.

Froude, James Anthony. *The Hundred Greatest Men.* Sampson, Low, Marston, Searle, and Rivington, 1880.

Froude, James Anthony. *Thomas Carlyle: A History of his Life in London 1834–1881.* Harper & Brothers, 1885.

Fussell, Paul. *The Great War and Modern Memory.* Oxford University Press, 1977.

Gabler, Neal. *Life, the Movie: How Entertainment Conquered Reality.* Alfred A. Knopf, 1998.

———. *Winchell: Gossip, Power and the Culture of Celebrity.* Alfred A. Knopf, 1995.

Gabor, Andrea. *Einstein's Wife: Work and Marriage in the Lives of Five Great Twentieth-Century Women.* The Viking Press, 1995.

Gardner, Howard. *Creating Minds: An Anatomy of Creativity Seen Through the Lives of Freud, Einstein, Picasso, Stravinsky, Eliot, Graham, and Gandhi.* Basic Books, 1993.

———. *Extraordinary Minds: Portraits of Exceptional Individuals and an Examination of Our Extraordinariness.* Basic Books, 1997.

Gardner, Howard, with Emma Laskin. *Leading Minds: An Anatomy of Leadership.* Basic Books, 1995.

Gardner, Ralph D. *Horatio Alger: Or the American Hero Era.* Arco Publishing Company, 1978.

Garment, Suzanne. *Scandal: The Crisis of Mistrust in American Politics.* Times Books, 1991.

Garraty, John A., and Marc C. Carnes, eds. *American National Biography.* Volumes 1–24. Oxford University Press, 1999.

Garraty, John Arthur. *The Nature of Biography.* Alfred A. Knopf, 1957.

Garrow, David J. *Bearing the Cross: Martin Luther King, Jr. and the Southern Christian Leadership Conference.* William Morrow, 1986.

Gay, Kathlyn, and Martin K. Gay. *Heroes of Conscience: A Biographical Dictionary.* ABC–CLIO, 1996.

Gay, Peter. *Freud: A Life for Our Time.* Anchor Books, 1989.

Geison, Gerald L. *The Private Science of Louis Pasteur.* Princeton University Press, 1995.

Gerdts, William H. *American Neo-Classic Sculpture: The Marble Resurrection.* The Viking Press, 1973.

Gergen, David R. *Eyewitness to Power: The Essence of Leadership: Nixon to Clinton.* Simon & Schuster, 2000.

Gerzon, Mark. *A Choice of Heroes: The Changing Faces of American Manhood.* Houghton Mifflin, 1992.

Ginzburg, Eugenia Semyonovna. *Journey into the Whirlwind.* Harcourt Brace Jovanovich, 1967.

———. *Within the Whirlwind.* Harcourt Brace Jovanovich, 1982.

Glendon, Mary Ann. *A Nation Under Lawyers: How the Crisis in the Legal Profession is Transforming American Society.* Farrar, Straus and Giroux, 1994.

Gomes, Peter J. *The Good Book: Reading the Bible with Mind and Heart.* William Morrow, 1996.

———. *Yet More Sundays at Harvard: Sermons for an Academic Year.* President and Fellows of Harvard College, 1997.

Goode, William J. *The Celebration of Heroes: Prestige as a Social Control System.* University of California Press, 1978.

Goodwin, Doris Kearns. *No Ordinary Time: Franklin and Eleanor Roosevelt: The Home Front in World War II.* Simon & Schuster, 1994.

Gordon, Lyndall. *T. S. Eliot: An Imperfect Life.* W. W. Norton, 1999.

Gordon, Mary. *Joan of Arc.* Viking Penguin, 2000.

Gorn, Elliott J. *Mother Jones: The Most Dangerous Woman in America.* Hill and Wang, 2001.

Graham, Billy. *Just as I Am: The Autobiography of Billy Graham.* HarperCollins, 1997.

Graham, Katharine. *Personal History.* Alfred A. Knopf, 1997.

Granatstein, J. L. *Who Killed Canadian History?* HarperCollins, 1998.

Green, Tim. *The Dark Side of the Game: The Unauthorized NFL Playbook.* Warner Books, 1996.

Greene, Theodore P. *America's Heroes: The Changing Models of Success in American Magazines.* Oxford University Press, 1970.

Grenier, Richard. *Capturing the Culture: Film, Art, and Politics.* Ethics and Public Policy Center, 1990.

Griffith, Elisabeth. *In Her Own Right: The Life of Elizabeth Cady Stanton.* Oxford University Press, 1985.

Grunwald, Henry. *One Man's America: A Journalist's Search for the Heart of His Country.* Doubleday, 1997.

Gurko, Leo. *Heroes, Highbrows, and the Popular Mind.* Bobbs-Merrill, 1953.

Gurstein, Rochelle. *The Repeal of Reticence: A History of America's Cultural and Legal Struggles over Free Speech, Obscenity, Sexual Liberation and Modern Art.* Hill and Wang, 1996.

Guttmann, Allen. *From Ritual to Record: The Nature of Modern Sports.* Columbia University Press, 1978.

Hadas, Moses, and Morton Smith. *Heroes and Gods: Spiritual Biographies in Antiquity.* Harper & Row, 1965.

Haight, Gordon S. *George Eliot, A Biography.* Oxford University Press, 1968.

———. *The George Eliot Letters,* Volume 8, 1840–1870. Yale University Press, 1978.

Halberstam, David. *The Best and the Brightest.* Random House, 1969.

———. *The Breaks of the Game.* Alfred A. Knopf, 1981.

———. *The Children.* Random House, 1998.

———. *The Fifties.* Villard Books, 1993.

Hallie, Philip P. *Lest Innocent Blood Be Shed: The Story of the Village of Le Chambon and How Goodness Happened There.* HarperPerennial, 1994.

Hamilton, Edith. *The Greek Way.* W. W. Norton, 1942.

———. *Mythology.* Little, Brown, 1969.

Handlin, Lilian. *George Bancroft, The Intellectual as Democrat.* Harper & Row, 1984.

Harris, Janet C. *Athletes and the American Hero Dilemma.* Human Kinetics, 1994.

Harsch, Joseph C. *At the Hinge of History: A Reporter's Story.* University of Georgia Press, 1993.

Hart, Charles Henry, and Edward Biddle. *Memoirs of the Life and Works of Jean-Antoine Houdon, the Sculptor of Voltaire and of Washington.* Charles Henry Hart and Edward Biddle, 1911.

Hart, Michael H. *The 100: A Ranking of the Most Influential Persons in History.* Hart Publishing, 1978.

Hawthorne, Nathaniel. *The Scarlet Letter.* New American Library, 1959.

Heckscher, August. *Woodrow Wilson.* Scribner, 1991.

Hedrick, Joan D. *Harriet Beecher Stowe: A Life.* Oxford University Press, 1994.

Hemingway, Ernest. *A Farewell to Arms.* Simon & Schuster, 1995.

———. *For Whom the Bell Tolls.* Simon & Schuster, 1995.

Henry, William A., III. *In Defense of Elitism.* Doubleday, 1994.

Hensley, Jeannine. *The Works of Anne Bradstreet.* Belknap Press of Harvard University Press, 1967.

Herrmann, Dorothy. *Helen Keller: A Life.* Alfred A. Knopf, 1998.

Hersh, Seymour M. *The Dark Side of Camelot.* Little, Brown, 1997.

Hicks, David. *Norms and Nobility: A Treatise on Education.* Praeger, 1981.

Higginson, Thomas Wentworth, ed. *Harvard Memorial Biographies.* Seaver and Francis, 1867.

Highet, Gilbert. *The Immortal Profession: The Joys of Teaching and Learning.* Weybright and Talley, 1976.

Himmelfarb, Gertrude. *The De-Moralization of Society: From Victorian Virtues to Modern Values.* Alfred A. Knopf, 1995.

———. *On Looking into the Abyss: Untimely Thoughts on Culture and Society.* Alfred A. Knopf, 1994.

———. *One Nation, Two Cultures.* Alfred A. Knopf, 1999.

———. *Victorian Minds: A Study of Intellectuals in Crisis and Ideologies in Transition.* I. R. Dee, 1995.

Hinsdale, B. A. *Horace Mann and the Common School Revival in the United States.* Charles Scribner, 1913.

Hirsch, E. D., Jr. *The Schools We Need and Why We Don't Have Them.* Doubleday, 1996.

Hitchens, Christopher. *The Missionary Position: Mother Teresa in Theory and Practice.* Verso, 1995.

Hofstader, Richard. *The American Political Tradition and the Men Who Made It.* Vintage Books, 1989.

Holton, Gerald. *Einstein, History, and Other Passions.* AIP Press, 1995.

Homer. *The Iliad.* Translated by Robert Fagles. Penguin Classics, 1990.

Homer. *The Odyssey.* Translated by W. H. D. Rowse. Signet Classics, 1999.

Hook, Sidney. *The Hero in History: A Study in Limitation and Possibility.* Beacon Press, 1955.

Horne, A. D., ed. *The Wounded Generation: America after Vietnam.* Prentice-Hall, 1981.

Houghton, Walter E. *The Victorian Frame of Mind, 1830–1870.* Yale University Press, 1985.

Hughes, Robert. *Culture of Complaint: The Fraying of America.* Oxford University Press, 1993.

Ignatieff, Michael. *Isaiah Berlin: A Life.* Metropolitan Books, 1998.

Isaacs, Neil D. *Jock Culture USA.* W. W. Norton, 1978.

Jacobs, Wilbur R. *Francis Parkman, Historian as Hero: The Formative Years.* University of Texas Press, 1991.

James, Clive. *Fame in the 20th Century.* Random House, 1993.

James, Edward T., ed. *Notable American Women: 1607–1950.* Volumes 1–3. Belknap Press of Harvard University Press, 1971.

James, Henry. *Charles W. Eliot, President of Harvard University, 1869–1909.* Houghton Mifflin, 1930.

James, Marquis. *The Raven: A Biography of Sam Houston.* Blue Ribbon Books, Inc., 1929.

James, William. *Memories and Studies.* Longmans Green, 1911.

———. *Talks to Teachers on Psychology, and to Students on Some of Life's Ideals.* W. W. Norton, 1958.

———. *The Varieties of Religious Experience: A Study in Human Nature.* Doubleday, 1902.

———. *Writings: 1902–1910.* The Library of America, 1987.

Jeffers, H. Paul, ed. *The Bully Pulpit: A Teddy Roosevelt Book of Quotations.* Taylor Publishing Company, 1998.

Jefferson, Thomas. *Writings.* The Library of America, 1984.

Johns, Elizabeth. *Thomas Eakins, The Heroism of Modern Life.* Princeton University Press, 1983.

Johnson, Allen, ed. *Dictionary of American Biography.* Volumes I–XX. Charles Scribner's Sons, 1928.

Johnson, Dick, and Glenn Stout. *DiMaggio: An Illustrated Life.* Walker & Company, 1995.

Bibliography

Johnson, Paul. *The Birth of the Modern: World Society, 1815–1830*. HarperCollins, 1991.

———. *A History of the American People*. HarperCollins, 1997.

———. *Intellectuals*. HarperPerennial, 1988.

Johnson, Robert Underwood. *Your Hall of Fame*. New York University, 1935.

Johnson, Samuel. *Rasselas, Poems and Selected Prose*. Rinehart & Company, 1956.

Jones, James H. *Alfred C. Kinsey: A Public/Private Life*. W. W. Norton, 1997.

Kammen, Michael. *The Mystic Chords of Memory: The Transformation of Tradition in American Culture*. Vintage Books, 1991.

Kaplan, Fred. *Thomas Carlyle: A Biography*. Cornell University Press, 1983.

Karl, Frederick R. *George Eliot, Voice of a Century: A Biography*. W. W. Norton, 1995.

Kasich, John. *Courage Is Contagious: Ordinary People Doing Extraordinary Things to Change the Face of America*. Doubleday, 1998.

Kaufmann, Walter. *The Portable Nietzsche*. The Viking Press, 1954.

Kearns, Martha. *Käthe Kollwitz: Woman and Artist*. Feminist Press, 1976.

Keegan, John. *The Face of Battle*. The Viking Press, 1976.

———. *Fields of Battle: The Wars for North America*. Alfred A. Knopf, 1996.

Keller, Helen. *My Religion*. Doubleday, Page & Company, 1927.

Kennedy, Eugene. *Authority: The Most Misunderstood Idea in America*. The Free Press, 1997.

Kennedy, John F. *Profiles in Courage*. Harper & Row, 1964.

Kennedy, Maxwell Taylor. *Make Gentle the Life of the World: The Vision of Robert F. Kennedy*. Harcout Brace, 1998.

Kershaw, Ian. *Hitler 1889–1936: Hubris*. W. W. Norton, 1998.

———. *Hitler 1936–1945: Nemesis*. W. W. Norton, 2000.

Keyes, Dick. *True Heroism in a World of Celebrity Counterfeits*. NavPress, 1995.

Kilpatrick, William, Gregory Wolfe, and Suzanne Wolfe. *Books that Build Character: A Guide to Teaching Your Child Moral Values Through Stories*. Simon & Schuster, 1994.

Bibliography

Kilpatrick, William K. *Why Johnny Can't Tell Right from Wrong.* Simon & Schuster, 1992.

Kimmel, Michael. *Manhood in America: A Cultural History.* The Free Press, 1996.

King, Coretta Scott. *My Life with Martin Luther King, Jr.* Holt, Rinehart and Winston, 1969.

Klapp, Orrin E. *Heroes, Villains and Fools: The Changing American Character.* Prentice-Hall, 1962.

———. *Inflation of Symbols: Loss of Values in American Culture.* Transaction Publishers, 1991.

Klein, Mina C., and Arthur H. Klein. *Käthe Kollwitz: Life in Art.* Holt, Reinhart and Winston, 1972.

Kollwitz, Käthe. *The Diaries and Letters of Käthe Kollwitz.* Northwestern University Press, 1988.

Kovic, Ron. *Born on the Fourth of July.* Pocket Books, 1977.

Kramer, Hilton, and Roger Kimball, eds. *Against the Grain: The New Criterion on Art and Intellect at the End of the Twentieth Century.* I. R. Dee, 1995.

———. *The Future of the European Past.* I. R. Dee, 1997.

Kuehnemann, Eugen. *Charles W. Eliot: President of Harvard University, May 19, 1869–May 19, 1909.* Houghton Mifflin, 1909.

Lamb, Brian. *Booknotes: America's Finest Authors on Reading, Writing, and the Power of Ideas.* Times Books, 1997.

———. *Booknotes: Life Stories: Notable Biographers on the People Who Shaped America.* Times Books, 1999.

La Rochefoucauld. *Maxims.* Penguin Books, 1959.

Lasch, Christopher. *The Culture of Narcissism: American Life in an Age of Diminishing Expectations.* W. W. Norton, 1978.

Lash, Joseph P. *Eleanor and Franklin: The Story of Their Relationship Based on Eleanor Roosevelt's Private Papers.* New American Library, 1971.

Lawrence, William L. *Life of Phillips Brooks.* Harper & Brothers, 1930.

Leach, William. *Land of Desire: Merchants, Power, and the Rise of a New American Culture.* Pantheon Books, 1993.

Lee, David D. *Sergeant York: An American Hero.* University Press of Kentucky, 1985.

Leo, John. *Two Steps Ahead of the Thought Police.* Transaction Publishers, 1998.

Lesy, Michael. *Rescues: The Lives of Heroes.* Farrar, Straus and Giroux, 1991.

Leuchtenburg, William E., ed. *American Places: Encounters with History: A Celebration of Sheldon Meyer.* Oxford University Press, 2000.

Levin, David. *History as Romantic Art: Bancroft, Prescott, Motley, and Parkman.* Stanford University Press, 1959.

Levine, Arthur. *When Dreams and Heroes Died.* Jossey-Bass, 1980.

Lewis, David L. *King: A Critical Biography.* Praeger, 1970.

Lewis, David Levering. *W. E. B. Dubois: Biography of a Race: 1868–1919.* Henry Holt, 1993.

Lewis, R. W. B. *The Jameses: A Family Narrative.* Doubleday, 1991.

Linden-Ward, Blanche. *Silent City on a Hill: Landscapes of Memory and Boston's Mount Auburn Cemetery.* Ohio State University Press, 1989.

Linderman, Gerald F. *Embattled Courage: The Experience of Combat in the American Civil War.* The Free Press, 1987.

Lipset, Seymour Martin. *American Exceptionalism: A Double-Edged Sword.* W. W. Norton, 1996.

Lipsyte, Robert. *Sportsworld: An American Dreamland.* Quadrangle/New York Times Book Co., 1975.

Lipsyte, Robert, and Peter Levine. *Idols of the Game: A Sporting History of the American Century.* Turner Pub., 1995.

Lodge, Henry Cabot, and Theodore Roosevelt. *Hero Tales from American History.* Century Co., 1918.

Loewen, James W. *Lies Across America: What Our Historic Sites Get Wrong.* The New Press, 1999.

Longmore, Paul K. *The Invention of George Washington.* University of California Press, 1988.

Lopez, Claude-Anne. *Mon Cher Papa: Franklin and the Ladies of Paris.* Yale University Press, 1966.

———. *My Life with Benjamin Franklin.* Yale University Press, 2000.

Lord, Walter. *The Good Years: From 1900 to the First World War.* Harper, 1960.

Louganis, Greg, with Eric Marcus. *Breaking the Surface.* Random House, 1995.

Lucas, Stephen. *The Quotable George Washington.* Madison House, 1999.

Ludwig, Emil. *Genius and Character.* Harcourt, Brace, 1927.

Lutz, Tom. *American Nervousness, 1903: An Anecdotal History.* Cornell University Press, 1991.

Lynd, Robert S., and Helen Merrell. *Middletown: A Study in American Culture.* Harcourt Brace Jovanovich, 1956.

MacArthur, Brian, ed. *The Penguin Book of Twentieth-Century Speeches.* The Viking Press, 1992.

MacCracken, Henry Mitchell. *The Hall of Fame.* The Knickerbocker Press, 1901.

Machiavelli, Niccolo. *The Prince and the Discourses.* Random House, 1950.

Magnus, Philip. *Gladstone: A Biography.* E. P. Dutton, 1954.

Maier, Pauline. *American Scripture: Making the Declaration of Independence.* Vintage Books, 1998.

Manchester, William R. *American Caesar: Douglas MacArthur.* Little, Brown, 1978.

———. *Disturber of the Peace: The Life of H. L. Mencken.* Harper, 1951.

Mandela, Nelson. *Long Walk to Freedom: The Autobiography of Nelson Mandela.* Little, Brown, 1994.

Mann, Horace. *Lectures on Education.* Arno Press and *The New York Times,* 1969.

Manson, Marilyn, with Neil Strauss. *the long hard road out of hell.* Regan Books, 1998.

Maraniss, David. *When Pride Still Mattered: A Life of Vince Lombardi.* Simon & Schuster, 1999.

Marius, Richard C. *Thomas More: A Biography.* Alfred A. Knopf, 1985.

Markowitz, Jack. *A Walk on the Crust of Hell.* Stephen Greene Press, 1973.

Marling, Karal Ann, and John Wetenhall. *Iwo Jima: Monuments, Memories, and the American Hero.* Harvard University Press, 1991.

Martin, Waldo E., Jr. *The Mind of Frederick Douglass.* University of North Carolina Press, 1984.

Bibliography

Mathews, Jay. *Escalante: The Best Teacher in America*. Henry Holt, 1988.

Matthiessen, F. O. *American Renaissance: Art and Expression in the Age of Emerson and Whitman*. Oxford University Press, 1968.

Meggyesy, David. *Out of Their League*. Ramparts Press, 1970.

McCain, John, with Mark Salter. *Faith of My Fathers*. Random House, 1999.

McCullough, David. *Brave Companions: Portraits in History*. Prentice Hall Press, 1992.

———. *John Adams*. Simon & Schuster, 2001.

———. *Mornings on Horseback*. Simon & Schuster, 1981.

———. *Truman*. Simon & Schuster, 1992.

McFeely, William S. *Frederick Douglass*. W. W. Norton, 1991.

———. *Grant: A Biography*. W. W. Norton, 1981.

McGinley, Phyllis. *Saint-Watching*. The Viking Press, 1969.

McGinniss, Joe. *Heroes*. The Viking Press, 1976.

McGuffey, William Holmes. *The Annotated McGuffey: Selections from the McGuffey Eclectic Readers 1836–1920*. VanNostrand Reinhold, 1976.

McMurtry, Larry. *Crazy Horse*. A Lipper/Viking Book, 1999.

McPherson, James M. *For Cause and Comrades: Why Men Fought in the Civil War*. Oxford University Press, 1997.

Medved, Michael. *Hollywood vs. America*. HarperPerennial, 1993.

Melikov, Gregor. *The Immortals of America in the Hall of Fame*. G. Melikov, 1942.

Menchu, Rigoberta. *I, Rigoberta Menchu: An Indian Woman in Guatemala*. Verso, 1984.

Mencken, H. L. *The Vintage Mencken*. Vintage Books, 1990.

Mencken, H. L., ed. *A New Dictionary of Quotations on Historical Principles from Ancient and Modern Sources*. Alfred A. Knopf, 1989.

Messerli, Jonathan. *Horace Mann: A Biography*. Alfred A. Knopf, 1972.

Miller, Arthur. *Death of a Salesman*. The Viking Press, 1958.

Miller, Arthur, with Robert A. Martin, ed. *The Theatre Essays of Arthur Miller*. The Viking Press, 1978.

236

Bibliography

Miller, Merle. *Plain Speaking: An Oral Biography of Harry S. Truman.* Berkley Publishing Corporation, 1974.

Miner, Joshua L. *Outward Bound U.S.A.: Learning Through Experience in Adventure-Based Education.* William Morrow, 1981.

Moore, Doris Langley-Levy. *The Late Lord Byron: Posthumous Dramas.* Lippincott, 1961.

Morello, Theodore, ed. *The Hall of Fame for Great Americans at New York University: Official Handbook.* New York University Press, 1967.

Morgan, Edmund S. *The Genius of George Washington.* Anderson House, 1980.

Morgan, Joy E. *Horace Mann: His Ideas and Ideals.* The National Home Library Foundation, 1936.

Morison, Elting E., ed. *The Letters of Theodore Roosevelt.* Harvard University Press, 1951.

Morison, Samuel Eliot. *Christopher Columbus, Mariner.* Little, Brown, 1955.

———. *John Paul Jones: A Sailor's Biography.* Time-Life Books, 1964.

———. *The Young Man Washington.* Harvard University Press, 1932.

———. *Vistas of History.* Alfred A. Knopf, 1964.

Morris, Edmund. *Dutch: A Memoir of Ronald Reagan.* Random House, 1999.

———. *The Rise of Theodore Roosevelt.* Coward, McCann & Geoghegan, 1979.

Morris, Ivan I. *The Nobility of Failure: Tragic Heroes in the History of Japan.* Holt, Rinehart and Winston, 1975.

Morris, Michael. *Madam Valentino: The Many Lives of Natacha Rambova.* Abbeville Press, 1991.

Mosley, Leonard. *Marshall, Hero for Our Times.* Hearst Books, 1982.

Muller, Melissa. *Anne Frank: The Biography.* Metropolitan Books, 1998.

Nagel, Paul C. *The Adams Women: Abigail and Louisa Adams, Their Sisters and Daughters.* Oxford University Press, 1987.

———. *Descent from Glory: Four Generations of the John Adams Family.* Oxford University Press, 1983.

———. *John Quincy Adams: A Public Life, A Private Life.* Alfred A. Knopf, 1997.

Bibliography

Nash, Gary. *History on Trial: Culture Wars and the Teaching of the Past.* Alfred A. Knopf, 1997.

Neuharth, Al. *Confessions of an S. O. B.* Doubleday, 1989.

Nevins, Allan. *The Emergence of Lincoln: Douglas, Buchanan, and Party Chaos: 1857–1859.* Charles Scribner's Sons, 1950.

——. *The Emergence of Lincoln: Prologue to Civil War: 1857–1861.* Charles Scribner's Sons, 1950.

——. *The Gateway to History.* Quadrangle Books, 1963.

Niebuhr, Reinhold. *Faith and History: A Comparison of Christian and Modern Views of History.* Charles Scribner's Sons, 1949.

Nisbet, Robert. *History of the Idea of Progress.* Transaction Publishers, 1994.

Nuland, Sherwin B. *Doctors: The Biography of Medicine.* Vintage Books, 1989.

Nye, Joseph S., Jr., et al., eds. *Why People Don't Trust Government.* Harvard University Press, 1997.

Nye, Russell B. *George Bancroft: Brahmin Rebel.* Alfred A. Knopf, 1944.

Oates, Stephen B. *Let the Trumpet Sound: The Life of Martin Luther King, Jr.* Harper & Row, 1982.

Oriard, Michael. *Dreaming of Heroes: American Sports Fiction, 1868–1980.* Nelson-Hall, 1982.

Orwell, George. *A Collection of Essays.* Harcourt Brace Jovanovich, 1953.

Pachter, Marc, ed. *Telling Lives: The Biographer's Art.* New Republic Books, 1979.

Painter, Nell Irvin. *Sojourner Truth: A Life, A Symbol.* W. W. Norton, 1996.

Pamplin, Robert J. *American Heroes: Their Lives, Their Values, Their Beliefs.* Master Media, 1995.

Parkman, Francis. *The Discovery of the Great West: La Salle.* Holt, Rinehart and Winston, 1956.

Partington, Angela, ed. *The Oxford Dictionary of Quotations.* Revised Fourth Edition. Oxford University Press, 1996.

Peabody, Francis Greenwood. *Reminiscences of Present-Day Saints.* Houghton Mifflin, 1927.

Peale, Norman Vincent. *The Power of Positive Thinking.* Prentice-Hall, 1956.

Pearson, Carol S. *The Hero Within: Six Archetypes We Live By.* Harper & Row, 1989.

Perret, Geoffrey. *Old Soldiers Never Die: The Life of Douglas MacArthur.* Random House, 1996.

Perry, Ralph Barton, et al. *The Thought and Character of William James.* Harper Torchbooks, 1964.

Peterson, Merrill D. *The Jefferson Image in the American Mind.* University Press of Virginia, 1998.

———. *Lincoln in American Memory.* Oxford University Press, 1994.

Pipes, Richard. *Struve: Liberal on the Left: 1870–1905.* Harvard University Press, 1970.

———. *Struve: Liberal on the Right: 1905–1944.* Harvard University Press, 1988.

Plutarch. *Makers of Rome: Nine Lives of Plutarch.* Penguin Books, 1965.

Pogue, Forrest C. *George C. Marshall.* The Viking Press, 1963.

Polster, Miriam. *Eve's Daughters: The Forbidden Heroism of Women.* Jossey-Bass, 1992.

Pope, Alexander. *Selected Works.* Random House, 1948.

Price, Eva Jane. *China Journal 1889–1900: An American Missionary Family During the Boxer Rebellion.* Charles Scribner's Sons, 1989.

Pringle, Henry F. *Theodore Roosevelt: A Biography.* Harcourt, Brace and Company, 1931.

Powel, Harford, Jr. *Walter Camp, The Father of American Football, An Authorized Biography.* Little, Brown, 1926.

Powell, Colin L., with Joseph E. Persico. *My American Journey.* Random House, 1995.

Quinn, Susan. *Marie Curie: A Life.* Simon & Schuster, 1995.

Rader, Benjamin G. *American Sports From the Age of Folk Games to the Age of Spectators.* Prentice-Hall, 1983.

Randall, Willard Sterne. *A Little Revenge: Benjamin Franklin and His Son.* Little, Brown, 1984.

Rampersad, Arnold. *Jackie Robinson: A Biography.* Alfred A. Knopf, 1997.

Remini, Robert V. *Andrew Jackson and His Indian Wars.* The Viking Press, 2001.

———. *Daniel Webster: The Man and His Time.* W. W. Norton, 1997.

———. *The Life of Andrew Jackson.* Penguin Books, 1990.

Reston, James. *Deadline: A Memoir.* Random House, 1991.

Reynolds, Donald Martin. *Masters of American Sculpture: The Figurative Tradition from the American Renaissance to the Millennium.* Abbeville Press, 1993.

———. *Monuments and Masterpieces: Histories and Views of Public Sculpture in New York City.* Macmillan, 1988.

Rice, Grantland. *The Tumult and the Shouting: My Life in Sport.* A. S. Barnes, 1954.

Richardson, Robert D., Jr. *Emerson: The Mind on Fire: A Biography.* University of California Press, 1995.

Roberts, Randy, and James S. Olson. *John Wayne: American.* The Free Press, 1995.

Robertson-Lorant, Laurie. *Melville: A Biography.* Clarkson/Potter Publishers, 1996.

Robinson, John C. *Death of a Hero, Birth of the Soul: Answering the Call of Midlife.* Tzedakah Publications, 1995.

Robinson, Ray. *Iron Horse: Lou Gehrig in His Time.* W. W. Norton, 1990.

———. *Matty: An American Hero: Christy Mathewson of the New York Giants.* Oxford University Press, 1993.

Rodman, Dennis, with Tim Keown. *Bad As I Wanna Be.* Delacorte Press, 1996.

Roe, Frederick William. *Victorian Prose.* The Ronald Press Company, 1947.

Rogers, Mary Beth. *Barbara Jordan: American Hero.* Bantam Books, 1998.

Rogers, Will. *The Autobiography of Will Rogers,* ed. Donald Day. Houghton Mifflin, 1949.

Rose, Mike. *Possible Lives: The Promise of Public Education in America.* Houghton Mifflin, 1995.

Rose, Phyllis. *Parallel Lives: Five Victorian Marriages.* Alfred A. Knopf, 1983.

Rosenberg, Philip. *The Seventh Hero: Thomas Carlyle and the Theory of Radical Activism.* Harvard University Press, 1974.

Rosenfeld, Harvey. *Raoul Wallenberg: Angel of Rescue: Heroism and Torment in the Gulag.* Prometheus Books, 1982.

Ross, Walter Sanford. *The Last Hero: Charles A. Lindbergh.* Harper & Row, 1976.

Rovin, Jeff. *Adventure Heroes: Legendary Characters from Odysseus to James Bond.* Facts on File, Inc., 1994.

——. *The Encyclopedia of Super Villains.* Facts on File Publications, 1987.

——. *The Encyclopedia of Superheroes.* Facts on File Publications, 1985.

Ryan, Kevin, and Karen E. Bohlin. *Building Character in Schools: Practical Ways to Bring Moral Instruction to Life.* Jossey-Bass Publishers, 1999.

Sale, Kirkpatrick. *The Conquest of Paradise: Christopher Columbus and the Columbian Legacy.* Alfred A. Knopf, 1990.

Salinger, J. D. *The Catcher in the Rye.* Bantam Books, 1964.

Salinger, Pierre. *P.S. A Memoir.* St. Martin's Press, 1995.

Salisbury, Harrison E. *Heroes of My Time.* Walker, 1993.

Samuelson, Robert J. *The Good Life and Its Discontents: The American Dream in the Age of Entitlement, 1945–1995.* Times Books, 1995.

Schickel, Richard. *Intimate Strangers: The Culture of Celebrity.* Doubleday, 1985.

Schlesinger, Arthur M., Jr. *A Life in the Twentieth Century: Innocent Beginnings, 1917–1950.* Houghton Mifflin, 2000.

——. *A Thousand Days: John F. Kennedy in the White House.* Houghton Mifflin Company, 1965.

Schopenhauer, Arthur. *Essays and Aphorisms.* Penguin Books, 1970.

Schwartz, Barry. *George Washington: The Making of an American Symbol.* The Free Press, 1987.

Schwarzkopf, H. Norman, and Peter Petre. *It Doesn't Take a Hero: The Autobiography of General H. Norman Schwarzkopf.* Bantam Books, 1992.

Sewall, Gilbert T. *American History Textbooks: An Assessment of Quality.* Educational Excellence Network, 1987.

Shaw, Peter. *The Character of John Adams.* W. W. Norton, 1977.

Shay, Jonathan. *Achilles in Vietnam: Combat Trauma and the Undoing of Character*. Atheneum, 1994.

Shelden, Michael. *Orwell: The Authorized Biography*. HarperCollins, 1991.

Sheldon, Charles Monroe. *In His Steps*. Grosset & Dunlap, 1935.

Silber, John. *Straight Shooting: What's Wrong with America and How to Fix It*. Harper & Row, 1989.

Silverman, Kenneth. *The Life and Times of Cotton Mather*. Harper & Row, 1984.

Simon, Linda. *Genuine Reality: A Life of William James*. Harcourt Brace, 1998.

Simonton, Dean Keith. *Greatness: Who Makes History and Why*. Guilford, 1994.

Simpson, Alan K. *Right in the Old Gazoo: A Lifetime of Scrapping with the Press*. William Morrow, 1997.

Simpson, Harold B. *Audie Murphy: American Soldier*. Hill Jr. College Press, 1975.

Smelser, Marshall. *The Life that Ruth Built, A Biography*. University of Nebraska Press, 1975.

Smiles, Samuel. *Self-Help: With Illustrations of Conduct and Perseverance*. John Murray, 1958.

Smith, Page. *The Rise of Industrial America: A People's History of the Post- Reconstruction Era*. McGraw-Hill, 1984.

———. *The Shaping of America: A People's History of the Young Republic*. McGraw-Hill, 1980.

Smith, Rex Alan. *The Carving of Mount Rushmore*. Abbeville Press, 1985.

Smith, Richard Norton. *The Harvard Century: The Making of a University to a Nation*. Simon & Schuster, 1986.

———. *Patriarch: George Washington and the New American Nation*. Houghton Mifflin, 1993.

Snow, C. P. *Variety of Men*. Penguin, 1969.

Solomon, Maynard. *Beethoven*. Schirmer Books, 1977.

———. *Mozart: A Life*. HarperCollins, 1995.

Solzhenitsyn, Aleksandr. *The Gulag Archipelago 1918–1956: An Experiment in Literary Investigation*. Harper & Row, 1973.

Sorenson, Theodore C. *Kennedy*. Harper & Row, 1965.

Sprawson, Charles. *Haunts of the Black Masseur: The Swimmer as Hero*. Jonathan Cape, 1992.

Steckmesser, Kent Ladd. *The Western Hero in History and Legend*. University of Oklahoma Press, 1965.

Steel, Ronald. *Walter Lippmann and the American Century*. Little, Brown, 1980.

Stephanopoulos, George. *All Too Human: A Political Education*. Little, Brown, 1999.

Sterling, Dorothy. *Lucretia Mott: Gentle Warrior*. Doubleday, 1964.

Stevenson, Burton. *The Home Book of Quotations—Classical and Modern*. Dodd, Mead, and Company, 1967.

Stockdale, James Bond. *Thoughts of a Philosophical Fighter Pilot*. Hoover Institution Press, 1995.

Stoll, David. *Rigoberta Menchu and the Story of All Poor Guatemalans*. Westview Press, 1999.

Strachey, Lytton. *Biographical Essays*. Harcourt Brace, 1933.

———. *Eminent Victorians*. Random House, 1918.

Stump, Al. *Cobb: A Biography*. Algonquin Books of Chapel Hill, 1994.

Sullivan, Mark. *Our Times: America at the Birth of the Twentieth Century*, ed. Dan Rather. Scribner, 1996.

Swindell, Larry. *The Last Hero: A Biography of Gary Cooper*. Doubleday, 1980.

Sykes, Charles J. *A Nation of Victims: The Decay of the American Character*. St. Martin's Press, 1992.

Templeton, John Marks, with James Ellison, eds. *Riches for the Mind and Spirit*. HarperSanFrancisco, 1990.

Theroux, Phyllis. *The Book of Eulogies: A Collection of Memorial Tributes, Poetry, Essays, and Letters of Condolence*. Scribner, 1997.

Thomas, Emory M. *Robert E. Lee: A Biography*. W. W. Norton, 1995.

Thornton, John F., and Katharine Washburn, eds. *Dumbing Down: Essays on the Strip Mining of American Culture*. W. W. Norton, 1996.

Tillich, Paul. *The Courage To Be*. Yale Univeristy Press, 1952.

Townsend, Kim. *Manhood at Harvard: William James and Others.* W. W. Norton, 1996.

Trevelyan, G. M., ed. *Carlyle: An Anthology.* Longmans, Green and Co., 1953.

Trevor-Roper, H. R. *The Last Days of Hitler.* Macmillan, 1947.

Trilling, Lionel. *Matthew Arnold.* Columbia University Press, 1949.

Tuchman, Barbara W. *Practicing History: Selected Essays.* Alfred A. Knopf, 1981.

——. *The Proud Tower: A Portrait of the World Before the War, 1890–1914.* Macmillan, 1966.

Tuleja, Tad. *The New York Public Library Book of Popular Americana.* Macmillan, 1994.

Tunis, John R. *Sports, Heroes and Hysterics.* The John Day Company, 1928.

Twitchell, James B. *Carnival Culture: The Trashing of Taste in America.* Columbia University Press, 1992.

——. *For Shame: The Loss of Common Decency in American Culture.* St. Martin's Press, 1997.

Ulrich, Laurel Thatcher. *Good Wives: Image and Reality in the Lives of Women in Northern New England, 1650–1750.* Vintage Books, 1991.

——. *A Midwife's Tale: The Life of Martha Ballard, Based on Her Diary, 1785–1812.* Vintage Books, 1991.

Unger, Harlow Giles. *John Hancock: Merchant King and American Patriot.* John Wiley & Sons, 2000.

——. *Noah Webster: The Life and Times of an American Patriot.* John Wiley & Sons, 1998.

Untermeyer, Lewis, ed. *The Poems of Henry Wadsworth Longfellow.* The Heritage Press, 1943.

Updike, John. *Picked-Up Pieces.* Alfred A. Knopf, 1976.

——. *The Same Door: Short Stories.* Alfred A. Knopf, 1959

——. *Self-Consciousness: Memoirs.* Alfred A. Knopf, 1989.

Van Doren, Carl. *Benjamin Franklin.* The Viking Press, 1938.

Vidal, Gore. *United States: Essays 1952–1992.* Random House, 1993.

Wagenknecht, Edward. *Henry Wadsworth Longfellow: Portrait of an American Humanist*. Oxford University Press, 1966.

Wall, Joseph Frazier. *Andrew Carnegie*. Oxford University Press, 1970.

Ward, John William. *Andrew Jackson: Symbol for an Age*. Oxford University Press, 1955.

Ware, Susan, ed. *Forgotten Heroes: Inspiring American Portraits from Our Leading Historians*. The Free Press, 1998.

―――. *Letter to the World: Seven Women Who Shaped the American Century*. W. W. Norton, 1998.

Warner, Marina. *Joan of Arc: The Image of Female Heroism*. Alfred A. Knopf, 1981.

Washington, George. *Writings*. The Library of America, 1997.

Washington, James M., ed. *A Testament of Hope: The Essential Writings and Speeches of Martin Luther King, Jr.* HarperCollins, 1991.

Waugh, Joan. *Unsentimental Reformer: The Life of Josephine Shaw Lowell*. Harvard University Press, 1997.

Wecter, Dixon. *The Hero in America: A Chronicle of Hero-Worship*. Charles Scribner's Sons, 1941.

Weems, Mason. *A History of the Life and Death Virtues and Exploits of General George Washington*. Grosset & Dunlap, 1927.

Weisberger, Bernard A. *Booker T. Washington*. New American Library, 1972.

Werbell, Frederick E., and Thurston Clarke. *Lost Hero: The Mystery of Raoul Wallenberg*. McGraw-Hill, 1982.

West, Thomas G. *Vindicating the Founders: Race, Sex, Class, and Justice in the ' Origins of America*. Rowman and Littlefield Publishers, 1997.

Whitehead, Alfred North. *The Aims of Education and Other Essays*. The Free Press, 1967.

Whittier, John Greenleaf. *The Complete Poetical Works of John Greenleaf Whittier*. Houghton Mifflin, 1894.

Wilford, John Noble. *The Mysterious History of Columbus: An Exploration of the Man, the Myth, the Legacy*. Alfred A. Knopf, 1991.

Wills, Gary. *Cincinnatus: George Washington and the Enlightenment*. Doubleday, 1984.

————. *John Wayne's America: The Politics of Celebrity*. Simon & Schuster, 1997.

Wilson, A. N. *Eminent Victorians*. W. W. Norton, 1990.

————. *Jesus: A Life*. W. W. Norton, 1993.

Wilson, Clyde N., ed. *Dictionary of Literary Biography: American Historians 1607–1865*. Volume 30. Gale Research Company, 1984.

Wilson, David Alec, and David Wilson MacArthur. *Carlyle in Old Age 1865–1881*. E. P. Dutton, 1934.

Wilson, Edward O. *Consilience: The Unity of Knowledge*. Alfred A. Knopf, 1998.

————. *Naturalist*. Island Press, 1994.

————. *On Human Nature*. Harvard University Press, 1978.

Wilson, James Q. *The Moral Sense*. The Free Press, 1993.

Winchell, Walter. *Winchell Exclusive*. Prentice-Hall, 1975.

Wingfield-Stratford, Esme. *Those Earnest Victorians*. William Morrow & Co., 1930.

Winik, Jay. *April 1865: The Month that Saved America*. HarperCollins Publishers, 2001.

Winsor, Justin. *Christopher Columbus and How He Received and Imparted the Spirit of Discovery*. Houghton Mifflin, 1892.

Wolf, Michael J. *The Entertainment Economy: How Mega-Media Forces Are Transforming Our Lives*. Times Books, 1999.

Wood, Gordon S. *The Radicalism of the American Revolution*. Alfred A. Knopf, 1992.

Woods, Ralph L. *World Treasury of Religious Quotations*. Hawthorn Books, Inc., 1966.

Woodward, W. E. *George Washington, the Image and the Man*. Boni and Liveright, 1926.

Wright, Esmond, ed. *Benjamin Franklin: His Life as He Wrote It*. Harvard University Press, 1990.

————. *Franklin of Philadelphia*. Belknap Press of Harvard University, 1986.

Wright, Nathalia. *Horatio Greenough: The First American Sculptor*. University of Pennsylvania Press, 1963.

Wright, Robert. *The Moral Animal: Why We Are the Way We Are: The New Science of Evolutionary Psychology and Everyday Life*. Pantheon Books, 1994.

Yaeger, Don, with Jerry Tarkanian. *Shark Attack: Jerry Tarkanian and His Battle with the NCCA and UNLV.* HarperCollins, 1992.

Yewell, John, et al. *Confronting Columbus: An Anthology.* McFarland & Co, 1992.

Ziegler, Philip. *Mountbatten.* Alfred A. Knopf, 1985.

Zhisui, Dr. Li. *The Private Life of Chairman Mao: The Memoirs of Mao's Personal Physician.* Random House, 1994.

Zinn, Howard. *A People's History of the United States.* Harper & Row, 1980.

————. *You Can't Be Neutral on a Moving Train: A Personal History of Our Times.* Beacon Press, 1994.

Zinsser, William, ed. *Extraordinary Lives: The Art and Craft of American Biography.* American Heritage, 1986.

Articles

Acocella, Joan. "Burned Again," *The New Yorker,* November 15, 1997.

Ahmed, Akbar. "The Hero in History," *History Today,* March 1996.

Altick, Richard. "Eminent Victorianism," *The American Scholar,* Winter 1995.

Atlas, James. "Hero Worship: Longing for a New Lone Genius," *The New York Times,* April 28, 1996.

Bailey, Thomas A. "The Mythmakers of American History," *Journal of American History,* June 1968.

Bernheim, Rachel Oestreicher. "A Study of Heroes," The Raoul Wallenberg Committee of the United States.

Birkerts, Sven. "Losing Ourselves in Biography," *Harper's,* March 1995.

Bowden, Charles. "Being Max Cleland," *Esquire,* August 1999.

Boyce, Nell. "Hugh Thompson," *U. S. News & World Report,* August 20–27, 2001.

Boyer, Peter O. "Admiral Boorda's War," *The New Yorker,* September 16, 1996.

Bibliography

Brookhiser, Richard. "A Man on Horseback," *Atlantic Monthly*, January 1996.

Browne, Malcolm. "Polar Heroes in History's Cold Eye," *The New York Times*, May 12, 1996.

Caldwell, Gail. "TV's New Blue Line," *The Boston Globe*, May 18, 1997.

Dalton, Kathleen. "Why America Loved Teddy Roosevelt, or, Charisma Is in the Eyes of the Beholders," *The Psychohistory Review 8*, no. 3, Winter 1979.

Denby, David. "Buried Alive," *The New Yorker*, July 15, 1996.

Denenberg, Dennis. "Move Over, Barney, Make Way for Some Real Heroes," *American Educator*, Fall 1997.

Fimrite, Ron. "A Flame that Burned Too Brightly," *Sports Illustrated*, March 18, 1991.

Fishwick, Marshall. "Making of a Hero," *Saturday Review*, August 1, 1964.

Gergen, David. "Finding Heroes after Atlanta," *U. S. News & World Report*, August 12, 1996.

Glazer, Nathan. "Monuments in an Age Without Heroes," *The Public Interest*, Spring 1996.

Goodman, Ellen. "Politics: Up Close and Too Personal," 8th Annual John S. Knight Lecture, February 29, 1996.

Gurstein, Rochelle. "The Case of Thomas Carlyle: Published Letters, Private Life, and the Limits of Knowledge," *American Scholar*, Summer 2001.

Hanson, Christopher. "Where Have All the Heroes Gone?" *Columbia Journalism Review*, March 1996.

Hitt, Jack. "Battlefield: Space," *The New York Times Magazine*, August 5, 2001.

James, Caryn. "Going the Extra Mile to Give Heroes Blemishes," *The New York Times*, November 26, 1996.

———. "Sex Icon Once, Oddity Now," *The New York Times*, November 8, 1991.

Kamp, David. "The Tabloid Decade," *Vanity Fair*, February 1999.

Krauthammer, Charles. "The End of Heroism," *Time*, February 10, 1997.

Marius, Richard C. "Many an Extravagant Prank and Mummery: Wilson, Race, and the Brahmin Historians," *Soundings*, Winter 1993.

Bibliography

Medlock, Ann. "Bringing Back Heroes," *Education Week,* June 21, 1995.

Neimark, Jill. "The Culture of Celebrity," *Psychology Today,* May 1995.

Nevins, Allan. "Is History Made by Heroes?" *Saturday Review,* November 5, 1955.

Perutz, M. F. "The Pioneer Defended," *New York Review of Books,* December 21, 1995.

Plumb, J. H. "Disappearing Heroes." *Horizon,* Autumn 1974.

Podhoretz, Norman. "Heroism in a Politically Correct Age," *National Review,* January 26, 1998.

Price, Reynolds. "The Heroes of Our Times," *Saturday Review,* December 1978.

Ravitch, Diane. "Tot Sociology," *American Scholar,* Summer 1987.

Rubin, Richard. "The Mall of Fame," *Atlantic,* July 1997.

Samuelson, Robert. "The American Sports Mania," *Newsweek,* September 4, 1989.

Schlesinger, Arthur M., Jr. "The Decline of Greatness," *Saturday Evening Post,* November 1, 1958.

Sewall, Gilbert T. "World History: An Appraisal," *Education Week,* June 13, 2001.

Siegel, Ed. "Where Are the Heroes?" *Boston Globe,* January 26, 1997.

Simon, William E. "A Sport in Search of Heroes," *Wall Street Journal,* May 9, 1996.

Spears, Monroe K. "William James as Culture Hero," *Hudson Review,* Spring 1986.

Starobin, Paul. "A Generation of Vipers: Journalists and the New Cynicism," *Columbia Journalism Revew,* March–April 1995.

Steinweis, Alan. "Hitler and Carlyle's 'Historical Greatness,'" *History Today,* June 1995.

Swartz, Clifford. "Heroes," *Physics Teacher,* December 1991.

Talese, Gay. "The Silent Season of Hero," *Esquire,* July 1966.

Thomas, Clarence. "The Benevolent State and the Need for Heroes," *The Weekly Standard,* October 23, 1995.

Bibliography

Weeks, Linton. "Books that May Make Parents Blush: Fiction Aimed at Teens Features Grown-Up Themes," *Washington Post,* May 11, 2001.

Wood, Gordon S. "The Greatness of George Washington," *Virginia Quarterly,* Spring 1992.

Zweig, Paul. "The Hero in Literature," *Saturday Review,* December 1978.

Author Interviews

Stephen Ambrose, Ted Anderson, Joseph Badaracco, Bernard Bailyn, W. Jackson Bate, Daniel Bell, Rachel Bernheim, Mildred Blackman, David Blight, Sue Bloland, Derek Bok, Sissela Bok, Peter Boyer, Douglas Brinkley, Richard Brookhiser, William F. Buckley Jr., James Cash, William Cleary, I. Bernard Cohen, Anne Colby, Robert Coles, Harvey Cox, William Crout, Mario Cuomo, Kathleen Dalton, Drewes Days, Edwin DeLattre, Dennis Denenberg, Alan Dershowitz, Chris Douglas, Michael Dukakis, Mary Maples Dunn, Marian Wright Edelman, Alan Edelstein, Richard Elmore, Allen Fern, Chester Finn, David Fish, Andrew Foster, James Freedman, Paul Gagnon, John Kenneth Galbraith, Howard Gardner, Henry Louis Gates, Peter Gay, Nathan Glazer, Mary Ann Glendon, Charles Glenn, Peter Gomes, Ellen Goodman, Stephen J. Gould, Pat Graham, Allen Guttmann, David Halberstam, Joseph Harsch, Richard Hawley, Ron Heifetz, Thomas Hibbs, David Hicks, E. D. Hirsch, Stanley Hoffmann, Gerald Holton, Sam Huntington, Tony Jarvis, Susan Moore Johnson, Marvin Kalb, Wendy Kaminer, Michael Kammen, Phil Katz, Dick Keyes, William Kilpatrick, Reyman Klave, Joe Klein, Ed Koch, Bill Kovach, Peter Kreeft, Anthony Kronman, Rosette Lamont, Sara Lawrence-Lightfoot, Richard Lipsyte, William Macomber, Richard Marius, David McCullough, Wendel Meyer, Dean Miller, John Miller, Martha Minow, Joel Monell, Robert Mooney, Jerome Murphy, Gregory Nagy, Georgia Nugent, Joseph Nye, Keith Olbermann, Marc Pachter, George Panichas, Orlando Patterson, Vito Perone, Richard Pipes, Art Powell, Robert Putnam, Diane Ravitch, Ned Rorem, Ralph Rourke, Neil Rudenstine, Walter Rutkowski, Kevin Ryan, Richard Ryerson, Arthur Schlesinger Jr., George Scialabba, Gilbert Sewall, Dan Shaughnessy, Hugh Sidey, John Silber, Alan Simpson, Ted Sizer, Christine Sommers, John Spong, Mark Starr, Krister Stendahl, Sheldon Stern, Sandra Stotsky, Michael Sugrue, Richard Tedlow, Richard Thomas, Stephen Truitt, Helen Vendler, Susan Ware, Charles Willie, E. O. Wilson, James Q. Wilson, Chris Winship, Alan Wolfe.

Recommended Readings

For the nineteenth century, the key book is Thomas Carlyle's *On Heroes, Hero-Worship and the Heroic in History*. The prose is not easy but the insights are brilliant and the profiles interesting. I also recommend Ralph Waldo Emerson's essays, "The Uses of Great Men" and "Heroism," and his profiles in the book *Representative Men*.

For the twentieth century, there are two key books on our changing attitudes toward heroes: Marshall Fishwick's *American Heroes: Myth and Reality* and Dixon Wecter's *The Hero in America: A Chronicle of Hero-Worship*.

Two brilliant essays on heroism are Daniel Boorstin's "From Hero to Celebrities: The Human Pseudo-Event" in his book *The Image: A Guide to Pseudo-Events in America;* and Arthur Schlesinger Jr.'s "The Decline of Greatness." Boorstin's essay is packed with insights, still widely quoted, and relevant. Schlesinger looks at the 1950s and makes a powerful case for the importance of great individuals.

In our own time there are two books on the loss of public heroes: Alan Edelstein's *Everybody Is Sitting on the Curb: How and Why America's Heroes Disappeared* and Dick Keyes's *True Heroism in a World of Celebrity Counterfeits*. Edelstein's book is written from a sociological perspective, Keyes's book from a Christian one. The best essays in defense of heroes that I have read are Joseph Epstein's "Knocking on Three, Winston" in his book *With My Trousers Rolled;* and John Silber's "Of Mermaids and Magnificence" in his book *Straight Shooting: What's Wrong With America and How to Fix It*.

Before September 11, 2001, not many intellectuals wrote about heroes. Robert Coles was an exception. In speeches, articles, and his recent *Lives of Moral Leadership*, he celebrates heroes. Gertrude Himmelfarb criticizes debunking professors and praises heroes in her essay "Of Heroes, Villains, and Valets." Nathan Glazer wrote about America's diminishing respect for great statues of heroes in the essay "Monuments in an Age Without Heroes." James O. Freedman, former president of Dartmouth College, regularly talked to incoming freshmen about heroes. He has collected some of his talks in his book *Idealism and Liberal Education*. I also recommend Clarence Thomas's essay "The Benevolent State and the Need for Heroes."

Acknowledgments

I am grateful to Jerome Murphy at the Harvard Graduate School of Education for his encouragement. I would also like to thank Joel Monell at the School of Education, for good conversation; and Linda DeLauri, for assistance with grant proposals. I am grateful to Peter Gomes, whose sermons at Harvard's Memorial Church gave me confidence and courage.

Much of this book was written in the main reading room of Harvard's Widener Library, where Fred Burchsted and Sarah Phillips were indefatigable in answering my questions and finding the sources of obscure quotations. I am indebted as well to the librarians at the Nantucket Atheneum, where I write during the summer: Sharon Carlee, Joan Rouillard, Chris Turrentine, and Betsy Tyler. I would also like to thank Nantucket historian Bob Mooney, who frequently found me hunched over my books in the Atheneum, for inviting me to speak in the hall where Frederick Douglass had first spoken.

During the early stages of my research, former colleague David Faus lured me out of the library by having me talk about heroism to high school students in Virginia. That was the beginning of a journey that would help shape this book. Also early on, Nancy Heckscher was especially helpful by setting up many school visits in Philadelphia.

I am grateful to all the people listed in my author interviews, who generously gave their time to talk to me about heroism, and to countless students whose probing questions forced me to come to terms with a complex subject.

For supporting my research and lectures, I would like to thank the Lynde and Harry Bradley Foundation and its director of academics, international, and cultural programs, Dianne Sehler; the F. M. Kirby Foundation; the Intercollegiate Studies Institute and its prep school program director, Jason Duke; and the Olin Foundation and its executive director, Jim Piereson.

With tact, patience, and skillful guidance, Brendan Cahill, my editor at Grove/Atlantic, Inc., pushed me to improve each draft. It was his inspiration that provided the structure for this book. I never realized what a difference a copy editor could make until Janet Baker marked up the manuscript. I am also grateful to Andrew Miller and Morgan Entrekin at Grove/Atlantic, Inc., for believing that a book on heroism was a good idea at a time when heroism was not in fashion.

I would like to thank my former high school English teacher, Jack Pickering, for reading early chapters of this book and testing my ideas; my former colleague Arthur Naething, for patiently reading the manuscript more than once; and my friend Paul Dickson, for introducing me to the world of publishing.

I will be forever grateful to my former colleague and good friend, Pamela Wetherill, who from the beginning believed in the project, read every word of the last few drafts, questioned every assertion and fact, and saved me from many errors.

I am indebted to my mother, Harriet Gibbon, who taught me to eschew self-pity and to persevere; and to my father, Ralph Gibbon, who taught me by example that a person could be at the same time realistic and idealistic.

My sons, Sean and Brendan, pitched in with their suggestions and offered constant encouragement.

Finally, this book is dedicated to my wife, Carol, who helped shape every page and kept me going at every stage with her enthusiasm, optimism, and support.

Index

sexuality, 94, 96, 97, 115, 145,
153, 157; of heroes and, 107–
10; presidents and, 106, 107,
109; sexual revolution (since
1960s), 107–8, 170
Shakespeare, William, 5, 6, 11,
72, 161, 168; Carlyle on, 25,
26; as hero, 150; on virtues,
142
Shakespearean Tragedy
(Bradley), 10
Shaw, Col. Robert Gould, 46–
47, 53, 55
Shays's Rebellion, 132
*She Said Yes: The Unlikely
Martyrdom of Cassie Bernall*
(Bernall), 152
Sheik, The (movie), 96
Sherman, Gen. William T., 163,
181
shero, 10
Shumaker, Lt. Com. Bob, 55
Silence of the Lambs (movie), 145
Simpsons, The (television show),
154
Sinatra, Frank, 9
Skinner, B. F., 162
Slaughterhouse-Five (Vonnegut),
64
slavery, 2, 5, 10, 16, 183; in
ancient world, 7; campaign
against, 34; democracy and,
91; emancipation of slaves,
125; extension of, 158;
founding fathers and, 134;

Geo. Washington and, 88,
123–24; Thom. Jefferson and,
123–24; Underground
Railroad, 162; women
against, 45, 46. *See also*
abolitionism
Small, William, 122
Smelser, Marshall, 84
Smithsonian Institution, 87, 89
social justice, 10
Socrates, 109
soldiers, xxi, xxv, 8, 67, 108,
160, 170; fallen in Civil War,
21; in Hall of Fame for Great
Americans, 16
Solomon, Maynard, 109
Solzhenitsyn, Aleksandr, 164,
171, 178
Sousa, John Philip, 16
Spanish-American War, 45, 57,
58, 60–61, 76, 127
Spencer, Herbert, 58
sports. *See* athletes; *specific
games*
Stalin, Joseph, xxii, 7, 26, 168–
69, 176
Stand and Deliver (movie), 168
Standish, Burt L. *See* Patten,
Gilbert
Stanton, Elizabeth Cady, 2, 44,
46, 47, 49, 180, 183
"Star-Spangled Banner, The"
(national anthem), 79
Statuary Hall (Washington,
D.C.), 118